THE WESTERN FRONT: REIMS, VERDUN AND THE ARGONNE

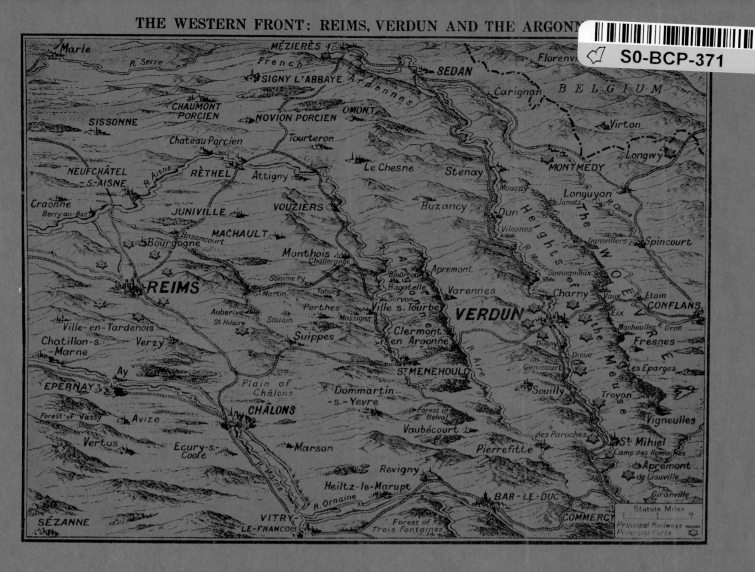

THE WESTERN FRONT: ALSACE & THE VOSGES

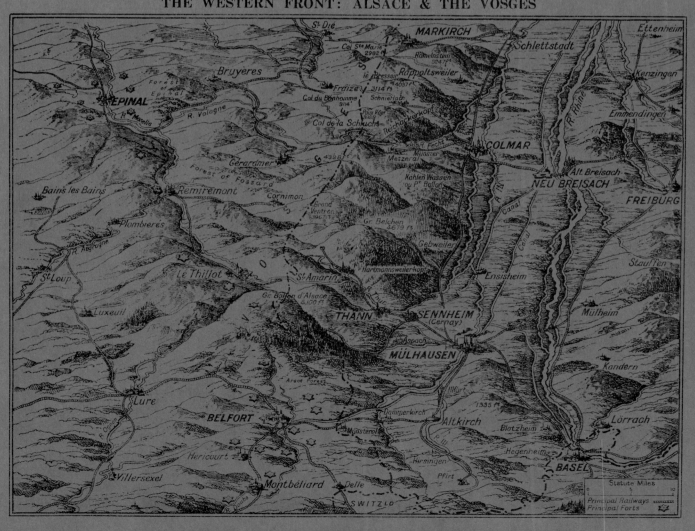

THE GREAT BATTLES
OF WORLD WAR I

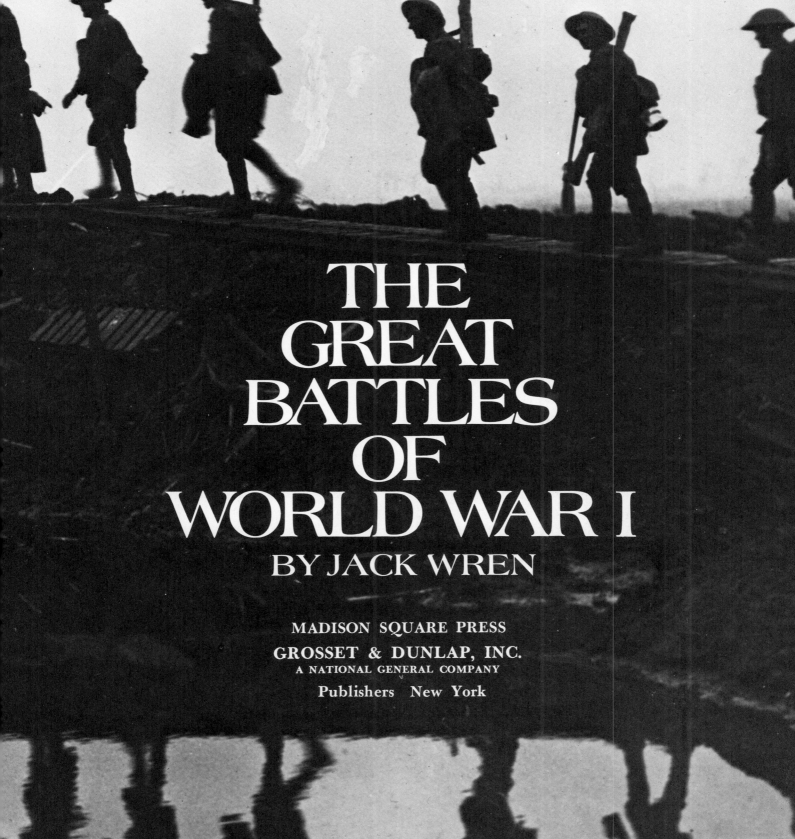

THE GREAT BATTLES OF WORLD WAR I

BY JACK WREN

MADISON SQUARE PRESS

GROSSET & DUNLAP, INC.

A NATIONAL GENERAL COMPANY

Publishers   New York

PUBLISHED SIMULTANEOUSLY IN CANADA.
LIBRARY OF CONGRESS CATALOG CARD NUMBER: 70-123464
ISBN: 0-448-02037-8

Printed in the United States of America.

Book design by Kay Ward.

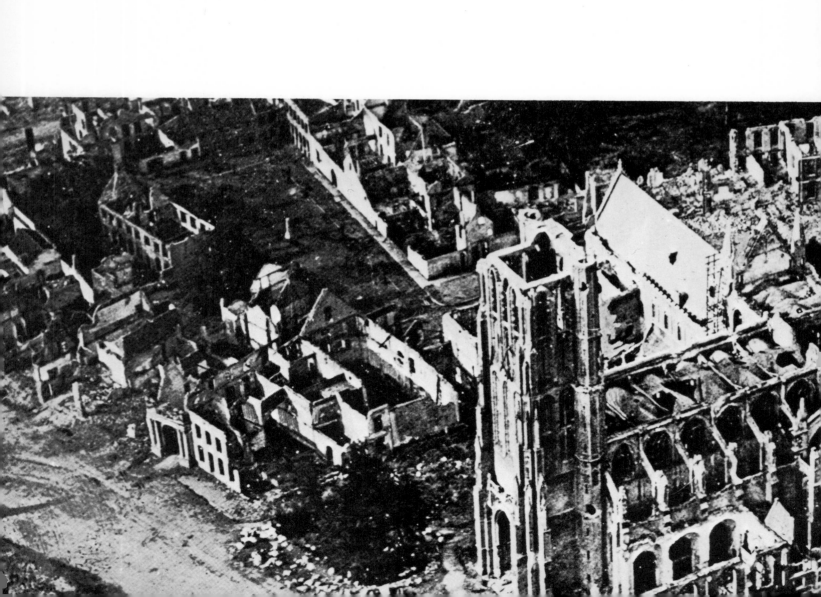

Contents

THE GREAT BATTLES
OF WORLD WAR I

Emperor Francis Joseph of Austria

Foreword

World War I was the first great global conflict; it involved twenty-eight nations on six continents. Almost 65,000,000 men were mobilized. Although mortality figures will never be accurately known, studies estimate that between 10,000,000 and 13,000,000 combatants perished in battle or from wounds and disease directly related to the War, and some 21,000,000 were wounded in varying degrees of severity. The War ended several ancient monarchies, and radically changed the alignment of power even among the victors.

By 1917 the 300-year-old Romanoff dynasty was so debilitated that it expired without a twitch. At the War's end Germany was in chaos, her cities wracked by civil war, and hungry civilians joined disillusioned troops to drive the Kaiser into exile. The Austro-Hungarian Empire was reduced to a shadow of its former greatness. Both England and France lost their status as first-class powers, and America emerged as the strongest financial and industrial nation in the world.

Determined to remain neutral, Woodrow Wilson had been reelected President in 1916 largely on the slogan, "He kept us out of war," but Germany ironically succeeded where England and France had failed. Her campaign of unrestricted submarine warfare finally drove America to join the Allies.

Kaiser Wilhelm II of Germany

King Albert of the Belgians

All European nations accepted war as an "instrument of national policy." In such an explosive atmosphere, each country needed an ally or confederate, for none felt strong or secure alone. During the years preceding the Great War, six European nations had aligned in two opposite camps. The Triple Entente—England, France, and Russia—faced the Triple Alliance of Germany, Austria-Hungary (together known as the Central Powers), and Italy. Commercial rivalries and localized wars erupted with ominous regularity, and any territory left unprotected was quickly seized.

Europe knew tension and relaxation but not tranquility. Two Moroccan crises, in 1905 and 1911, almost embroiled England and France against Germany. Austria's voracious appetite led her to annex Bosnia-Herzegovina in 1908. Three years later Italy dispossessed the Ottoman Empire from Tripoli. In the First Balkan War, in 1912, the Turks suffered another humiliating defeat, this time by the combined action of Bulgaria, Greece, and Serbia. In a return engagement the following year—but with a different alignment of belligerents—Bulgaria was defeated by an alliance of Greece, Romania, Serbia, and Turkey.

Among the Allied powers, France yearned to regain Alsace and Lorraine, lost to Germany in 1871. As self-appointed protector of her "Slav brothers," Russia frowned at Austria's aggression in the Balkans.

Prime Minister Nikola Pasic of Serbia

King George V of England

And the Czar's ambition to extend Russian influence to Constantinople worried all the powers. At the same time England and France blocked German and Italian ambitions in Africa.

Proud of her reputation as "Mistress of the Seas," England could in truth boast that the sun never set on the British flag. With a population of only 43,000,000, Britain ruled about twenty-five percent of the world's area containing 425,000,000 people. London was too deeply absorbed in consolidating her intercontinental empire to plot war, but Kaiser Wilhelm's growing naval might was a matter of gnawing concern to the policy makers at Whitehall.

Prewar Germany enjoyed the most spectacular industrial development of all European nations, and attained high economic and cultural levels. Despite the German Reichstag, civilians played a rubber-stamp role in foreign policy which caused this body to be dubbed "the figleaf of autocracy" by August Bebel, its leading socialist member. As a result, German foreign policy was characterized by the brinkmanship of Kaiser Wilhelm and his General Staff, wed to the precept of Prussian General Karl von Clausewitz: "War is a continuation of politics by other means." Backed by this powerful and aggressive ally, Austria would commit what she planned as a localized aggression against Serbia—and thus spark the great conflagration.

President Raymond Poincaré of France

Czar Nicholas II of Russia

1. Assassination
at Sarajevo

1. Assassination at Sarajevo

Sarajevo — the start of the royal visit.

For Archduke Francis Ferdinand, heir to the Hapsburg throne, and for his wife Sophie, June 28, 1914, promised to be an auspicious day. It was their fourteenth wedding anniversary and to celebrate it they had undertaken a special visit to Bosnia-Herzegovina, annexed some six years earlier.

Countess Sophie Chotek had won the Archduke's heart when she was a lady-in-waiting to his cousin Archduchess Isabella. However, in the eyes of Emperor Francis Joseph she was little better than a chambermaid. Distressed at his nephew's choice of a wife beneath royal status, the aged emperor fussed for a year before granting permission for the marriage. And as a price for his consent, he compelled Francis Ferdinand to renounce any right of rank or succession for his offspring. As a result, the three children, Ernst, Maximilian, and Sophie, as well as their mother, were continually snubbed in the ancient court of the Hapsburgs.

In 1909 Emperor Francis Joseph relented slightly and gave Sophie the title of Duchess of Hohenberg, thus allowing her to attend court functions at the Schönbrunn Palace. Even so court etiquette banned her from riding in the archducal carriage with her husband, nor could she sit with him in the royal box at the theater. And at court ceremonies the folding door was opened only halfway when Sophie made her entrance.

The visit to the Bosnia-Herzegovina province was motivated by the Archduke's desire to have his wife accorded the regal honors denied her in Vienna. As Inspector General of the Armed Forces, he would observe the annual maneuvers of the two Austrian army corps stationed there, and then visit the capital, Sarajevo. Traveling with her husband in his military capacity, Sophie would receive equal homage. Francis Ferdinand was enormously pleased at this double anniversary gift.

Six touring cars, their hoods folded back, were at the railway station when the brief visit to Sarajevo began. In the first car were Fehim Effendi Curcic, Mayor of Sarajevo, and his police commissioner, Dr. Gerde. The second auto carried Francis Ferdinand with Sophie on his right. General Oskar Potiorek, Military Governor of Bosnia, sat in the left folding seat. Next to the chauffeur rode Count Harrach, aide-de-camp to the Archduke.

It was a warm, sunny Sunday as the royal motorcade drove slowly through the heavily thronged but sparsely protected streets. Thousands of troops in the area were at field maneuvers. (At the Archduke's request, Sarajevo had been declared off limits; Francis

Francis Ferdinand and his family. Maximilian stands next to his mother with the young Ernst at left. Sophie, named after her mother, is in between.

6

Ferdinand did not want to associate his visit with a show of military power.) Only a thin cordon of gendarmes lined the route.

Milling Bosnians filled the streets in a festal mood, for June 28 was the feast of St. Vitus, or Vidovan, a special holiday to Balkan Slavs. Until 1912, Vidovan had been a day of national sorrow in remembrance of the Turkish victory at the battle of Kossovo in 1389, when the Kingdom of Serbia was destroyed and its Christian population enslaved. But since the Turkish defeat in the First Balkan War two years earlier, Vidovan had become a day of national jubilation.

From several accounts this joyous feeling was not dampened by the visiting Hapsburgs. Spectators applauded enthusiastically or politely, depending upon how they felt. Although the Archduke was not personally responsible for Bosnia's bondage, many viewed him as the symbol of Austrian oppression.

Lying in wait along the announced route were seven Serbian assassins, sworn to take the Archduke's life. The oldest was twenty-three; five were nineteen; and one was seventeen. Shortly after 10 A.M. the official cars entered Sarajevo. Taking advantage of the indifferent security, the conspirators positioned themselves along the main street, Appel Quay, parallel to the Miljacka River.

The first appeared as the motorcade crossed the Cumurja Bridge over the Miljacka in the City's center, and turned into Appel Quay. On the bridge stood Muhamed Mehmedbasic, the lone Muslim of the murder crew, but he did nothing. (Later he claimed a policeman stepped in front of him so that he was unable to throw his bomb.)

A short distance away Nedjelko Cabrinovic, aiming at the Archduke's plumed helmet, hurled his bomb. Spotting the gesture, the driver quickly accelerated and the bomb fell on the folded canvas hood and bounced to the ground where it exploded in front of the third car, blowing out its front tire. Flying fragments wounded Lieutenant Colonel Erik Merizzi, General Potiorek's adjutant, and several bystanders. Slightly injured was Countess Lanjus, Sophie's lady-in-waiting, who rode in the same car.

Swallowing the contents of a vial of cyanide, the would-be assassin leaped into the river, which was extremely low at that time. He was quickly fished out and within a few minutes several civilians dragged the vomiting youth along the river bank, drubbing him until policemen interceded. This Sarajevo-born printer was wretchedly ill from the poison, but managed to keep his wits and revealed nothing about the plot. Francis Ferdinand was more concerned over the injured victims than he was about Cabrinovic. "Come on," the Archduke urged, "the fellow is insane; let us go on with the program."

While the wounded were taken to a hospital, the party sped to City Hall, passing three more conspirators who made no attempt at assassination. Mayor Curcic, who rode in the lead car, apparently had not heard the explosion above the din and clamor of the crowds. As he was about to read his prepared welcome speech, he was startled by a tight grip on his arm. "Mr. Mayor," the furious Archduke hissed, "one comes here for a visit and is received with bombs! This is outrageous!" After a pause, he simmered down: "All right, now you may speak."

Still unaware of what occurred and confused by his visitor's outburst, Curcic gave a speech of extravagant praise, concluding: "God maintain His Royal and Imperial Apostolic Majesty, Our Most Gracious Lord Francis Joseph, Emperor and King." Meanwhile, Sophie had calmed her husband who responded graciously to the mayor's compliments and closed, "I assure you of my unchanged regard and favor."

This bizarre scene was described a quarter century later by the son of a local official, who had been present at the ceremony. Interviewed by Dame Rebecca West, who visited Sarajevo to collect material for her book on Yugoslavia, *Black Lamb & Grey Falcon*, the man recalled:

". . . we were all silent, not because we were impressed with him (Francis Ferdinand) for he was not at all our Bosnian idea of a hero. But we all felt awkward because we knew that

---

Gavrilo Princip (right) with co-conspirators. Trifko Grabez is at left and Djuro Sarac in the middle. The wan and sallow look of the three men is due partly to the imperfect photography of the time, partly to tuberculosis, from which several of the conspirators suffered.

when he went out he would certainly be killed. No, it was not a matter of being told. But we knew how the people felt about him and the Austrians, and we knew that if one man had thrown a bomb and failed, another man would throw another bomb, and another after that if he should fail. . . . It gave a very strange feeling to the assembly."

Immediately after the ceremony, Francis Ferdinand dispatched a telegram to the Emperor. He then asked General Potiorek whether they should continue with the announced afternoon plans and was assured that another attempt would be unlikely. Before resuming their schedule to visit the National Museum, however, the Archduke insisted on seeing the bomb victims at the military hospital. He urged Sophie not to accompany him. "No," she insisted, "I must go with you."

Outside City Hall cars were waiting to drive the party in the same order as before, except for one change in seating. Instead of sitting in the front next to the driver of the Archduke's car, Count Harrach stood on the left running board with hand on sword hilt to protect the royal couple. Since the first bomb had been hurled from the left side, the Count adopted this stance to prevent a possible repetition.

As the cortege reached a bridge immediately beyond City Hall, it passed within several feet of another plotter but he froze. The motorcade was scheduled to drive along the Quay to the hospital. However, the Mayor's driver had not been told of the changed plans and turned right into Francis Joseph Street toward the museum. He was obediently followed by the Archduke's chauffeur, who was also unaware of the altered schedule.

Seconds after the wrong turn was made, General Potiorek ordered the driver to reverse and turn in the opposite direction. The car stopped directly in front of Gavrilo Princip, the most determined of the conspirators. Quickly drawing a small Belgian pistol the nineteen-year-old slayer, only five feet away, fired point-blank twice. Count Harrach, still standing at the ready on the opposite running board, could only gape in horror.

The first bullet entered the Archduke's neck, clipping his jugular vein. Sophie's abdomen was pierced by the second slug, which severed an artery. For a few stunned moments the couple remained erect, staring glassily ahead. Believing them unharmed, but in danger of another attempt, Potiorek cancelled the hospital visit, and ordered the driver to return to the Military Governor's residence. As the car reversed to make the turn, Harrach leaned closer to speak; blood spurted from the Archduke's mouth onto his aide's right cheek.

At this, Sophie cried out, "For heaven's sake! What happened to you?" She then tumbled slowly from her seat, her face resting on her husband's knees. Summoning his remaining strength, the Archduke implored: "Sophie dear! Sophie dear! Don't die; stay alive for our children!" As his green-plumed general's helmet toppled off, Harrach held him up and asked, "Is your Imperial Highness suffering very badly?" In a steadily weakening voice the Archduke murmured, "It is nothing." He repeated these words a few times then lapsed into a coma. Shortly after 11 A.M. the Archduke and Archduchess were dead from internal bleeding.

After the double homicide, Princip raised the gun to his head, but a bystander grabbed his arm while police closed in. During a brief struggle he managed to gulp cyanide from a vial but, as in Cabrinovic's case, he developed intense cramps, retched, and vomited. The poison was either too dilute or too old.

Emperor Francis Joseph, at his summer villa at Bad Ischl near Salzburg, learned of the murder from his seventy-seven-year-old aide-de-camp Count Edouard Paar, who wrote the message on a pad as he heard it over the telephone. As he read the news, the aged monarch closed his eyes. "Horrible!" he then muttered. "The Almighty cannot be provoked with impunity. A Higher Power has restored the order which unfortunately I was unable to maintain," indicating the crime, however terrible, offered a desirable solution to problems confronting the Hapsburgs. He was apparently expressing awe at the Divine Retribution that

Two views of the capture of Princip. At the top, one policeman grabs him while another restrains passersby. Below, the prisoner is under control (although his coat seems partly ripped off) and is on his way to prison.

punished his heir for morganatic transgression against the dynasty.

Later that day the German Emperor received the news aboard his yacht *Hohenzollern*, while celebrating the nineteenth anniversary of the Kaiser Wilhelm (later renamed Kiel) Canal, which connected the North and Baltic seas. In a launch that drew alongside, an admiral folded his message in a gold cigarette case and pitched it toward waiting hands. Wilhelm was genuinely fond of Francis Ferdinand, his friend and hunting companion. Upon reading the report, he paled and retreated to his stateroom in silence.

Messages of sympathy came from all parts of the world. President Woodrow Wilson sent a telegram of "sincere condolences of the Government and people of the United States and my own expression of profound sympathy." King George V of England announced his court would observe seven days of mourning. Not to be outdone, Czar Nicholas displayed his sorrow for twelve days.

Sarajevo was quiet the rest of that fateful Sunday. Early the next morning roving bands of Croats and Muslims sacked the Serbian quarter to revenge the murder. Homes, schools, shops, and clubs were damaged and their occupants assaulted. Troops brought into the city by General Potiorek quickly established order, but not before some fifty persons were injured. The only death was that of a rioter who fell at the hands of Serbians defending themselves.

To the world at large this outbreak signified the end of a local incident. Seeming evidence of Austria's pacific intentions was offered when Finance Minister Leon von Bilinski allotted funds to repay the Serbs for injury and property damage, an act that drew angry objections from General Potiorek.

The Black Hand

Only one of the conspirators escaped, but the police more than compensated for the loss. By chance their dragnet of suspects and subversives included one Danilo Ilic, a member of the conspiracy. Until then Princip and his fellow prisoner steadfastly maintained that they alone had committed the crime. But the terrified Ilic,

who was twenty-three years old, offered to exchange information for his life. (Under Austrian law the death penalty applied only to criminals twenty years and older, and Ilic believed that both prisoners had confessed and implicated him.) By July 5, three other plotters were arrested. But Ilic had not admitted all— just enough to satisfy the police.

Although six prime suspects were firmly in hand, maladroit officials learned little. The Austrian government relinquished the case to a local police judge, Leo Pfeffer, who interrogated the six indifferently and haphazardly. Quickly assessing Pfeffer's incompetence, the prisoners kept changing answers and shifting explanations and thereby thoroughly confusing him. Their evasions and lies were shrewdly planned. Placed in separate but contiguous

cells, the six communicated with each other by tapping coded messages on their walls. Throughout the hot and crucial month of July, numerous leads emerged from their contradictory answers, but not a single one of them was followed up.

Pfeffer did learn that the bombs, pistols, and cyanide were brought from Serbia by a Milan Ciganovic, but he never detected the conspirators' connection with the Serbian terrorist society Union or Death, better known as the Black Hand. Founded in 1911 "to realize the national ideal, the unification of all Serbs," its members were mostly army officers and government officials. The judge also did not know that his six prisoners were tools of this homicidal band.

Colonel Dragutin Dimitrijevic, director of the Black Hand, was also the chief of the Serbian Army's Intelligence department. Nicknamed *Apis*, "the Bee," Dimitrijevic was a driven and driving staff officer who accepted violence almost as an end in itself.

Francis Ferdinand had been marked for death because he proposed upon becoming Emperor to supplant "dualism" with "triadism," giving Bosnia equal status with Austria and Hungary. Such a policy threatened the Black Hand's objective of a South Slav Union, for these reforms would diminish Slavic resentment and hostility toward the monarchy. Without deepseated discontent, Apis reasoned, Serbia would not be able to unite the Balkan peninsula.

Apis was no novice at terrorism. In 1903, at the age of twenty-six, he had been a ringleader

The royal funeral procession in Trieste. The bodies were taken to the mouth of the Neretva River where they were placed on the battleship *Viribus Unitis*. The ship then brought them to Trieste where they were sent inland by train. Because Hapsburg protocol denied Sophie burial in the royal crypt, they were interred under the chapel of the family castle of Francis Ferdinand.

Sarajevo

City Hall, from which Francis Ferdinand went to his death. The orange and buff striped building is now the library of the University of Sarajevo

View of the City Hall fronting on Appel Quay and the Miljacka River. The bridge in the center is the Princip Bridge, originally the Latin Bridge.

The Princip Bridge. The building at left housed Schiller's Delicatessen in 1914 and since 1953 has been a museum. Just the top of the plaque can be seen.

in the assassination of King Alexander Obrenovic and Queen Draga of Serbia. Breaking into the palace at night, the plotters had dragged the couple from a secret alcove, repeatedly shot and hacked both, then hurled the blood-smeared corpses from an upper story.

To forestall future heirs' of this dynasty claiming the throne, Apis personally murdered all surviving royal relatives within his reach. For good measure he also slew all the cabinet ministers who failed to flee the country. In 1911 he sent a youthful terrorist to Vienna to kill the emperor but the mission fizzled.

In the flux of Serbian rivalries, Prime Minister Nikola Pasic had prudently infiltrated the Black Hand with his own agents, one of whom informed him at the beginning of June, 1914, that Apis had marked Francis Ferdinand for death. Pasic issued a secret order for the arrest of the assassins at the Serbian frontier, but it was thwarted by guards belonging to the Black Hand.

The Prime Minister then notified Vienna through his ambassador, but in a manner so vague as to cause no alarm. Envoy Jovan Jovanovic, a Pan-Serb nationalist, conferred briefly with Austrian Finance Minister Bilinski, who was so lulled or unimpressed that he dismissed the matter without reporting it to his government. Whether Pasic's ambiguous warning was intentional or motivated by dread has never been established. A clear-cut warning, after all, might well have prompted the Austrian police to arrest the plotters, directing Black Hand suspicion to himself.

A veteran at intrigue and assassination, Pasic was gifted in the art of survival. In the 1880s he had fled Serbia for Austria when he faced death for an attempt on the life of King Milan. Following the assassination of King Alexander in 1903, Pasic returned to Serbia, which he ruled until his death in 1926 with few recesses. Pasic knew his Serbs well, and anticipated that

many would hail the assassins as heroes. He also knew that if his betrayal of the Black Hand conspirators became known, his political career—probably his life—would terminate abruptly. Pasic held his peace. Later on, in 1920, he had the bones of Gavrilo Princip, who had died on April 28, 1918, and those of his two fellow-murderers, transferred from a prison grave to a sepulcher of honor in a Sarajevo cemetery. The bridge where Princip shot the couple was named after him, and the assassin's footprints were embedded in the sidewalk where he stood at the fateful moment. A memorial erected in honor of the Archduke and his wife at the murder scene was replaced by a black marble plaque on the building wall facing the footprints, inscribed in gold: "On this historic spot, Gavrilo Princip initiated freedom on St. Vitus day, June 28, 1914."

During his eight remaining post-war years Pasic, the "Old Fox of the Balkans," persistently declined to disclose his knowledge of the murder plot or why he failed to act resolutely against what he must have anticipated would be a *casus belli*. This silence combined with his glorification of Princip suggests the Serbian regime was far from blameless.

Professional terrorists rarely die in bed. Almost invariably they acquire powerful enemies who settle final accounts. Apis was no exception. By the end of 1916, Pasic moved to destroy him and the Black Hand. After the Serbian Army had been mauled by the Austrians and retreated to Greece, Apis was arrested in Salonika and tried by a military tribunal. Among his co-defendants was Muhamed Mehmedbasic, the only Sarajevo conspirator who escaped. In a manifest frame-up, the Black Hand chieftain was accused of plotting the overthrow of Pasic's regime and signing peace with the nation's foes. Two days short of the third anniversary of the Sarajevo assassination, its organizer faced a firing squad of Serbian rifles.

ᴥᴥᴥᴥᴥᴥᴥᴥ

Europe on the eve of the War. Although Italy was nominally the ally of Germany and Austria-Hungary, the nature of the aggression against Serbia gave her the option of remaining neutral, which she did until 1915, when the Allies outbid the Central Powers for her services. Turkey joined the War later in 1914, Bulgaria in 1915, Romania in 1916. Greece flipflopped back and forth. Albania, Spain, Holland, Switzerland, and the Scandinavian countries remained neutral.

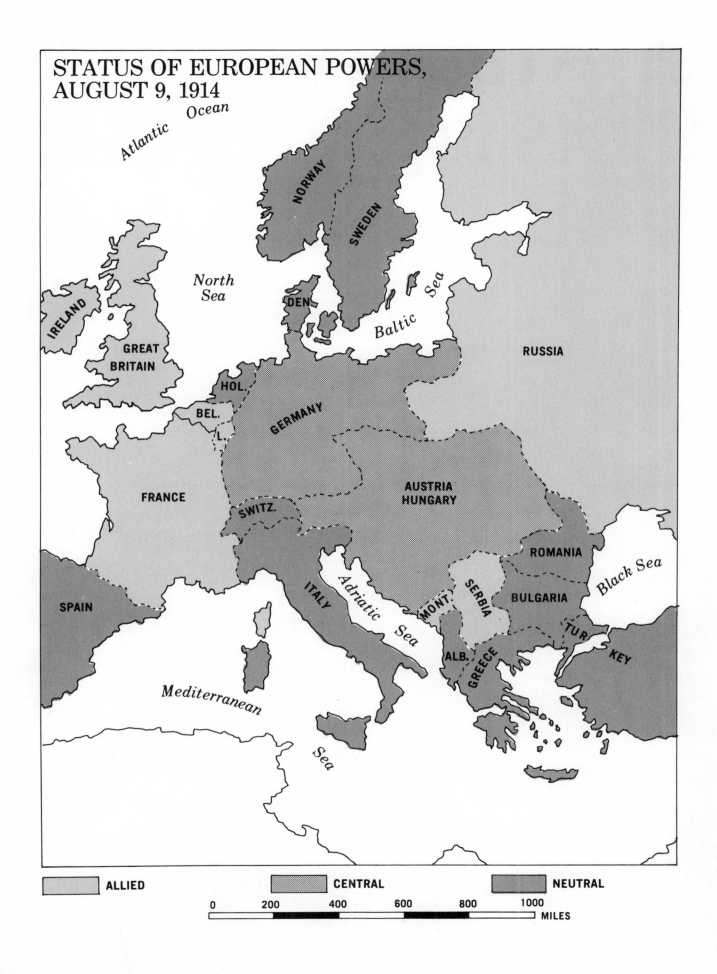

STATUS OF EUROPEAN POWERS,
AUGUST 9, 1914

Atlantic Ocean

NORWAY

SWEDEN

North Sea

IRELAND

GREAT BRITAIN

DEN.

Baltic Sea

RUSSIA

HOL.

BEL.

L.

GERMANY

FRANCE

SWITZ.

AUSTRIA HUNGARY

ROMANIA

Black Sea

SPAIN

ITALY

Adriatic Sea

MONT.

SERBIA

BULGARIA

ALB.

GREECE

TUR KEY

Mediterranean

Sea

| | ALLIED | | CENTRAL | | NEUTRAL |

0   200   400   600   800   1000
MILES

2. Austria
Plots Aggression

Kaiser Wilhelm II.

2. Austria Plots Aggression

For more than a week following the assassination, the Austrian Foreign Office remained silent, but much of the press and other agencies drummed up anti-Serbian sentiment. Viennese billboards proclaimed: *Alle Serben müssen sterben*, "All Serbians must die." But these seemed to be passing eruptions. Two days after the slain heir-presumptive and his wife were buried, Emperor Francis Joseph returned to his summer villa, without having attended the burial.

Faithful Count Paar, Francis Joseph's aide-de-camp, brushed aside any suggestion that his monarch looked forward to a conflict. "This is just another of those tragic occurrences," he explained, "which have been so frequent in the Emperor's life. I don't think he considers it in any other light." Paar was alluding to the tragedy at Mayerling in 1889, when Crown Prince Rudolph shot and killed his seventeen-year-old mistress, Baroness Vetsera, then committed suicide, and to the assassination, nine years later, of the Empress Elisabeth by an anarchist.

Paar apparently did not realize that events were taking a new turn in Vienna. After Apis, the man most elated at the Archduke's demise was Count Leopold von Berchtold, the Austrian Foreign Minister, who had long sought an opportunity to destroy Serbia. He was joined by the Austrian Chief of Staff, General Baron Franz Conrad von Hötzendorf. Several years earlier, Conrad had prodded the Emperor to

wage a preventative war against Serbia, but had been rebuffed.

Berchtold (Poldi to his intimates) was a dandified fop whose ministerial qualifications were an aristocratic, wealthy, and influential family. He now had recourse to a document against Serbia, previously prepared and held for an opportune occasion. But before approaching the point of no return, he called on Kaiser Wilhelm for support. On July 5, the German Emperor and his chancellor, Theobald von Bethmann-Hollweg, assured Berchtold that Austria could "count on it with certainty that Germany would stand behind her as an ally and a friend."

That same day, General Conrad visited the Austrian monarch, seeking his nod for war, but the eighty-two-year-old ruler still had full command of his senses: ". . . and how can we wage war if they all jump on us, especially Russia?" To which the General replied: "But do we not have German re-insurance?" Eying him quizzically, the cautious sovereign asked, "Are you sure of Germany?"

To get the requisite assurance, Count Alexander Hoyos, Berchtold's chef-de-cabinet, entrained for Berlin with a query from Francis Joseph to Kaiser Wilhelm, to be transmitted by the Austrian envoy in Berlin, Count Marish Szögyeny. Could Austria, Francis Joseph asked, rely on Germany if she proceeded against Serbia? At a pleasant Sunday luncheon with the Kaiser, Szögyeny received an answer. No

Count Leopold von Berchtold (right) confers with the Italian Minister of Foreign Affairs, the Marchese di San Giuliano. The Austro-German strategy was to persuade the Italians to fight on their side if possible, otherwise to keep them neutral.

Helmuth von Moltke, Germany's
Chief of the Imperial General Staff
in 1914 and the principal architect
of the two-front war — against both
France and Russia.

record was made of the conversation, but Ambassador Szögyeny reported that "even if matters went to the length of war between Austria-Hungary and Russia, we could remain assured that Germany, in her customary loyalty as an ally, would stand at our side."

None of the Kaiser's ministers attended the repast. Admiral Alfred von Tirpitz was vacationing in Switzerland. Chief of Staff Helmuth von Moltke was drinking the waters at Karlsbad. Later that day Chancellor Bethmann-Hollweg was the first ranking official to hear the news. Next day the other ministers were told of their Emperor's binding commitment. Although none demurred, Wilhelm seemed eager to assuage any uneasiness. "I do not believe in any serious warlike developments," he commented to the naval chief. "The Czar will not place himself on the side of regicides. Besides, neither Russia nor France is prepared for war."

Upon settling matters of the day, Wilhelm's white and gold yacht sailed northward for a twenty-day cruise through the Norwegian fiords. With their Kaiser away, most ministers also went on vacation. Later, Winston Churchill would dryly note that Wilhelm's pledge was "a blank check valid against the resources of the whole German Empire, to fill out at pleasure."

When Francis Joseph received the Kaiser's blank check, his peaceful sentiments abruptly deserted him. "Now we can no longer turn back," he muttered. "It will be a terrible war."

Count Istvan Tisza, the Hungarian Prime Minister, feared an invasion of Serbia would invite war with Russia. He also suspected, with good reason, that an annexed Serbia would reduce Hungary's position to that of a very junior partner with Austria in the Dual Monarchy. Berchtold solemnly averred that Serbia would remain independent, yet his file contained plans for dismembering Serbia. Deceived by Berchtold, Tisza reluctantly agreed to support Austria.

Alfred von Tirpitz, the organizer of the
German navy. He advocated a naval
showdown with the British fleet as well as
all-out submarine warfare. He resigned his
post in 1916, two months before the
Battle of Jutland.

Theobald von Bethmann-Hollweg,
Chancellor of the German Empire.

Count Berchtold.

A German artillery reserve unit, photographed in 1911. The signs on the cannons ("To London" and "To Paris") leave little doubt that the German army was both well prepared and motivated when war came in 1914.

At exactly 6 P.M. on July 23, the Austrian Envoy, Baron Vladimir von Giesl, handed his nation's ultimatum to the Serbian government. The date and hour were determined in advance for strategic reasons. Eight days before, French President Raymond Poincaré and Premier René Viviani had cruised to Saint Petersburg for a state visit. They were scheduled to begin their return trip on the afternoon of July 23, and Berchtold wanted them well out to sea when his demands were made.

So determined was the Austrian Minister to defeat and crush Serbia that his ultimatum precluded the remotest possibility of negotiation. One of the harshest demands was for unlimited access into Serbia and interference by Austrian bureaucrats in directing the investigation of the Sarajevo conspiracy. In light of Austria's total ignorance of Apis and his Black Hand, this intrusion into Serbia's domestic affairs was a deliberate provocation on the part of the Austrians.

Another clause insisted that Belgrade disclaim "the unhealthy propaganda" generated against Austrian subjects, a measure to be taken under Austrian overseers. Berchtold and his confederates gave Serbia a mere forty-eight hours to knuckle under. Wilhelm was relaxing aboard his yacht in northern waters when news of the ultimatum reached him next morning. After reading the text, he assumed an air of light-hearted banter. "A spirited note, what?" he quipped to his naval aide, Admiral von Müller.

Several minutes before the forty-eight hour deadline, a tall dignified man with a flowing white beard appeared at the Austrian Embassy. Prime Minister Pasic brought his government's reply. The document bore much evidence of anguished debate among the ministers. It had been amended and reamended until the last moment. The only typewriter had been jammed into disrepair by an exhausted secretary. Copies in Pasic's envelope were handwritten.

It was certainly not diplomatic practice for a prime minister, however small his realm, to act as messenger. As the time came to deliver the document, Pasic had turned to his ministers who, by their misery, left no doubt the task was his. Ambassador Giesl surmised the contents before Pasic announced respectfully:

"Part of your demands we have accepted . . . for the rest we place our hopes on your loyalty and chivalry as an Austrian general."

The Serbian government's reply was propitiatory and hopeful. It reminded Vienna of her peaceful attitude during the Balkan wars. Serbia was prepared to condemn officially the actions of individuals who were anti-Austrian, but she could not accept two demands that violated her sovereignty. If Austria was dissatisfied, Belgrade offered to submit to arbitration before the Hague Court.

Wilhelm accepted this reply. Since Serbia had prostrated herself, he declared, the cause of war had evaporated. Austria should take a mortgage on Serbia as a "hostage territory," he recommended, until she fulfilled her pledge. Russian Foreign Minister Sergei Sazonov also accepted Serbia's reply, and offered to negotiate with Vienna. But Austria was determined to destroy Serbia; a diplomatic victory would not suffice. Even before the forty-eight hour limit of the ultimatum, Austrian troops were mobilized along the Serbian frontier.

News of the break with Serbia, following publication of the ultimatum, caused alarm on the continent. Russia notified Austria that an attack against Serbia would cause prompt mobilization. Since Berchtold planned only a localized assault against Serbia, he relied on his German ally to force Russia to back down. His misunderstanding of recent history only hastened the conflict.

In 1908, St. Petersburg had watched in helpless anger while Austria annexed Russia's "little Slav brothers," Bosnia and Herzegovina. At that time the Czarist regime was still exhausted from its defeat by Japan in the war of 1904–1905, followed by revolutionary uprisings that were suppressed with great difficulty in 1906. But by 1914 Russia felt sufficiently recovered to mobilize.

Berchtold's aggressiveness was buoyed by the highest German figures. General von Moltke insisted "the unusually favorable situation

---

Russia managed to mobilize her troops at a speed that astonished and troubled the Central Powers. The vast numbers of men involved were brought to staging areas by cart, horse, or by train.

German forces mobilizing in Berlin. In 1914 troops marched cockily through the city with bands playing and sightseers cheering. As the War dragged on, these scenes lost this aura of festivity.

should be used to strike," stressing that "France's military situation is nothing less than embarrassed, that Russia is anything but confident; moreover the time of the year is favorable."

Berlin's Foreign Minister Gottlieb von Jagow believed Austrian boldness plus German support would "most likely keep Russia quiet." To this threat the Czar's Foreign Minister, Sazonov, responded ominously: "Russia cannot allow Austria to crush Serbia and become the predominant power in the Balkans." By now the Kaiser felt that bluff and threats were getting out of hand and urged discussions to resolve the dispute. But his own military juggernaut was gathering momentum and could not be stopped.

Because Russia's alliance with France would aggravate the crisis, British Foreign Minister Edward Grey entered the situation on July 26th, suggesting a meeting of Germany, France, England, and Italy to arbitrate the Austro-Serbian feud. Berlin flatly rejected his offer, contending the issue concerned only the two countries involved. The central thrust of Austro-German strategy was to localize the conflict, allowing Austria to destroy Serbia while German military muscle deterred Russia from acting.

On July 27, Grey again suggested mediation. Possibly at the Kaiser's urging, Chancellor Bethmann-Hollweg recommended in a letter to Berchtold that he reconsider Grey's overture. Refusal to agree, he added, would lead world opinion to believe Austria and Germany were deliberately starting a war. By way of reply, Austria declared war against Serbia on July 28. The following day Berchtold replied, regretting he could not consider Grey's suggestion because it was "overtaken by events."

To assure his Emperor's signature on the declaration of war, Berchtold placed a report before him alleging that Serbian soldiers had fired at Austrian troop transports on the Danube. The document ended with proud defiance, ". . . the more so as Serbian troops have already attacked a detachment of Imperial and Royal troops at Temes-Kubin." Not one Serbian shot had been fired. It was a complete lie contrived to propel the reluctant monarch into war.

Point of No Return

All hopes of "localization" were abandoned when Russia ordered general mobilization on July 29. Two days later Berlin dispatched ultimatums to Saint Petersburg and Paris. Russia was ordered to "suspend every war measure against Austria and ourselves within twelve hours," and "definitely notify us of this." Foreign Minister Sazonov explained the time period was too brief to end mobilization, but Russian troops would not move beyond their frontier so long as negotiations continued among them.

Czar Nicholas, who had no taste for war, wired Wilhelm: "Understand that you are obliged to mobilize, but wish to have the same guarantee from you as I gave you that these measures do not mean war, and that we shall continue negotiating . . . ." Berlin replied with a declaration of war on August 1.

The ultimatum to France demanded to know her attitude "in a Russo-German War." Giving Paris eighteen hours to answer, Berlin brandished her mailed fist, adding, "mobilization will inevitably mean war." The German militarists had long planned a preventive war against France. As their overall plans were devised for a two-front conflict, one way or another France was to be forced into battle. If she announced neutrality, the Berlin envoy was ordered to demand that the fortresses of Verdun and Toul be placed under German military control.

Although France had only eighteen hours to reply, Germany waited until August 3 to declare war. Wilhelm and his Chancellor — unlike the General Staff — were beset by doubts of a two-front war, and began to seek means of avoiding it. They seized British Minister Grey's latest recommendation that so long as hope existed for a peaceful solution among Russia, Austria, and Germany, France should remain militarily neutral.

Toward this end the French civil government ordered border troops to withdraw more than six miles behind the frontier as evidence of peaceful intent. But German patrols began crossing into France four days before war was declared.

A French sentry at Belfort in the morning of August 2 challenged a German cavalry patrol

Not every thought was bent on war, even in Germany in 1914. Here an army unit is overtaking pitchmen advertising "Captain Kleinschmidt's Polar Journey," currently playing at the Astoria Theater.

Sir Edward Grey, the Foreign Secretary of Great Britain. He is probably best remembered for his remark on the eve of the War: "The lamps are going out all over Europe. We shall never see them lit again in our time."

Grave Parisians examine the latest poster on a billboard devoted to
military news: the conscription of horses, mares, and mules of both
sexes — an essential step in mobilizing the French forces.

led by a lieutenant, who promptly fired at the soldier. The poilu aimed his rifle and fired three times, killing the officer. Corporal André Peugeot then dropped his gun, staggered a few steps and fell dead—the first soldiers killed on the Western Front. When open hostilities were announced on August 3, Chancellor Beth-mann-Hollweg was ready with a pretext. He accused France of sending a pilot to drop "bombs on the railway at Karlsruhe and Nuremberg."

Prince Karl Lichnowsky, German Ambassa-dor to London, was an ardent advocate of peace between his nation and the West. In a telegram to Berlin, expressing wishful thinking rather than fact, he said Grey's suggestion "would appear to mean that, in case we did not attack France, England would remain neutral and would guarantee France's neutrality." Facing Chief of Staff Moltke, the elated Kaiser an-nounced, "We march, then, with all our forces, only toward the east."

Moltke was distressed. According to his memoirs, he urged his sovereign to banish such thoughts, for "this was impossible. The ad-vance of armies formed of millions of men . . . was the result of years of painstaking work. Once planned, it could not possibly be changed." He was pained by the Kaiser's brusque retort, "Your uncle would have given me a different reply," referring to Moltke the elder, the grand strategist of German military victories in the nineteenth century.

Wilhelm finally yielded to Moltke's en-treaty, but insisted that crossing the frontiers of Luxembourg and France be postponed for twenty-four hours. Moltke lamented in his diary: "It was a great shock to me, as though something had struck my heart." By nightfall his heartache vanished as "good news" from London clearly indicated that England would not guarantee neutrality. The relieved Chief of Staff promptly ordered invasion timetables set in motion. His forces operated with such a high degree of efficiency that German troops entered Luxembourg a full day ahead of schedule.

Waiting for news. Berliners are assembled outside a newspaper office in the Alexanderplatz, waiting for the latest dispatch from the front. High on his pedestal, his back turned, is the statue of Bismarck.

While Britain hoped the continental dispute would resolve in peaceful agreement, her irresolute Cabinet offered neither guidance nor leadership. A strong warning might have stopped Germany. In a meeting at his office, French President Poincaré told the British Ambassador: "If England will make an immediate declaration of her intention to support France, there will be no war and Germany will at once modify her attitude." But London temporized until her only choice was to join the fray.

Since the Franco-German border was too strongly fortified for an easy invasion, German troops first invaded Luxembourg on August 2, over the protest of the ruler of that tiny principality. That same day Berlin demanded that Belgium permit unlimited passage of German forces to invade France. This was in violation of a pact signed in 1839 by England and Germany, among other nations, underwriting Belgium's perpetual neutrality. King Albert's response to this demand was unequivocal. Belgium "would not sacrifice her honor as a nation and at the same time betray her duty to Europe." She "would repel by all means in her power every attack on her rights."

Britain's signing the Belgian neutrality pact was motivated by more than just a lofty concern for a small, weak state. Her maritime dominance could not abide having a major land power (such as Germany) control a vital stretch of channel coast, including the first-rate port complex of Antwerp. When the Germans invaded Belgium on August 4, England officially entered the conflict, the only nation to declare war against Germany. British dominions Canada, Australia, and New Zealand became belligerents, and South Africa joined in January, 1915.

Bethmann-Hollweg was furious with Britain for going to war over "a scrap of paper," as he termed London's pledge to perpetuate Belgian neutrality. His clumsy remark would be exploited by Allied propagandists with devastating effect.

Several days after the hostilities began, his predecessor, Prince Bernhard von Bülow, inquired with an air of bewilderment, "How did it all happen?" Raising his long, thin arms in helpless gesture, Bethmann-Hollweg muttered, "Ah, if only I knew." Confessing even a lack of hindsight did not abash the Chancellor. A few moments later, he switched to soothsaying: "I count on a war of not more than three, or perhaps at the very most four, months, and I am basing our whole policy on that."

The combat lineup soon included other nations. Montenegro joined Serbia against Austria. Turkey, long alarmed at Russia's designs on Constantinople, aligned herself with the Central Powers. Italy announced neutrality, claiming that Austria and Germany had voided their treaty by committing aggression, and in 1915 declared war against her former partners. Bulgaria soon entered the Central Powers' camp; all the Balkan countries were eventually drawn in.

In the Far East, Japan was pledged to support her ally England, a treaty she happily exploited by ejecting the German garrison from the strategic Chinese port city of Kiaochow in Shantung province. India, a colony of England, was automatically committed. Within three years the United States would enter, the last of the global powers to become enmeshed.

Germany's Crown Prince (at right in doorway)
and the King of Saxony, reviewing a detachment
of goose-stepping infantry.

3. Strength
and Strategy

Uhlans, advancing.

3. Strength and Strategy

Universal military service and improved railway networks enabled most of the belligerents to mobilize reserves behind their professional armies quickly. In a matter of months, Germany raised her standing army from 791,000 to 5,000,000; Austria-Hungary, 450,000 to 3,350,000; France 790,000 to 4,000,000; and Russia, 1,200,000 to 6,000,000. England had no large standing army; the British Expeditionary Force (BEF) of 160,000 was later increased to 975,000, including Dominion and Colonial troops.

The opposing armies were organized in similar formations, but their units varied in size. A division ranged from 12,000 to 22,000 men. One division was normally commanded by a major-general. Two or more divisions ranked as a corps, led by a lieutenant-general. Two or more corps became an army headed by a general. Some nations, especially Germany, designated their armies numerically. Armies, corps and divisions had a general staff of four or five sections, usually comprising administration, intelligence, operations, supply, and training.

In descending order, a division consisted of two or more brigades, each commanded by a brigadier-general, sometimes called a brigadier; a brigade represented two or more regiments, each under a colonel; a regiment equalled three or more battalions, each headed by a lieutenant-colonel; a battalion was formed by four companies, each commanded by a major or captain; and a company was made up of four platoons, each under the command of a lieutenant.

Most of the fighting was done by infantry, cavalry, and artillery, but technological advances produced service troops that equalled, and often exceeded, the number of front-line troops. The less industrially developed nations, such as Austria and Russia, continued their reliance on outmoded concepts of warfare. Cavalry, a hangover from the nineteenth century, played a major role only in the first months of the conflict. A cavalry brigade usually consisted of three regiments amounting to 9,200 troops and 9,800 horses.

Cavalry in those days represented the military elite. German Uhlans, wearing ornate helmets, dashed into action with spears and sabers flying, only to be mowed down by massed fire. French and English horsemen fared no better. Machine guns and high-explosive shells soon relegated horses to relative rear-line safety and to transport use, compelling their former riders to battle ingloriously on foot.

Artillery was formed into batteries of four to eight guns. Three to four batteries comprised a

A huge gun from the famed Skoda works in Plzen (often written Pilsen), Bohemia. The city also has given its name to the light, carbonated beer that it pioneered and made famous.

Armor and
Armaments

The Germans were the first to introduce battle helmets. Here shown are the various stages of manufacture from steel disk to finished helmet, patterned on those of the Imperial Roman Legions.

The body armor (left) given out to the Italian forces was primitive to the point of being medieval.

German armor (right) found in the Argonne in 1918, modelled by an American officer.

The interior of the vast Krupp armament plant in Essen, Germany.

Early German horse-drawn howitzer.

British body armor of 1917.

group, or battalion; two or three groups equalled a regiment. Range of fire had increased by this time far enough to enable artillery to rain shells on targets well beyond anything the soldiers manning the guns could see, so airplanes and balloons were used to spot enemy targets and report hits and misses.

Initially, the Germans and Austrians excelled in cannon. The Krupp works in Essen, Germany, and the Skoda works in Bohemia were the most redoubtable armament factories in all Europe. France's 75-mm. gun was light, mobile, and the fastest cannon in existence, but this three-inch piece was effective only against exposed troops. It was inadequate for long-distance shelling and outmatched by the powerful German howitzer. Furthermore, the French General Staff eyed artillery as a secondary or inferior supplement to infantry; *esprit de corps*, they believed, would more than compensate for any technological deficiencies. (French vision had not progressed much beyond that of United States Civil War generals, who treated artillery as an unwanted stepchild.)

In 1914 Germany had 3,500 medium and heavy cannon compared to fewer than 300 guns for the French. Each German army corps had thirty-six 105-mm. howitzers plus sixteen 150-mm. howitzers. Germany also had more than 4,500 machine guns compared to France's 2,500, and was superior even in light artillery with more than 6,000 77-mm. guns to 3,500 French 75s.

Russia's greatest menace to the Central Powers lay in its 6,000,000 troops, but that much vaunted steamroller moved with ponderous inefficiency. The largely illiterate army consisted of brave men, but they were poorly trained by an officer staff of aristocrats and moneyed men with influence, whose knowledge of warfare was limited to the use of saber and sword. On the other hand, their talent for graft was highly developed.

Russia's handicap was further increased by her enormous land area and undeveloped railway system. Her access to seas was blocked by ice or enemy patrols. Often the front lines lacked artillery and machine guns. Many soldiers did not even have rifles—units frequently went into action with some men armed only with a bayonet tied to a stick.

When British historian Bernard Pares visited the front in 1915, a Russian soldier sadly remarked, "You know, sir, we have no weapon except the soldier's breast." To which another added, "This is not war, sir; it is slaughter." In the first war year, Russian casualties amounted to 2,000,000.

All physically fit German youth were subject to military service and no eligible youth, however influential his family, could avoid conscription. Two or three years' time was required, depending on the branch of service, followed by five and one half years in the regular reserves; then transfer to the Landwehr, a second reserve, for twelve years, and at the age of thirty-nine to the Landsturm, a last reserve, until their forty-fifth birthday. Behind these were units of men unsuitable for any service except limited duties in the rear and quiet sectors.

Unlike other nations, Germany developed a highly efficient cadre of officers and noncommissioned officers, capable of molding a mass of recruits and reserves into a superior fighting force. At the outbreak of hostilities, some 2,000,000 men were integrated around the nucleus of well-trained professional soldiers.

A close comradeship between German officers and men, unknown in the armies of the democratic nations, had been introduced by Field Marshal von Moltke in the nineteenth century and continued by his successors. German officers were as concerned about the welfare of their troops as they were with the maintenance of their well-oiled guns. During the conflict, when some commanders sent soldiers needlessly to death, the German generals were least inefficient and least wasteful with their troops.

Germany also had an initial advantage in small-arms weaponry. The infantry was armed with the Mauser rifle, so sturdy and accurate that even today it is one of the most popular guns among sportsmen. The German General Staff also understood the strategic value of the Maxim machine gun.

Austria-Hungary bore the disadvantage of a multilingual empire. Most officers were Germanic, but only twenty-five percent of its troops spoke German. The Dual Monarchy neither cared nor was able to unite its divers nationalities. "Often a platoon commander could not make himself intelligible to his motley collection," admits Austrian official history very frankly.

The Schlieffen Plan

In 1870, the French government of Emperor Louis Napoleon had effectively committed suicide by declaring war against Prussia. The Prussians had crushed the French Army in battles along their common frontier, then marched unopposed to surround and vanquish Paris. To eliminate any future French military threat, the new united Germany annexed Alsace and the part of Lorraine containing the fortress city of Metz, leaving France exposed to future invasion.

French military engineers then proceeded to construct a chain of fortresses that centered around four cities along the 150-mile Franco-German border. Beginning at the southeast, where the Swiss Alps present an impregnable barrier, massive concrete fortresses radiated from Belfort, Epinal, Toul, and Verdun. One wide gap was planned between Epinal and Toul as a huge trap into which the enemy was expected to enter, then be annihilated by cross fire from well-protected concrete encasements. Some twenty miles north of Verdun were Luxembourg, Belgium, and the rugged Ardennes forest.

Confronted with this formidable bastion, Count Alfred von Schlieffen, the German Chief of Staff from 1891 to 1906, had devised a strategy of invading France through the wide, level plains of Belgium. This small, industrialized country offered an easy route with abundant railways, roads, rivers, and canals and her border with France was unfortified. General Schlieffen was incensed at her fortified strongholds in Liège and Namur, facing Germany, which prompted him to complain that Belgium's military defenses were devised ". . . to prevent Germany from invading its territory, but toward France it left its frontiers open." That the reason lay in fear of Germany but not of France the General pretended not to know.

An able strategist, Schlieffen was one of the best-read men in military history. He drew much of his inspiration from the Battle of

British artillery firing at night. As the men are not wearing helmets the picture would seem to date from 1914.

German Reservists

The lowest echelon, the "schipper," kept out of regular service by reason of bad health or some sort of disability. Clad in nondescript "fatigue" uniforms, they performed cleanup jobs in safe areas.

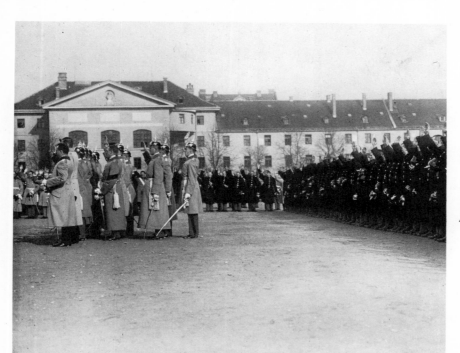

A reserve unit takes the oath.

Members of the Landwehr, the second line of reservists, pose by the soup kettle. Judging by the paunch on some of them, their commitment was more to the table than it was to the trenches.

Members of the Landsturm ranged in age from 39 to 44. Above, a Landsturm contingent is shown on its way to occupation duty in Antwerp. These forces also tilled the land to grow food for the army, as is shown in the picture at right.

Cannae (216 B.C.), where Hannibal had defeated the stronger Romans by encircling both wings and rear. General Schlieffen's similar plan centered on Metz, the German city nearest the French border, 178 miles from Paris.

With the fortified area as a pivot, seventy-nine divisions forming the right wing would blitz through Belgium into France, immediately followed by secondary reserves such as the Landwehr. The smaller left wing of eight divisions would remain at the Franco-German border. Sweeping in a pivotal movement akin to an enormous revolving door, the German forces would spread to the French coastal areas, enveloping Paris from the north, west, and south, then would wheel eastward.

If the French soldiers left their Lorraine fortresses to drive the eight stationary German divisions toward the Rhine, so much the better. In this event, the eastern-moving Germans would hammer the French from the rear. The French fortress guns faced only Germany and could not be turned westward against Germans attacking from France.

General Schlieffen charted his strategy to include a British expeditionary force of 100,000 "operating in conjunction with the French." Taking into account that Russia's primitive railway system would result in a snail-like pace of mobilization, Schlieffen programmed only ten divisions for the Eastern Front to delay Czarist troops until France was overwhelmed. On his deathbed, the great tactician reportedly urged: "It must come to war . . . make the right wing strong."

His successor, General Moltke, altered the plan to meet what he considered different conditions. Instead of reinforcing the right wing, he reduced its strength by one-third and added eight divisions to the left wing—a fortunate stroke for France. Because of other obstacles and delays, Moltke so shortened the German line of invasion pivoting from Metz, that

Resignation and disgust register on these men in another bout with General Mud. The combination of frustration, boredom, tension, and fear resulted in extremely high suicide rates among the troops.

his troops passed to the east of Paris without enveloping it. Weeks later, when the Germans attempted to capture Paris in a frontal assault, they were repulsed in the Battle of the Marne.

School of Attack

Although the French fortress system was the best of its day, increasing numbers of younger officers had begun to question the static defensive strategy that dominated the General Staff. This new school of attack found their spokesman in Colonel Loiseau de Grandmaison, whose views influenced General Joseph Joffre, elevated to Chief of General Staff in 1912.

The doctrine of attack to the bitter end was officially accepted in early 1914, and called Plan XVII because it was the seventeenth plan approved since 1870. It contained no provision for even makeshift earthworks or fortifications. Colonel Grandmaison was clear and to the point: "For attack only two things are necessary: to know where the enemy is and to decide what to do. What the enemy intends to do is of no importance."

Early combat experiences revealed that Plan XVII was a disaster. The French forces made

Troops board British transports heading for combat.

The Schlieffen Plan. Here is shown the vast cartwheel envisioned by ▶ Schlieffen to circle around and behind Paris, then come up and attack the French fortress system from the rear.

their appearance on the battlefield in the best nineteenth-century formation with smartly groomed officers, wearing white gloves, marching sixty feet in advance of their troops, who wore dusk-blue jackets and scarlet trousers. Regimental pennants and brass bands accompanied them to strike fear and terror in enemy hearts.

Observing the resultant carnage, a British officer recalled: "Whenever French infantry advance, their whole front is at once regularly covered with shrapnel and the unfortunate men are knocked over like rabbits. They are very brave and advance time after time to the charge through appalling fire, but so far it has been of no avail. No one could live through the fire that is concentrated on them. The officers are splendid. They advance about twenty yards ahead of their men as calmly as though on parade, but so far I have not seen one of them get more than fifty yards without being knocked over."

Plan XVII soon became another dead leaf in French military history. Perhaps its fitting epitaph was the bullet-shattered body of Colonel Grandmaison, slain in a madcap infantry charge. At appalling cost in lives and territory, the French General Staff was finally forced to recognize that defensive measures also play an integral role in modern warfare.

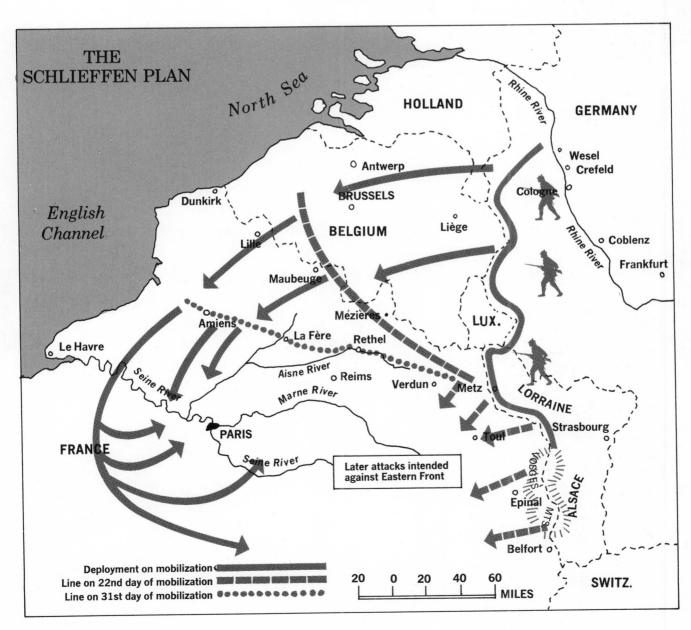

4. Invasion of Belgium

General Gérard Leman.

4. Invasion of Belgium

Germany's complex railway system, planned and developed by the Army, had officers assigned to supervise every line. No rail section, down to the shortest spur, could be laid or altered without the approval of the Chief of General Staff. The two-way tracks running to the western border allowed 550 trains daily to cross the Rhine bridges; in twenty days they transported more than 3,100,000 men in 11,000 trains. Every ten minutes, during the first two weeks of war, a long, troop-laden train rolled across the bridge at Cologne.

More than 1,200,000 of these soldiers were to form the swinging arm that would sweep through Belgium and Luxembourg into France. Because Holland's neutrality would not be violated, despite Schlieffen's plan, this enormous body of men had to advance through an area about seventy-five miles wide. The timetable allowed no margin for delay—troop advance had been scheduled to crush France before she had time to mobilize fully.

But no invasion of Belgium could succeed without conquering Liège, the strongly fortified gateway beyond which lay open plains—and France. Four rail lines from Germany converged at this strategic city then fanned out. Liège is built astride the Meuse River on a high slope, with a view commanding all approaches. Twelve powerful forts—six on either side of the river—ringed an area some ten miles in diameter. Their mutual-support system was limited

by three-mile gaps between each fort, but mobile troops to be dispatched as needed were considered effective substitutes.

On the morning of August 4, German advance units approached Visé on the Meuse River, only to discover that the bridge had been demolished and that Belgian soldiers were massed on the western bank. General Otto von Emmich, commanding two cavalry divisions and six infantry brigades, soon elected a suitable alternative. Two cavalry regiments rode three miles south where they forded the river. Fearing encirclement, the Belgian defenders at Visé quickly retreated southward toward Liège. By evening the German infantrymen had also crossed the Meuse at Visé and were heading toward the citadel.

Within hours of their invasion the Germans began shooting civilians in retaliation against sniper fire. Hostages were rounded up to be executed; homes were shelled or burned down. If house-to-house fighting developed, field guns quickly leveled the village. "Our advance in Belgium is certainly brutal," wrote Moltke to

---

The Belgian nightmare of 1914 consisted in part of German troops, row after row, day after day, from morning until night, boots thudding methodically along the dusty roads, ceasing only at nightfall to be replaced by chorus after lusty chorus of patriotic German songs late into the night. And in the morning, more endless rows of marching boots.

The ruins of Fort Loncin, pounded to bits by the new German siege gun.
The solitary soldier to the left of center gives some feeling of the scope and
enormity of the devastation.

General Conrad, "but we are fighting for our lives and all who get in the way must take the consequences."

German strategy envisioned an almost uninterrupted march through Belgium, expecting little if any resistance. In her eighty-three years of existence, King Albert's nation had never fought a war, and because of Belgium's security as a "perpetually neutral state" militarism was scorned. But Kaiser Wilhelm's saber-rattling had impelled the Belgian government to introduce military conscription in 1913, a measure that further diminished the already low esteem for the army. Until 1910 the army didn't even have a general staff.

King Albert's newly mobilized army consisted of 165,000 troops, about half of them deployed between Liège and Brussels. Belgian strategy relied on the forts of Liège and Namur to delay the enemy until French and British forces could arrive. General Gérard Leman, commander of Liège, was sent reserves which raised his manpower to 40,000, and was ordered by Albert to defend Liège "to the end."

The Liège fortifications had been planned by General Henri Brialmont, an outstanding military engineer, about twenty-five years before their completion in 1913. Shaped as flat, triangular buttes of reinforced concrete with steel gun cupolas, they bristled with 400 weapons ranging from machine guns to 8-inch cannon. The structure itself was designed to withstand bombardment by shells up to this size. Turrets in each corner of a triangle were armed with rapid-firing guns of smaller caliber.

Each fort was circled by a thirty-foot-deep dry moat; powerful searchlights were added to prevent a surprise night attack. As with the heavy guns, these lights could be lowered beneath the surface where subterranean tunnels interconnected the system. All the guns dominated the four rail lines leading from Germany. General Leman retained 25,000 fortress troops, and sent one division to strengthen King Albert's army situated on the Gette River covering Brussels.

Still believing that the Belgians would surrender without further struggle, von Emmich sent an emissary under a flag of truce demanding the surrender of Liège; otherwise, he announced, the city would be bombed from the air. Heeding his King's order, Leman refused.

55

Within hours German cannon rained shells on the eastern forts and the city itself, but did little more than chip away some concrete. The next day, a diesel-powered zeppelin flew over from nearby Cologne and dropped thirteen bombs, killing nine civilians. Thus began a new dimension in warfare.

Waves of German troops charged again and again, particularly the eastern forts of Fléron and Evegnée, only to be cut down by combined artillery and machine-gun fire as corpses piled up waist high before the forts. All the Meuse bridges above and below Liège were destroyed and troops attempting to cross the Meuse in pontoons were raked with gunfire.

Only one German assault was even partly successful. When the 14th Infantry Brigade's commander was slain, his troops encountered General Erich Ludendorff, the Second Army's Deputy Chief of Staff, who promptly assumed command. The following night Ludendorff led his troops into Liège by way of the gap between forts Fléron and Evegnée. But the forts were still manned by Belgians; Liège had been invaded but was far from conquered.

Continual artillery and infantry assaults against the forts were ineffective until August 10, when von Emmich captured the first one. Within twenty-four hours the second fort fell.

The Germans then moved up a cannon that would reduce the forts to rubble and astonish the world. Until then the British 13.5-inch naval gun was the largest of its kind. But Krupp's gunsmiths had designed a siege howitzer of 16.5-inches (420-mm.) which hurled a one-ton shell nine miles. Each armor-piercing projectile had a delayed–action fuse timed to explode only after the target had been penetrated. This howitzer was one kind of huge cannon nicknamed "Big Bertha" after Bertha von Krupp, wife of the munitions maker. (Another huge gun was to make its surprise appearance later in the war.)

By August 16, eleven of the twelve forts had

"Big Bertha," the Germans' revolutionary 420-mm. howitzer, the largest cannon in the world in 1914, responsible for the destruction of the fortifications around Liège. Neither British nor French Intelligence had an inkling of the existence of the gun before it was used at Liège.

56

Invasion of Belgium

German officers encamped near Visé enjoy the spoils of victory — local produce and wines.

German propaganda: After General Emmich had conquered Liège, the Germans released a picture of him on horseback. Originally the picture had shown him, on a previous visit, with the King of the Belgians.

The Dutch-Belgian frontier. A Dutch sentinel
(left) stands guard on one side of the line, a
German sentry on the other.

Rearguard Germans with Belgián prisoners.

Belgians engaged in the defense of Liège.

Fort Fléron before the War. The sloping
icy-looking surface is the *glacis*, meant to impede
any frontal assault.

been battered into submission. Later that day a direct hit destroyed Fort Loncin, Leman's command post, and struck him unconscious. He, in contrast to civilians, was treated gallantly by his captors. Von Emmich refused to take his sword, and accepted a message for transmittal to King Albert. On August 20, the victorious German troops marched into Brussels.

Estimates vary of the delay caused by Leman's resistance. British military historians place the setback at "four or five days." Other sources suggest the invaders were only a day or two behind schedule. "Liège was lost," records British official history, "but by delaying the German advance it rendered transcendent service to the cause of Belgium's Allies."

The first pictures of the Germans in Brussels. Above, in front of the office of the coal merchant L. Vanderelst in the Chaussée de Louvain and left, beneath the emblem of the Singer Sewing Machine Company. At right, Hussars, wearing their bearskin hats, relax in the sun.

5. Battle
of the Marne

General Joseph Joffre.

5. Battle of the Marne

As the month of August wore on, German Supreme Headquarters, or *Oberste Heeresleitung* (OHL), became accustomed to almost hourly reports of victory. Four separate engagements during August, called the Battles of the Frontiers, involved almost 3,500,000 troops; lasting little more than ten days, the Germans resoundingly beat the main Allied armies. Meanwhile, eager to recover their lost provinces, the French First and Second armies crossed the border into Alsace-Lorraine on August 14, only to be driven back.

Because Joffre assumed the Germans, strapped for troops, could not move west of Luxembourg, the French Third, Fourth, and Fifth armies were ordered to advance through the Ardennes Forest on August 22. French headquarters was confident that the Germans would avoid the difficult Ardennes terrain; as a consequence no thought was given to reconnaissance or any other preparation for full-scale battle. An order to all commanders read that, "No serious opposition need be anticipated on August 22. . . . The enemy will be attacked wherever encountered." The School-of-Attack policy still dominated French tactics.

Joffre thought the Germans had no more than eighteen divisions; their actual strength amounted to twenty-five, combined into the Fourth and Fifth armies that formed the pivot wheeling through Belgium into France. Unlike the French, the German advance units scouted the Ardennes and posted guards as the main body entered the forest. Reconnaissance had already warned them of the approaching French. In a flanking attack the Germans fell upon the unsuspecting French, forcing them to retreat hastily the next day.

On August 22–23, at the Battle of Mons, General Alexander von Kluck's First Army drove back the British Expeditionary Force (BEF) as well as the French forces that had been rushed to the area in support of the Belgians. And at the Sambre River, the French Fifth Army was routed by the German Second and Third armies. The heaviest fighting was compressed within four days, August 20 through 23. French casualties for the ten days amounted to 300,000, the greatest losses being inflicted upon the young officer-disciples of Colonel Grandmaison.

Meanwhile the German armies were moving southward toward the Marne River and Paris, mauling any Allied troops in their path. On August 26, Kluck's First Army overtook the BEF at the Battle of Le Cateau and forced it into debilitating rear-guard actions. Three days later OHL shifted headquarters from Coblenz to Luxembourg. As the Imperial train rolled westward, the Kaiser's aide, Admiral von Müller noted that his sovereign ". . . positively revelled in blood," pointing with glee at "piles of corpses six feet high."

Confident of victory, neither Moltke nor his staff weighed the possibility of an Allied withdrawal to prepared positions; they assumed the

French infantrymen pursuing a train. The uniforms are those of 1914, with caps instead of helmets. However, the picture looks as if it has been staged.

Women and old men tend the famous grapevines of Champagne. The younger men, now soldiers, pass by heading for combat.

French and English were conclusively whipped. Reports from spies indicated that while civilians were deserting Paris, troops were arriving, but Moltke failed to transmit this intelligence to the two key field generals, Kluck and Karl von Bülow, commander of the Second Army.

As the distance grew between OHL and its armies, radio communication became more haphazard. In those early war days OHL was limited to one crude wireless (later radio) receiving set; the First Army was restricted to one transmitter. Consequently, only the most urgent messages were sent. Nor was the field telephone system any more efficient. It was not devised for use over long distances and sabotage and incidental damage resulted in constant disruption. Soon Kluck was compelled to make his own

---

General Sir John French inspects volunteers in Liverpool. The BEF at the start of the War was completely volunteer. The British did not introduce conscription until early in 1916.

German troopers poised and tense on the side of a hill, waiting to attack.

decisions but was unable to tell Moltke what he was doing. The retreating French, however, were able to use their civilian telephone system as well as their shortened field communications.

Paris had long played a strategic role in the defense of France. All major railway lines converged and passed through this political and cultural center protected by a ring of fourteen inner and twenty-five outer forts. But little thought was given to the defense of Paris until the French were forced to retreat at the Sambre River. Four divisions and one brigade of Territorials, each with two squadrons of cavalry, a separate cavalry brigade, and six artillery groups (seventy-two cannons) comprised the Paris garrison. Although these forces were soon doubled, the garrison was poorly commanded, and inadequately trained and equipped to successfully resist an assault by Kluck's First Army.

Minister of War Adolphe Messimy ordered General Joffre on August 25, to send "an army of three corps as a minimum . . . to the Entrenched Camp of Paris to assure its protection . . . if our armies are forced to retreat." That Messimy remained ignorant of the actual situation was probably due to Joffre's habit of withholding unfavorable news from the government. The next day the military crisis became acute, driving the government into a state of near panic, but suggestions that the capital be abandoned were rejected, for the fall of Paris would presage the collapse of France. Dissatisfied with the performance of General Augustin Michel, military governor of Paris, Messimy replaced him with General Joseph Gallieni—a stroke of great fortune for France.

Joffre had refused Messimy's order for three army corps, contending he needed every man to halt the German advance. Troops would be sent, he promised, only if and when Paris was immediately menaced. (Actually Joffre recommended that Paris be declared an open city and surrendered without struggle to the Germans.) At the same time he ordered General Maurice Sarrail to evacuate Verdun and only Messimy's firm rejection of this proposal saved France from calamity. By August 31, the government made plans to depart for Bordeaux, leaving the capital in the Army Zone. Gallieni was still entrusted with the city's defense, but was now subordinate to Joffre. Messimy was

replaced by Alexandre Millerand, whose pressing request for more troops only moved Joffre to respond, "the German army will not be before Paris for some days."

The French commander in chief's turtlelike imperturbability maddened those who saw need for prompt decisions in the heat of battle. However crucial the situation, Joffre continued to relish at least two gourmet-prepared meals daily, and he kept to his habit of retiring at exactly 10 P.M. for a night of uninterrupted slumber. It was a rare general who dared disturb him with any kind of news. Even when the Germans opened their campaign at Verdun in 1916, the courier who conveyed the news was curtly told that Joffre was asleep and would not be wakened.

Joffre also avoided the telephone. His orders were issued through it by aides, who also answered all incoming calls, thus giving him an opportunity to think. Sometimes, when an important minister demanded that he personally take the call, Joffre would shuffle forward. Aside from listening, he offered neither reply nor comment; in fact he almost never committed himself in any manner. He exhibited equal distrust toward any dispatch or official memorandum, in the manner of a foxy rustic who suspiciously refuses to sign any written paper. Joffre's immediate reaction, according to a contemporary, was to "turn it inside out and examine every detail, always afraid of landing in some trap or pitfall."

When Colonel Carence, intelligence chief at the War Ministry, visited Joffre in early 1915 to secure his approval for desperately needed heavy artillery, the commander in chief listened benignly, occasionally nodding his massive head. Encouraged, Carence continued to pour forth facts and figures. With a growing sense of dismay, the Colonel realized he was engaged in a monologue; Joffre uttered not a word in response. He finally gave the exhausted intelligence officer a paternal pat of dismissal, commenting ambiguously, "You always loved your guns; that's excellent."

The Defense of Paris

General Gallieni was a different breed—an imaginative strategist whose boundless energy

German atrocities were wildly overstated in Allied propaganda yet German "justice" was harsh and quick. Above, a Belgian patriot hanged in Louvain, August 24, 1914; below; Frenchmen, possibly partisans, shot by the Germans in 1914.

The ruins of a village along the Marne, victim of German shellfire.

Zouaves parade before leaving for battle. Originally composed of Algerian troops, by this time they were recruited solely among the French. Only the distinctive Algerian uniforms were retained.

A German grenadier photographed sometime after the institution of trench warfare. Grenades of sorts had made their appearance as early as the Thirty Years War, but until World War I they were neither particularly effective nor much used.

Invasion of France

High German officers review troops on the Western Front.

French dead in the Battle of the Marne. The picture was taken at the village of Vitry-le-François, some twenty miles up the river from Châlons-sur-Marne.

belied his sixty-five years and failing health. (In earlier times he had been governor-general of Madagascar, where Joffre was his subordinate.) To the semideserted city of Paris he issued a memorable proclamation: "The members of the government of the Republic have left Paris to give a new impetus to the national defense. I have been entrusted with the duty of defending Paris against the invader. This duty I shall carry out to the end." In a later aside, Gallieni remarked: "The government has left for Bordeaux and left me alone in the presence of a population that has been deceived until now by lying communiqués."

Within a few hours a small army of men began to construct trenches and barricades and reinforce the ring of forts. Recalling the siege of 1870, when starving inhabitants ate animals from the zoo and household pets, Gallieni filled the city's racetracks and parks with cattle, sheep, pigs, goats, and horses. Profiteering was firmly checked because, he said, "it was not only necessary that Paris should not want for bread, but that it should eat the same bread." Liquor supplies were placed under stringent supervision. Arrangements were made for the removal of any machinery or equipment that might be useful to the enemy. Explosive charges were planted under eighty bridges spanning the Seine, the Oise, and the Marne rivers, as well as under the Eiffel Tower.

But Gallieni did not content himself merely with Paris' defense. An aviator returning late on September 3 reported that the German columns were changing their line of march. Early the next morning air and cavalry reconnaissance confirmed that the Germans had indeed revised their plan to assault Paris frontally, and had veered southeast beyond the capital's outskirts. A brief study of the map showed Gallieni that the Germans' new course offered a splendid opportunity for a flanking attack. "I dare not believe it," he cried, "it is too good to be true."

As the five German armies neared Paris, the spasmodic radio linkage with OHL ended abruptly. Except for the First and Second armies, which marched together, no commander could accurately locate the others and now Moltke's alteration of the Schlieffen plan was beginning to exact its price. The strategy was originally planned to weaken the German left

flank deliberately and lure the French right wing out of its fortified entrenchment to be assaulted in turn from the rear by the pivoting German right wing. But the German generals on the left, facing the French fortress system, persuaded Moltke to reinforce their ranks, a shift that contradicted Schlieffen's scheme by forcing the French soldiers to remain safely in their underground stronghold. Moltke also weakened his right wing by detaching two army corps (four divisions) to the Eastern Front against the Russians.

Because the invasion was a gigantic swooping cartwheel movement, the outermost troops (Kluck's First Army and Bülow's Second Army) necessarily drove themselves faster and harder to keep in line with the inner ranks, taxing their strength. Lacking combat intelligence, Kluck had only a hazy notion where he stood in relation to the Allies. Completely unaware that the French Sixth Army was approaching his right flank, he accepted Bülow's proposal that they execute a joint inward wheeling sweep to attack the French Fifth

Army. The Schlieffen plan then became further deformed as Kluck and Bülow marched in front and to the *east* of Paris, instead of behind and to its *west*. This maneuver also shortened the right wing by eighty miles.

Meanwhile, Gallieni had sent a messenger on September 3 to Joffre who had just arrived at Bar-sur-Aube, some 120 miles southwest of Paris, to tell him of the favorable situation and win consent for a counteroffensive. In despair of Joffre's ability to make an early decision, Gallieni himself raced by car to Melun, where the British were quartered, hoping to win their support.

Sir John French, the British commander, was away from headquarters. Even his chief of staff was absent. A bizarre scene ensued. Fretful and distressed by their month of defeats, the British staff brusquely told their unwelcome visitor that if England had had a glimmering of French military incompetence, she decidedly would not have joined the war. The irate Britons were in no mood to make discriminating judgments, and Gallieni presented an un-military appearance, squinting through a pince-nez that fluttered precariously, as he argued for British support. The staff's skepticism increased as they gazed at his unkempt uniform, shaggy mustache, black buttoned boots, and yellow leggings. Later an English general would comment that "no British officer would be seen speaking to such a—comedian."

Soon Archibald Murray, French's chief of staff, returned, but evinced "great loathing" for Gallieni's plan against the German right flank, and told him no decision could be made anyway in the absence of Sir John French. Gallieni wasted three valuable hours waiting vainly for the British commander to return. He left with nothing more than the promise of a telephone call later, which amounted to an admission that the British would resume their retreat the next day. This decision was in part due to Joffre's message to the British commander: "My intention in the present situation," he wrote, "is to retire behind the Seine. In case of the German armies continuing their movement toward the S-S-E . . . perhaps you

German infantrymen on the advance.

will agree that your action can be most effectively applied on the right bank of this river, between the Marne and the Seine." Since its author was unable to grasp the need for resolute action, the British could not be completely faulted for separating themselves from the Germans.

Early on September 4, Gallieni's message was placed before Joffre, who waited four hours before approving the deployment of Maunoury's Sixth Army against the Germans. For some unfathomable reason, the commander in chief insisted the attack be made south of the Marne. In the late afternoon he learned that General Franchet d'Esperey's Fifth Army was prepared to join the offensive and could begin active combat in the morning of September 6 but, aside from eating a long, leisurely dinner, Joffre made no decisions and issued no orders.

At midday, September 5, as Kluck's army passed east of Paris, in view of the Eiffel Tower, his right rear flank was attacked by forward units of Maunoury's army. The British were too far south to be an immediate threat, so Kluck shifted two army corps from this sector to strengthen the corps struggling to fend off the French. A thin cavalry screen was substituted to cover the twenty-mile-wide breach facing the British. Maunoury requested reinforcements—a plea that inspired Gallieni to organize the first motorized column in the history of warfare, the Marne taxicabs.

The combat-ready Seventh Division had just arrived in Paris, but no rail transport to the front was available. Even a forced march would get them there too late. Gallieni, responding characteristically, issued a decree requisitioning "all self-propelled vehicles, including taxis." In every quarter of Paris, police halted taxis and ordered the passengers out; they commandeered some 700 vehicles. Throughout the night, the two-cylinder taxis rumbled toward

German communications center. Despite the seeming efficiency and (for the time) sophisticated equipment, the Germans' communications were a shambles.

A Renault two-cylinder taxicab, veteran of the Marne. Some 700 taxis transported 3,000 troops to turn the battle into a victory for the Allies.

General Joseph Gallieni, the hero of the Battle of the Marne. He served as military governor of Paris and later as Minister of War although suffering from cancer of the prostate that required constant care.

the front. It took only two trips to transport the entire division. The Germans immediately felt the intensified pressure against their rear flank. Had Gallieni been provided with the two additional army corps he had so urgently requested several days earlier, but which had arrived only in dribs and drabs, the German armies south of the Marne might have been completely encircled.

While Kluck was preoccupied with repelling Maunoury's forces, the twenty-mile-wide rift in the southern sector enabled Franchet d'Esperey's soldiers to strike at Bülow's exposed flank. Then Kluck learned that the British were approaching the center of the gap between Maunoury and d'Esperey, a signal for him to plan his retreat. General French and his troops arrived on September 9.

Prince Rupprecht, commanding the German Sixth Army facing France on the east, was unable to aid the invaders at the Marne. The powerful guns of the French fortresses at Toul and Epinal, backed by the First and Second armies of Generals Auguste Dubail and Noël de Castelnau, decimated his ranks of Bavarians and constrained the Prince to notify OHL on September 8 that his army could advance no farther. Nor did the German Crown Prince, facing General Sarrail's Third Army northeast of Verdun, fare better. Murderous gunfire from Verdun's forts ground Prince Wilhelm's Fifth Army to a halt. Two other German armies, the Fourth under the Duke of Württemberg, and the Third under General Max von Hausen, were fought furiously in the marshes of Saint Gond by the forces of Generals de Langle de Cary and Ferdinand Foch.

Much of this combat was a bewildering series of savage skirmishes, fought in and out of small villages where the terror-stricken inhabitants found themselves caught in the cross fire. Deprived of the victory they so desired, the Germans lunged in a colossal bayonet charge against Foch's army at dawn on September 8. At least one army corps was forced to retreat, but a solid phalanx of French artillery left the battlefield piled high with German corpses. This battle is memorable for Foch's legendary defiance: "My flanks are turned; my center gives way; I attack!"

The German withdrawal from the Marne region began not long thereafter. By after-

noon it became general and continued through September 11, when the Germans arrived at previously selected positions along the north bank of the Aisne River. The Marne battle had consisted largely of fierce, brief, confused frays and engagements along a 200-mile front. Allied and German casualties have been sketchily estimated at 250,000 each. German losses by capture during the battle and the fifty-five-mile retreat amounted to 15,000 men and 40 guns. To avoid a debacle at the Marne, the Germans retired in an orderly manner, successfully repulsing the Allied pursuers.

Morale remained good among the German troops, but despair overwhelmed the High Command. The defeat had shattered the mystique of German invincibility; simultaneously, it eclipsed the career of Moltke, who had been so responsible for the War in the first place. And Kaiser Wilhelm's ego had been bruised. Assured by Moltke that Prince Rupprecht's Bavarians would capture Nancy, Wilhelm had appeared with a glittering cohort of white-and-gold-uniformed cuirassiers wearing ornate helmets and embossed breastplates, waiting to make his triumphal entry. But the French artillery had raked every assault wave with such lethal accuracy that even Moltke was appalled by the slaughter. On September 11, he ordered Rupprecht to end the suicidal charges. Nancy remained unconquered.

Failing his sovereign weighed heavily on Moltke, who wrote his wife next day: "Things are going badly. The battles east of Paris are turning against us . . . the great hopes that the beginning of the war gave us have been dashed . . . .We shall finally wear ourselves out in this struggle on two fronts! What a difference from the brilliant beginning of our campaign! Now it is a cruel disillusion. And we must pay for all this devastation."

Dugouts before Verdun. The large gate at right would lead into the interior of the fort which honeycombed the hill with galleries. The massive guns were on the other side, facing Germany.

Colonel Bauer, a German staff officer, recorded an unforgettable scene: "Desperate panic seized severely the entire army, or to be more correct, the greater part of the leaders. It looked . . . its worst at the supreme command. Moltke completely collapsed. He sat with a pallid face gazing at the map, dead to all feeling, a broken man. General von Stein (Moltke's deputy) certainly said, 'We must not lose our heads,' but he did not take charge. He was himself without confidence and gave expression to his feelings by saying, 'We cannot tell how things will go.' "

For losing the Battle of the Marne, Moltke was dismissed as Supreme German Commander in a humiliating manner. According to former Chancellor von Bülow: "Later, in tears, Moltke assured me that his health was then (September, 1914) so impaired that the agony of these days felt 'indescribable.' The Emperor . . . abruptly relieved Moltke of his command, to confer it on his War Minister, General von Falkenhayn. Provisionally this had to be kept secret, so as not to alarm the country. That is why Moltke, now a puppet, was still, for the look of the thing, obliged to be present every day at discussions of strategy, at which nobody asked his advice or paid him any attention whatsoever. He was forced to sit without a word at the side of his former rival, now his successor. Later he told me that: 'Dante's Hell cannot contain in it such torments as I was forced to undergo at that time.' "

If Sir John French had heeded Gallieni's proposal for immediate united action, the Battle of the Marne might have ended disastrously for the Germans. Cyril Falls in *The Great War* writes: "Most British historians have done their utmost to make as good a story as possible of the B.E.F.'s advance. In fact it was a crawl. The chief blame must undoubtedly fall upon the head of Sir John French, who never seems to have sensed that he was moving into what was virtually a void, and never drove his troops forward. Undoubtedly too there was among French and British troops alike a certain caution, degenerating at times into timidity.

"Commanders could not believe that the tide had turned and kept wondering whether or not they were walking into a gigantic ambush. Anyhow the British infantry's advance measured only about eight miles a day from September 7 to 9, when half as much again, a mere 12 miles, would have been enough to sever Kluck's three corps from the rest of the German array and enable the British to attack them in the rear while Maunoury was attacking them frontally."

Six weeks of war had resulted in agonizing losses for the French army. Troop strength at the outset was in excess of 1,250,000. At mid-September 600,000 of these had been killed, wounded, or taken prisoner, a paralyzing blow to a nation already comparatively poor in manpower. By the end of the year, French casualties would rise to 750,000.

Germany had entered the war with eighty-seven divisions (as against seventy-two for the French and British). Schlieffen's plan had specified ninety-seven divisions just for the conquest of France, and seventy-nine of these were to form the vast assault wheel through Belgium. Moltke had assigned seventy-eight divisions to the west and fifty-three for the wheeling attack. He further weakened these by transferring two corps (four divisions) to the Eastern Front. German armies would pay a stupendous price for their leader's misjudgment.

French *cuirassiers* (cavalrymen) at the Gare du Nord in Paris. At top, they are entraining on the line leaving Paris for Soissons, Laon, and Hirson. At bottom: Waiting in front of the station. The wine bottle was no doubt intended to spread cheer during the journey.

6. The Eastern Front, 1914

Grand Duke Nicholas.

6. The Eastern Front, 1914

The Battle of Tannenberg

Russia shared a common border with Germany and Austria-Hungary that extended for more than 1,100 miles. Poland, then a Russian province, formed a 250-mile-wide salient that jutted 200 miles to the westward, abutting Germany on the west and northwest and Austria-Hungary on the south. Its western border was only 180 miles from Berlin. To its north was East Prussia, eighty miles of German territory sandwiched between Poland and the Baltic Sea. A successful Russian drive could sever it from all Germany. The Hapsburgs also had a vulnerable province, Galicia, whose rich lands were separated from the rest of Austria-Hungary by the Carpathian Mountains. The strategy of the Eastern-Front belligerents was designed to meet these geographic conditions.

Russian military plans, formulated with French assistance, provided for two contingencies. If Germany first attacked France, Russia would strike concurrently against East Prussia and Austrian Galicia. The other plan was purely defensive, in case Germany directed its initial thrust against Russia. The Austrians also had two plans. One envisioned war only with Serbia, which would be attacked by three of the six Austrian armies, the others being earmarked for Galicia to fend off the Russians. Another was for war with both Russia and Serbia, in which event only two armies would march against Serbia, with four armies stationed on the Galician front.

East Prussia was guarded by fortified zones intended to prevent the Russians from advancing beyond the Polish frontier. Strong points were built along the upper Vistula River, and around the capital, Königsberg. Across the eastern border was the fifty-mile-wide cluster of Masurian Lakes, a natural barrier severely limiting Russian paths of invasion. Austria utilized the Carpathians to install a hedge of defensive works from Cracow through Lemberg (now Lvov) to the Romanian frontier. Between Russia and its Polish province, centering around Pinsk, were the Pripet Marshes, 38,000 square miles of swampland, scrub forest, and a few dirt roads.

Germany's railway complex included seventeen lines into East Prussia, permitting five hundred trains each day; such a system could transport a huge army in a short time. Multiple rail spurs diverged from the main lines to numerous frontier areas, expediting rapid shifts of troops to meet sudden emergencies.

Troops of General Alexander Samsonov's Second Army wait at a railway station for transportation toward East Prussia.

Austria had built seven rail lines through the Carpathians with a daily capacity of two hundred and fifty trains into Galicia. Russia had only six rail lines from major interior cities to Warsaw, and too few branches to be of any military value.

To block an invasion from the west, the Russian railway gauge was wider than that used by the Germans. Frontier zones were intentionally left as semi-desolate wastelands, broken by stretches of forest and thickets, and unpaved roads that became mud fields during heavy rains. One result was that as the Russian Army neared these frontier areas, its movement slowed to the pace of horse and wagon. The transport system imposed immense strain on an already unwieldy military machine. Matters would worsen when the unprepared Russians rashly invaded East Prussia, at the insistence of France, to reduce German pressure on the Western Front.

General Ivan Jilinsky, who had served as Chief of the Russian General Staff until 1913, and who would command the armies in the field, pledged France that 800,000 Russians would be combat ready two weeks after mobilization. By mid-August more than 650,000 men were in readiness, a feat that amazed and

worried the Germans. Early German victories in the west caused the French to barrage Russia with pleas to strike at the enemy.

Barely two days after the outbreak of war, French emissary Maurice Paléologue urged his hosts to mount an offensive in East Prussia. The Czar's uncle, the Grand Duke Nicholas, commander in chief, and a dedicated Francophile, assured the ambassador, "I may not even wait for all my corps to be assembled. As soon as I feel strong enough I shall attack." The eager Russians, however, neglected to provide sufficient food, supplies, or transport facilities for their army.

Jilinsky's forces, amounting to thirty infantry and eight cavalry divisions, were divided into two armies under Generals Alexander Samsonov and Pavel Rennenkampf. Rennenkampf commanded the First (Vilna) Army and Samsonov the Second (Warsaw) Army, named after their city bases. To invade East Prussia, both would be confined to fixed routes on either side of the Masurian Lakes region, Rennenkampf proceeding along the northern border, crossing the frontier on August 17, with Samsonov scheduled to follow two days later by way of the southern fringe.

Years earlier Schlieffen had spent much time at the Masurian Lakes, pondering the most effective measure against this type of maneuver. Concentrate full strength against the Russian army that first appears, he commanded, then attack the other. This tactic was brilliantly simple, but General Max von Prittwitz, commander of the German Eighth Army in East Prussia, dreaded making decisions. A combination of timidity and faulty intelligence misled him to divide his forces, then begin a frontal instead of flank attack against Rennenkampf's First Army. The battle was joined on August 20, in the vicinity of Gumbinnen (now Gusev); General August von Mackensen's XVII Corps bore the brunt. Fearful of encir-

Cavalry troops belonging to General Pavel Rennenkampf's First Army ride through an East Prussian community, probably Gumbinnen (the present Russian town of Gusev).

84

clement, Rennenkampf was on the verge of retreating when he learned the Germans had withdrawn. Samsonov reached the frontier that same day, his troops and horses hungry and exhausted, his Second Army clearly unfit for immediate battle.

When Samsonov's troops and their spent condition were reported to Prittwitz, he was unaccountably seized with misgiving. Later that day he told two subordinates: "I suppose, gentlemen, you have received this fresh news from the southern front? The army is breaking off the battle and retiring behind the Vistula." Protests that victory was certain were of no

avail. The decision was final, snapped Prittwitz, and left. Meanwhile, Colonel Max von Hoffmann outlined a plan of attack to Count Waldersee, Prittwitz' Chief of Staff; namely, a strike against Samsonov's left flank. Three divisions would be withdrawn from the Gumbinnen sector to buttress local forces.

Assigned as operations officer to the Eighth Army on the first day of mobilization, Hoffmann conspicuously outshone his colleagues. He was the General Staff's expert on Russia, whose language he spoke and read easily. Over the years he had amassed a fund of knowledge about his enemies, particularly the antagonism

General Alexander Samsonov.

General Pavel Rennenkampf.

General Ivan Jilinsky.

between Rennenkampf and Samsonov. During the Russo-Japanese War Hoffmann had been present as an official observer when he inadvertently witnessed a memorable fracas. On the station platform at Mukden, Manchuria, two hot-eyed Russian commanders were heaping abuse on each other. Suddenly they switched to fists until one knocked the other down. (Samsonov, the winner, had instigated the fight. When his battle-weary Siberian Cossacks had been forced to cede a valuable coal mine to Japanese troops, Rennenkampf had repeatedly ignored orders to lend support with his cavalry division.) Hoffmann guessed that Rennenkampf again would decline to aid Samsonov and this time would tarry in the Gumbinnen area.

Reports that the Russians were transmitting uncoded messages were greeted with deep suspicion by German senior officers. Only Hoffmann believed that this was not a ruse—he had had ample time to observe Russian laxity in Manchuria. Papers found on a dead Russian officer of Jilinsky's staff revealing planned routes and deployment were confirmed by the interception of such messages. Russian field armies were without codes or cryptographers. Training operators for this function seemingly had not occurred to the Russian High Command.

Several hours afterward Prittwitz returned, heard, and approved Hoffmann's plan; retreat behind the Vistula was forgotten. The next day Samsonov's army ground to a halt. Two days later Prittwitz was busily adding final details to his campaign against Samsonov, when a thunderclap from OHL at Coblenz struck the Eighth Army. A telegram from Moltke informed Prittwitz that he and Waldersee were replaced by a new commander in chief and chief of staff—Generals Paul von Hindenburg and Erich Ludendorff. Thirty minutes later the benumbed Prittwitz and Waldersee were notified by a second telegram, coming almost as an afterthought, of their retirement.

The mystery was very soon solved. After Prittwitz had left his subordinates on August 20, he telephoned Mackensen of his intention to retire behind the Vistula, and then telephoned Moltke to report his decision. Upon returning to headquarters, he forgot to tell his staff of the phone calls. Thus no one telephoned Moltke of Prittwitz' decision to attack Samsonov. Moltke had long wanted to dislodge Prittwitz, a court favorite better known for his eating habits, which had earned him the nickname "Fatso," than for his military competence. Prittwitz' high rank was the Kaiser's reward to a spieler of tales and goatish gossip.

Ludendorff had been chosen to replace Waldersee as the Eighth Army's Chief of Staff in recognition of his action at Liège, where he had turned possible defeat into victory. He learned of his promotion on August 22, while with Bülow's Second Army near Namur, Belgium's strongest fortress city after Liège. In a grateful telegram OHL told him: "You may be able to save the situation in the East. I know of no person in whom I have such absolute trust. The Kaiser also has absolute confidence in you. Of course, you will not be held responsible for what has already happened in the East."

Soon Ludendorff was speeding toward Coblenz in a staff car. Along the way he noted for his diary: "I passed through Wavre. The day before it was a peaceful town. Now it was in flames. The populace fired on our troops." In Coblenz that evening, he was received by the Kaiser and Moltke who briefed him. Three hours later he was on a special train for the Eastern Front. Only one stop was scheduled, at Hannover, where the new commander of the Eighth Army would join him. General Paul von Hindenburg had been retrieved from retirement at sixty-eight years, about the same age as a number of other active commanders.

Hindenburg had not been invited to Coblenz for briefing or consultation. Upon accepting the appointment he had been told by telegram to board Ludendorff's train, which would reach Hannover before daybreak. This procedure reflected the rigid caste-consciousness of the Imperial German Army. Ludendorff was the man to whom the Eastern Front was being entrusted, but his lower-middle class origins, as shown by the lack of a "von" in front of his name, kept him from being named commander.

Ludendorff unwittingly almost aborted Hoffmann's plan, which he was to adopt and expand. Before leaving Coblenz, he notified all Eighth Army corps commanders to operate on their own initiative, ending Prittwitz' last vestige of authority. Generals August von Mackensen's XVII and Otto von Below's I Reserve Corps at Rennenkampf's front reduced the pace of their westward withdrawal and paused for a day's rest. A further delay occurred when the Eighth Army headquarters shifted from Allenstein to Marienburg where Hindenburg and Ludendorff would detrain.

General Friedrich von Scholtz' XX Corps was bested in a brief skirmish with Samsonov's troops on August 24, then one division was withdrawn to a stouter defense position. Misjudging this movement to be the entire Eighth Army in retreat, Samsonov ordered full pursuit, his uncoded message being intercepted by the German signal corps. Actually, Scholtz faced no immediate threat, for Samsonov's troops were far too tired to pursue. According to a radio intercept, one corps had slogged more than 150 miles in twelve days through ankle-deep dirt "roads."

Sensing a decisive coup, Mackensen and Scholtz retired toward the south, leaving only a token cavalry division to face Rennenkampf's twenty-four infantry divisions. Within two days masses of German soldiers traveled over the efficient railways more than 100 miles southwest, where upwards of nine divisions regrouped in a seventy-mile arc facing southeast. Samsonov continued to pursue the "retreating" enemy, heading toward the deliberately weakened center. Both wings had been strengthened to deliver staggering blows against Samsonov's two flanks as he moved into the soft, yielding center.

Reports from Russian cavalry scouts that the German alignment hinted at a flank assault, caused Samsonov to reduce the tempo of pursuit. He dispatched messages to Jilinsky, suggesting a temporary halt. Convinced that the Germans were in retreat according to Prittwitz' plan, Jilinsky saw Samsonov's caution as faintheartedness. From the safety of his headquarters at Volkvosik, nearly 200 miles behind the front, Jilinsky ordered Samsonov to stop "acting the coward and resume the offensive."

Moving through the night of August 25–26 toward the German center, Samsonov's right flank, about thirty miles from the rest of his army, collided with the two German corps that had marched from Gumbinnen. Fatigued but well fed, the Germans faced a weary and semistarved Russian army. After a short, confused battle, the Russians stumbled back while the Germans stared in relief, too tired to pursue.

Several companies of a Russian division, their backs to Lake Bossau, reeled into the water and some were drowned. German propagandists embellished this into the legend that Hindenburg had driven Samsonov's army into the marshes where they had perished by the tens of thousands. Ever alert to keep the record accurate where his own prestige was involved, Ludendorff brushed this aside as a "myth . . . no marsh was anywhere near." Doomsday for the Russian force began at sunrise August 27, when General Hermann von François's I Corps shelled Samsonov's left wing in the Usdau sector. German signal-corps operators intercepted messages from Samsonov imploring aid, but neither Jilinsky nor Rennenkampf acknowledged his pleas. Inevitably, the hungry and already demoralized Russians broke rank and fled in panic. Despite the precarious position of his troops, Samsonov ordered his center to attack, causing brief uneasiness among the Germans. But the hungry and dazed Russians allowed themselves to be rounded up like so many sheep. A forty-mile stretch of German troops merely pointed the way toward prisoner corrals for these brave men who had fought beyond the limit of endurance. The Russian Second Army was a total loss; two of its five corps commanders were captured and three were summarily dismissed for inefficiency. Samsonov avoided their fate. In the late afternoon of August 28, he wandered alone into the woods, raised a pistol to his temple and pulled the trigger. His body, buried by the Germans, was released to his wife in 1916, through the Red Cross, for burial in his homeland.

The battle was a German triumph and a Russian disaster. More than 92,000 captives were taken. Those killed and missing have been estimated at 30,000. Some 500 of the Second Army's guns were destroyed or seized. Concerned about Samsonov's fate, Jilinsky directed Rennenkampf to locate the now non-existent Second Army. But Rennenkampf turned tail and fled, as the victorious Eighth Army zeroed in on his troops. In the Masurian Lakes campaign two weeks later, the Germans cleared East Prussia of all Russians.

German prisoners, guarded by Cossacks.

Austrian amputees, victims of the Eastern Front, learn how to walk again at a war hospital in Brest Litovsk.

German soldiers examine heavy machine guns captured from the Russians.

Rennenkampf's casualties amounted to 145,-000 compared to 10,000 Germans. Hysterical at such disproportionate losses, Rennenkampf deserted his army and drove full speed back to Russia. Furious at this act of cowardice, Jilinsky, in a telegram to the Grand Duke, urged his immediate dismissal. According to General Nosskov, garrison commander in Petrograd: "Rennenkampf . . . interrupted his advance, so as not to be obliged to come to Samsonov's aid.

He was even accused of treason: 'He is a German, what else can you expect from him?'" Not only did the commander in chief oust Rennenkampf in disgrace, he also cashiered Jilinsky "for losing his head and (being) unable to control operations."

Moltke carefully timed the news of the victory to offset the German reverses at the Marne. When the news was released, Hindenburg overnight became a demigod to a delirious

Lines of Russian prisoners of war, among the 100,000 taken at the Battle of Tannenberg. They presented a formidable problem in terms of food and shelter to their German captors.

90

nation. Hoffmann, who really deserved the credit for the victory, was overlooked, but Ludendorff, who had elaborated Hoffmann's strategy, won some share of the acclaim. Hoffmann's abilities were not, however, completely unnoticed. Promoted to major general, he succeeded Ludendorff as Chief of Staff on the Eastern Front, but his resentment of Hindenburg continued. Upon Hindenburg's departure to OHL, Hoffmann told visitors to the battleground in mock awe: "Here is where the Field Marshal slept before the battle; here is where he slept during the battle; and here is where he slept after the battle."

Hoffman also grasped the charismatic value of a heroic name. Ludendorff had moved on August 28 to a small village called Frögenau, under which name he issued orders in the hours preceding Samsonov's defeat. He and Hindenburg thought the battle should be

A detachment of Russian women
soldiers "dressing the line." The men
seem to be taking it all quite lightly.

General Hindenburg using a field
periscope. Hoffman is behind, at far
right. The man beside him is probably
Ludendorff.

The Russian Front

A German supply dump in Russia where ammunition and supplies were stored in vast quantities on sleighs. When the snow was too deep for horses to maneuver, the men had to pull the sleighs to the front.

named after this village. Less than two miles away was a tiny hamlet, Tannenberg. No name would be more appropriate, suggested Hoffmann, for this was the scene of battle in 1401 when the Teutonic knights were routed by Poles and Lithuanians. And Tannenberg is how it is remembered.

Victory was in the offing when Moltke notified Ludendorff that three corps and a cavalry division, detached from the Western Front, were on route to the East. Swayed by Prittwitz' apprehension, Moltke had weakened his right wing to provide needless support against the Russians—a decision that would give the Allies enough leverage to win at the Marne.

The Galician Campaign

General Conrad, the Austrian commander in chief, was more adept at starting a war than at fighting one. His prewar plan was to crush Serbia, simultaneously sending the mass of his army into Galicia to launch an offensive against Russia. But Conrad virtually nullified his chances for victory when he split his six armies for this two-front war. He further diminished those chances by assigning General Potiorek to the Serbian Front. Potiorek had never recovered from his failure, as governor of Bosnia, to protect Francis Ferdinand from assassination. Now apprehensive and timid, fearing possible assassination himself, he refused to appear before his troops and made his "decisions" far from the battle scene.

Since Bulgaria, Serbia's eastern neighbor, was still neutral in 1914, Austria was able to assault only Serbia's northern and western borders. This access was impeded by such natural barriers as the Danube, Sava and Drina rivers, which could be crossed only by boat or raft, and the mountainous areas that rose behind them. The vastly outnumbered Serbian Army had little alternative but to fight delaying actions until the Allies could come to its aid. General Radomir Putnik, the Serbian commander, pinched for artillery, automatic weapons, and transport, offset these deficits with battle-trained veterans of the recent Balkan wars. Above all, Putnik was adept at maneuvering an enemy to fight on terrain most favorable to himself.

Austrian women free men for military service by manning the fire brigade.

General Radomir Putnik.

94

Serbian women learning marksmanship.

A combination of boredom and tension characterizes these Austrians encamped near the Sava River.

A Serbian observer climbs up the shaft of an upended ammunition carriage in an attempt to check his guns' accuracy.

96

War casualties in a Serbian village near Belgrade. Ancient hatreds and rivalries led to brutal atrocities all along the Serbian-Austrian frontier.

The Balkans

Heavy field artillery in open terrain on the Balkan front. ▶

Mustachioed Montenegrins pose with other Allied officers.

Rugged Serbian mountaineers prepare to come to the defense of their country.

A group of Serbian prisoners. They are unusual as neither side showed much interest in taking prisoners.

Three Austrian armies consisting of nineteen divisions invaded Serbia on August 12. (Potiorek had misapplied one corps to occupation duty in Bosnia and squandered other troops in pursuing Montenegrins in the fastnesses of the mountains they knew so well.) Putnik stationed a few troops along the river borders and grouped the main body of his army in the arc formed by the confluence of the Drina and Sava. The Serbs kept rolling back under the Austrian attack until they reached a sector that met Putnik's tactical requirements.

Then, on August 16, Putnik struck along a thirty-mile front on the Jadar River. Before the sun set the surviving Austrians were fleeing headlong back to the Drina. Putnik then moved against the Austrian left flank which promptly broke and retreated with high casualties. The Austrian rout was all the more remarkable for at sixty-seven years, Putnik was a bedridden invalid, frequently in pain, who directed the campaign from his room.

Unaware of the severe blow against his troops, Conrad entrained for the Galician fortress city of Przemysl that night. He received the news on the next day, then ordered Potiorek to shift one corps of the Second Army from its Danube garrison to reinforce the Austrians facing the Serbs. Potiorek wanted the entire Second Army, but Conrad decided to send the balance of this force to Galicia. (The relief corps arrived at the battleground two days too late to be of any help to Potiorek.) The battle resumed at the Jadar the following day and continued for a week in sweltering heat. Fighting raged around Sabac until August 30.

Only desperate rearguard action enabled the Austrians to extricate themselves. Back on their own soil by September 1, the Austrians counted 40,000 casualties, whereas the Serbs were relatively unscathed. But the latter paid an appalling toll in a typhus epidemic communicated by Austrian troops—more than 70,000 soldiers and uncounted thousands of civilians had perished by April, 1915, when the plague subsided.

Conrad now turned his full attention to the Russians. All the initial advantages were his. Beginning at the Danube, some fifty miles east of Vienna, the Carpathian mountain range forms an 800-mile arc ending in southeastern Romania. Its width varies from 7 to 230 miles, and is about 70 miles at the center. Neither natural roads nor river valleys bisect this barrier, but the seven Austrian rail lines running through the mountains to Galicia could be defended with ease or blocked if necessary. North of the Carpathians were the fortified cities of Cracow, Przemysl, and Jaroslaw, further protected by the Vistula and San rivers.

If Conrad had entrenched his troops, no Russian charge could have crashed these barriers. But he was led to believe that the Russians had not yet mobilized adequate manpower and were vulnerable to attack. He planned a rapid offensive from Galicia to capture the rail line between Warsaw and Brest Litovsk, but obviously gave little thought to what the Russians might do if they actually were mobilized when his army collided with theirs. During the decade preceding the war, Russia had acquired every worthwhile Austrian military secret from its highly placed spy, Colonel Alfred Redl, who systematically betrayed his country even before his appointment as the Austro-Hungarian Army's Director of Intelligence. Redl was Chief of Staff of Austria's Eighth Army in 1913, when his espionage activity was accidentally exposed. But try as he might, Conrad could not radically alter his basic war plans to deceive the Russians without totally distorting his central strategy.

Conrad requested that the German Eighth Army start an offensive from East Prussia. He was refused by Moltke. The Hapsburg commander had wanted the Germans to sweep east of the Nieman River, then strike at the Russian right flank. He was so eager to bestow the first Austrian victory on his Emperor that he continued to believe that the Germans would indeed act when his army reached the Bug River.

Conrad rashly sent thirty divisions, grouped into three armies, toward Lublin on August 22. Galloping in the van were the colorfully uniformed Hussars, picturesque relics of the nineteenth century, eager to slay Cossacks. But no Cossacks were in sight. General Nikolai Ivanov kept his horsemen well in the rear and apparently isolated; actually they were positioned in the wide corridors separating the four Russian armies, to lure the Austrian units into positions where their flanks would be fully exposed.

The strategy of defense in depth is superbly

A solitary Russian soldier stands guard by a ruined gun cupola at the captured Austrian fortress of Przemsyl.

suited to Russia's vast expanses, and Ivanov simply varied the expedients used against Napoleon. When the Cossacks were seen by the invaders they turned and trotted eastward at a pace just fast enough not to be overtaken by the Austrians, who were thus lured into a perilously exposed position. Unlike the Russian commanders at Tannenberg, Ivanov and his fellow commanders, Aleksei Brusilov, Nikolai Russki, and the Bulgarian-born Radko Dmitriev, were able tacticians who planned and coordinated their battles in harmony.

By August 25, the Austrians were deep in Russian Poland. Brusilov, though outnumbered, then assailed the Austrian right wing, forcing it back into Galicia. Following closely on the enemy's heels, the Russians reached Lemberg (Lvov), the commercial and industrial center of the province, entering the city on September 3. Brusilov then divided his army, speeding its left wing to block the Carpathian passes against the retreating Austrians, and driving the center and right wing toward Przemysl. Meanwhile General Russki's army effectively wedged itself between the Austrian Third Army, which was turning tail, and its home base.

In a week-long battle at Rava Russkaya, Galicia's chief railway junction west of Lemberg, General Dmitriev's army pressed the Austrians so hard that they were compelled to rush their already battered Second Army from Serbia to provide support, but this thin reed arrived too late. Combined flanking charges by the Russians drove the Austrians back to the Carpathian line, leaving more than 150,000 at Przemysl, which fell after a six-month siege. When the Russians entered the city, most of its inhabitants were unable to stand. Hunger had reduced them to living skeletons. Meanwhile, Brusilov cut his own swath through the province of Bucovina and seized its capital Czernowitz, then moved on to Hungary.

Ivanov's victory in Galicia had exposed Silesia to a Russian invasion. Insofar as the Silesian plain led directly into the heart of Germany, Hindenburg felt he had to act and act quickly. On September 28, a specially formed German Ninth Army led by General August von Mackensen entrained to reinforce the Austrians.

Enraged at the defeat inflicted on his forces by the less well equipped Serbian Army, Conrad had Potiorek begin another invasion in November. Fighting was intermittent but brutal with few prisoners taken. Belgrade fell in the first days of December but even this triumph was brief. Putnik counterattacked, cleared the capital of Austrians, then drove them out of the country. Casualties were estimated at 175,000, shared about equally by both sides. Potiorek's incompetence was finally too much even for a regime in which *schlamperei* ("sloppiness") was a way of life. He was shelved and forgotten.

7. First Battle
of the Aisne

German trench — 1914

7. First Battle of the Aisne

When the Germans turned to face the pursuing Allies on September 13, they held one of the most formidable positions on the Western Front. Between Compiègne and Berry-au-Bac, the river winds westward and is about one hundred feet wide, ranging from twelve to fifteen feet deep. Low-lying ground extends a mile on each side, rising abruptly to a line of steep cliffs three to four hundred feet high, then gently leveling to a plateau. The Germans settled on the higher northern side two miles beyond the crest, behind a dense thicket that covered the front and slope.

Low crops in the unfenced countryside offered no natural concealment for the Allies. Deep narrow paths, cut into the escarpment at right angles, exposed infiltrators to extreme hazard. The forces on the northern plateau commanded a wide field of fire.

In a dense fog on the night of September 13–14, most of the BEF crossed the Aisne on pontoons or partially demolished bridges, landing at Bourg-et-Comin on the right and at Venizel on the left. At Chivres, east of Venizel, was an escarpment the Germans had selected as their strongest position. Meanwhile the French Fifth Army crossed the Aisne at Berry-au-Bac and captured the eastern tip of Chemin-des-Dames, a steep ridge named after the royal coach road Louis XIV had built for his daughters. Contact was established along the entire front. East of Chemin-des-Dames the French Fourth, Fifth, and Ninth armies made only

negligible progress beyond the positions they had reached on September 13.

Under the thick cover of the foggy night, the BEF advanced up the narrow paths to the plateau. When the mist evaporated under a bright morning sun, they were mercilessly cross-raked by fire. Those caught in the valley without the fog's protective shroud fared no better. A German combatant reports the carnage: "From the bushes bordering the river a second line of skirmishers sprang into view and advanced. There was at least ten paces distance from man to man. Our artillery flashed and hit at most a single man at a time. This second line held on and pushed always nearer and nearer. Two hundred yards behind the second line of skirmishers came a third wave and a fourth wave. Our artillery fired like crazy, but with little effect. Then a fifth and a sixth line of skirmishers came on, in good order, with the same deliberate spacing, and with excellent precision. It was a splendid display by a well-disciplined and courageous foe. We were all filled with admiration."

Trench Warfare Begins

It soon became clear that neither side could budge the other, and since neither chose to retreat, the impasse hardened into a stalemate that would lock the antagonists into a relative-

German infantrymen dig in with spades and crowbars. The ever efficient Germans supplied their troops with all sorts of equipment; the Allies, less foresighted, had to take tools from nearby farms.

A British gun crew in action early in the War. The man with the steering device at the far left "aims" the weapon, not very scientifically, by moving the shaft to the right or left, on instructions from the spotter. As the War progressed, the men ceased wearing the white hatbands that made them such conspicuous targets.

ly narrow strip for the next four years. On September 14, Sir John French ordered the entire BEF to entrench, but few digging tools were available. Soldiers scouted nearby farms and villages for pickaxes, spades, and other implements. Without training for stationary warfare, the troops merely dug shallow pits in the soil. These were at first intended only to afford cover against enemy observation and shell fire. Soon the trenches were deepened to about seven feet. Other protective measures included camouflage and holes cut into trench walls then braced with timber.

Trench warfare was also new to the Germans, whose training and equipment were designed for a mobile war to be won in six weeks, but they quickly adapted their weapons to the new situation. Siege howitzers now lobbed massive shells into Allied trenches. Skillful use of trench mortars, rifle grenades, and hand grenades (first used against English troops on September 27), enabled the Germans to inflict great injury upon Allied soldiers, who had neither been trained nor equipped with these weapons. Searchlights, flares, and periscopes were also part of German equipment intended for other purposes, but turned to effective use in the trenches.

A shortage of heavy weapons handicapped the British. Only their 60-pounders (four to a division) were powerful enough to shell enemy gun emplacements from the Aisne's south shore, and these guns were inferior to German cannon in caliber, range, and numbers. Four batteries of 6-inch guns (a total of sixteen) were rushed from England. Though a poor match against the German 8-inch howitzers, they helped somewhat—if not a great deal. "For every shell of this type which they would fire the Germans would fire twenty," reports one contemporary source. Defensive firepower was limited to rifles and to the two machine guns allotted to each battalion. The British regulars were excellent marksmen, but even their combined accuracy was no match for the German machine guns and grenades.

The British had equipped very few of their airplanes with radio sets, and those that were so equipped initially were used just to report troop movements. But it was only natural for aviators to recognize the advantage of directing, or spotting, artillery fire. On September 24,

Lieutenants B. T. James and D. S. Lewis, flying over the German lines, detected three well-concealed enemy gun batteries that were inflicting considerable damage on British positions. They radioed back the location of the batteries, then droned in a wide circle waiting to spot the gunners' exploding shells. Theirs were the first directional messages recorded from the air:

"4.2 p.m.   A very little short. Fire. Fire.

4.4 p.m.   Fire again. Fire again.

4.12 p.m.   A little short; line O.K.

4.15 p.m.   Short. Over, over and a little left.

4.20 p.m.   You were just between two batteries. Search 200 yards each side of your last shot. Range O.K.

4.22 p.m.   You have them.

4.26 p.m.   Hit. Hit. Hit.

4.32 p.m.   About 50 yards short and to the right.

4.37 p.m.   Your last shot in the middle of three batteries in action; search all around within 300 yards of your last shot and you have them.

4.42 p.m.   I am coming home now."

Antiaircraft fire was desultory and inaccurate. The BEF used only percussion shells of which, according to Canadian sources, "not one in several hundred ever hit its aerial target, and fell to earth frequently at some point in the British lines and there burst."

Race to the Sea

For a three-week period following the unexpected development of trench warfare, both sides gave up frontal assaults and began gradually trying to encircle each other's flank. The period is called the "Race to the Sea." As the Germans aimed for the Allied left flank, the Allies sought the German right wing. "As a result of this symmetrical maneuver," wrote Marshal Ferdinand Foch, "the northern wing moved at ever increasing

Belgian troops set up a
machine-gun nest in their attempt
to defend Antwerp.

German soldiers
file into Antwerp.

Even front-line troops need rest.
Here off-duty soldiers read or play cards.

Life in the German Trenches

An early — and primitive — slit trench.

The morning's duty — bringing up the ammo. The twists and turns are typical of the trenches dug by both sides.

Home away from home. Under the circumstances these soldiers have managed to make quite comfortable quarters for themselves. The rifle, of course, is always close at hand. In the lower bunk, at any rate, so is the bottle.

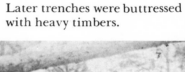

Later trenches were buttressed with heavy timbers.

speed up to the North Sea. In this way the sea marked the end of the maneuver, although it had never been its aim."

The Western Front thus became a fixed, curving, often zigzag, continuous trench system of more than 400 miles. From the Belgian channel town of Nieuport, the trench lines ran southward for some hundred miles, turning southeast at Noyon continuing past Reims, Verdun, Saint Mihiel, and Nancy; then cutting south again to the northern Swiss border twenty miles east of Belfort.

The BEF, left exhausted by the Aisne battle, remained relatively inactive. It was mainly the French who engaged the Germans in the "race" but the British grew increasingly alarmed as the Germans advanced. Winston Churchill, First Lord of the Admiralty, determined to prevent the Germans from capturing other channel ports which could be used as bases to attack English shipping. In late September he arrived in France to arrange the transfer of the BEF to the north. By October 10 all but one corps had reached their staging areas in the Saint Omer-Hasebrouck section, where the last unit joined the main body. The carefully camouflaged move was not detected by German air reconnaissance until October 8, too late to muster adequate forces against the British.

Meanwhile, the Belgian Army became a growing threat to German communication lines as the battle shifted northward. The Germans made plans on September 28 to capture the port of Antwerp and crush the Belgian forces. This important maritime city was encircled by an obsolete fortress system that could not withstand even 6-inch shells. An outer ring of eighteen forts ranged from seven to nine

miles from the city, an inner ring from one to two miles. Each fort was armed with two machine guns, but lacked both telephone communication and a means for observing gunfire. One 6-inch gun poked out at each mile, none of the forts had high explosive projectiles or smokeless gunpowder, and several thousand surrounding acres had been cleared to provide unobstructed fields of fire—defensive measures the invaders would exploit.

At daybreak on September 29, General Hans von Beseler, called from retirement at the age of sixty-five, arrayed six divisions in an arc facing the outer ring of forts. The heavy siege howitzers that had destroyed the defenses of Liège and Namur had been placed well beyond the range of Belgian artillery. Aided by aircraft spotting, German gunners quickly found their targets. Belgian guns belched dense, black smoke puffs revealing their exact locations, and the fields cleared by the defenders deprived the forts of any concealment. Two of the forts were quickly reduced to rubble; the others fell in methodical succession. Without waiting for the outcome, the Belgian government and 65,000 troops departed for Ostend that night, leaving an army of 80,000 to hold off the enemy. Next day the entire outer ring collapsed, prompting a mass evacuation of civilians to neutral Holland. A British Royal Marine Division joined the defending troops during the attack, but even this combined force was unable to stem the German drive. After six days of stubborn fighting, the remaining garrison retired across the Scheldt River to the southern border of Holland, while the rest of the Belgian Army retreated to the south, subsequently attaching itself to General Foch's Ninth Army.

The Belgian cavalry after its defeat at Antwerp crosses a bridge in Ghent on its way to join the French Ninth Army.

8. The Eastern Front, 1915

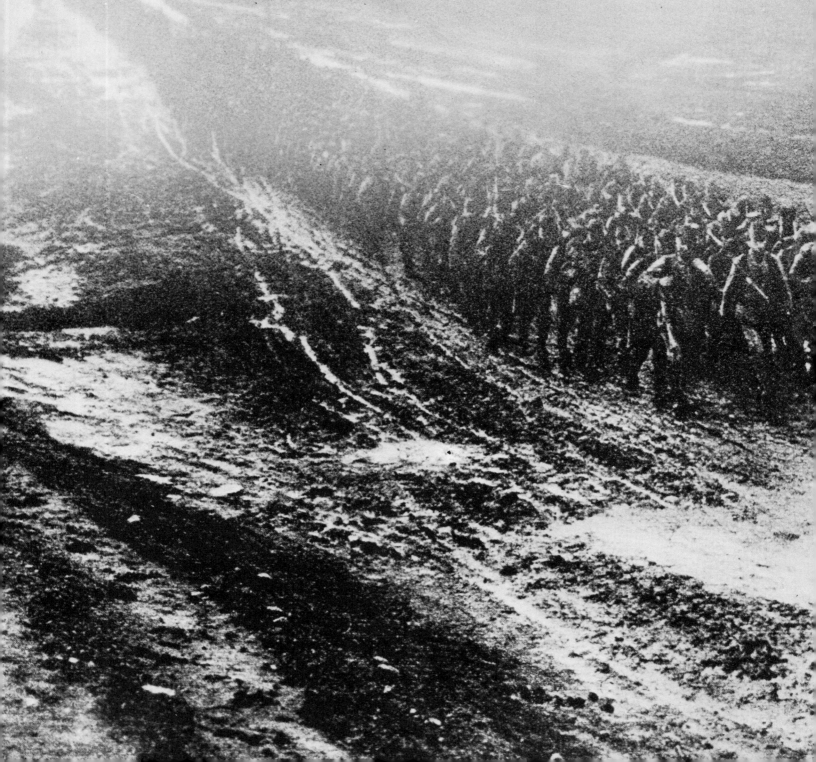

Rasputin.

8. The Eastern Front, 1915

The Dual Monarchy's military fortunes waned steadily. By April, 1915, Russia dominated every road into Hungary on a broad front along the Carpathians, and the Russian occupation of the fortress city of Przemsyl threatened the Austrian rear. Conrad came to the realization that his armies alone were not strong enough to budge the forces of Grand Duke Nicholas. In addition, Austria was periled by a crisis brewing in the south. Italy, although officially neutral, was beginning to shift away from Berlin and Vienna.

Not everything was going well for the Russians either. They had been driven from East Prussia in the winter battle of the Masurian Lakes where, on January 31, the Germans had used poison gas for the first time. Whatever the number of chlorine-gas shells fired at them, the Russians failed to make any mention of this new weapon. Perhaps sub-zero temperatures and poor design had nullified its effect.

New acclaim for the victors had won Hindenburg the rank of Field Marshal in command of all the forces in the East, and Ludendorff became his Chief of Staff. To the Germans these two represented an indivisible unity symbolized by the monogram HL. Both now contended that Russia could be defeated in a single campaign, provided enough troops were at hand. Falkenhayn disagreed. Convinced the war would be won on the Western Front, he decided to concentrate his main might there and only after Austria's plight was revealed did

he reluctantly transfer four army corps from France to Galicia.

These corps were formed into the Eleventh Army, led by General Mackensen, one of the victors at Tannenberg, and the Ninth Army, commanded by Field Marshal Prince Leopold of Bavaria. For sheer numbers, the battle array was impressive. More than 1,750,000 Russians were pitted against 1,300,000 Austro-German troops. That the Czarist army outnumbered its combined enemy was of little importance, however, for it was totally outclassed.

Not until combat began did the Germans fully realize the Russian Army's poor condition. More than one third of the Russian troops were without rifles. Many of the others were armed with Mexican, Japanese, or captured Austrian weapons, making impossible any efficient supply and distribution system. Troops were given cartridges that did not fit their guns, artillery lost in battle was replaced at such a low rate that battery guns were reduced by twenty-five percent, and commanders were even ordered not to fire more than three shells daily for each gun, in order to conserve ammunition.

The no-man's-land between the opposing armies was an open, hilly terrain, every acre of which was utilized for crops or for pasture by the inhabitants of the many villages in the area. Neither side interfered much with the day-to-day activities of the civilians, and when, several days before they began their offensive, the Germans evacuated all noncombatants from

Heavy German artillery at Lodz, Poland.

the area, the Russians were apparently unconcerned. The forward sentries faced each other at an average distance of 3,000 yards. Paying no attention to the deep entrenchments dug by the Germans, the Russians were satisfied with trenches only shallow enough to conceal kneeling soldiers. They also chose, as supporting positions, hills and villages—a serious tactical error in that the German guns found these positions the easiest targets.

Under the cover of night on April 30, German infantrymen advanced to positions where they could quickly overrun the front trenches, scattered shrapnel fire forcing the Russians to keep their heads low. At daybreak, the German artillery opened a thunderous, four-hour barrage, and German planes suddenly appeared and dropped the first bombs of the War. By noon, the first Russian lines had been captured. Hordes of soldiers, dazed by the barrage, simply stumbled forward with upraised arms.

The next day, specially trained troops attached to Prince Leopold's Ninth Army launched a limited gas attack to distract attention from Mackensen's preparations to capture Gorlice and Tarnow. Cylinder valves were opened and chlorine gas drifted with the breeze toward the Russian lines only to have a shifting wind carry the gas back to the Germans, who had not been equipped with gas masks. Mackensen's forces were unaffected by this setback; he was able to link up with the Austrian Fourth Army in a successful combined attack on the defense lines between Gorlice and Tarnow. Soon the Russians were in mass retreat in the Carpathian sector as Mackensen hammered them back along the entire Galician Front. At the end of May, his army alone had captured 153,000 prisoners and 300 pieces of artillery.

Covered by a single rifleman, Austrian soldiers advance in a trench along the Russian Front.

With the billowing smoke of a burning village behind them, German soldiers continue their advance into Russia.

118

Russian forces pass through the ruins of an ancient church as they advance in an unidentified sector of the Austrian Front.

Russian prisoners — probably Siberian — captured outside of Warsaw. A few are wearing their winter fur hats.

German forces in double column, with the officers in the center, plod into the province of Galicia to bail out their inept and overextended Austrian allies.

A German clergyman holds Sunday services in Poland in front of a portable altar flanked by stacked rifles and field guns.

The Germans now directed their efforts to the wide section between the rivers Bug and Vistula, where the bulk of the Russian Army was clustered. In a two-pronged drive, Hindenburg advanced southeast from East Prussia across the Narew River toward the Bug, while Mackensen moved northward toward the Lublin-Kholm area in line with Brest Litovsk. General von Gallwitz' Twelfth Army crowded the entire Russian First Army back against the Narew, while Prince Leopold's Ninth Army was nearing Warsaw.

The only alternative for the Grand Duke was to extricate his forces from the Warsaw salient, leaving an army of 100,000 reserves in the fortress town of Modlin to cover the retreat of the Russian First and Second armies. For a month the Germans pounded the brave but weakening defenders. Their defenses finally collapsed on August 20, fifteen days after the main body of Russians had decamped from Warsaw to the east bank of the Vistula. All the survivors were taken by the triumphant Germans who now occupied all of Poland and held 750,000 captives.

The Russian debacle had been foreseen by Major General Sir Alfred Knox, the British liaison officer with the Grand Duke's forces. Young recruits had been sent into battle after only four weeks of training, usually without having even handled, much less fired, a rifle. Unarmed reserves crouched in the rear waiting to grab a wounded or dead comrade's rifle. Instead of grappling with these and other critical military problems, the high-ranking Russian officers and officials ignored them.

Bulgaria declared herself with the Central Powers in September, and promptly joined Austria in an attack against Serbia. But because he did not want to spread his forces too thin, Falkenhayn discontinued all major German offensives in the East, reducing German activities on that Front to localized battles. At the end of 1915, the Eastern Front extended for 600 miles, from Riga on the Baltic Sea to Czernowitz near the Romanian border. Russian losses for the year had been more than one million dead or wounded and another million in captivity. Casualties during the five months of fighting in 1914 were another two million.

General von Hindenburg (back to camera) on an inspection tour of the front.

The Bulgarians joined the Central Powers in October, 1915, and in this early battle were savagely mauled by the Serbians.

Germans in Warsaw, which fell
to General Max von Gallwitz'
Twelfth Army in August.

Occasionally in "our battles with the Russians," Hindenburg wrote in his memoirs, "we had to remove the mounds of enemy corpses from before our trenches in order to get a clear field of fire against fresh assaulting waves."

In early September, Czar Nicholas dismissed the Grand Duke and assumed personal control. This was a political decision prompted by Czarina Alexandra and, as Nicholas called him, their "man of God, Gregory," a semiliterate Siberian peasant aptly named Rasputin (libertine). Rasputin's hypnotic ability to arrest the bleeding of the royal couple's hemophiliac son had won him the loyalty of the deeply superstitious and strong-willed Czarina, who exalted him as a modern Christ. Rasputin used her as his instrument to dominate the weak-willed Czar.

Alexandra's letters continually exhorted her husband to show "your reign of will and power . . . draw the reins in tightly that you let loose . . . I suffer over you as over a tender soft-hearted child . . . How I wish I could pour my will into your veins . . . Russia loves to feel the whip." How supple the Czar became at his wife's bidding was reflected in a letter signed,

Germans inspecting Russian dead, killed in their own barbed-wire entanglements.

"Tender thanks for the severe scolding . . . Your poor little weak-willed hubby."

A lecherous drunkard with a scarred head (from being clubbed for horse-stealing in his native town), Rasputin controlled or influenced most high appointments and virtually all contracts. He was widely hated for his power. Gripped by a mood to pray for the troops, Rasputin once wrote to the Grand Duke at his headquarters in Mogilev, inviting himself to visit the front. "Come at once that I may hang you!" replied Nicholas. To the dismay of the General Staff, Rasputin frequently sought the date of an offensive in advance "to pray for victory," a request that could not be denied since it came through the Czarina.

Military affairs bored the Czar. With a flourish of publicity, he established himself at the Grand Duke's former headquarters, but limited his martial duties to an hour a day. From 11 A.M. to noon he sat silently behind an ormolu-trimmed marquetry desk while his Chief of Staff, General Mikhail Alekseev, reported. When the Czar did speak it was usually to transmit some order or query from the Czarina. The campaigns were planned by the dedicated, hard-working Alekseev, and were announced in the Czar's name.

9. Ypres, 1915

9. Ypres, 1915

Ypres — the Cloth Hall.

Gas Warfare

Since the late autumn of 1914, the Western Front had become static, particularly in the Belgian province of Flanders where stubborn German attempts to break through were continually beaten back. Gains were measured in yards, which usually were retaken in another savage skirmish. In this sector was the ancient moated town of Ypres, behind an Allied line that formed a seventeen-mile-deep bulge, beginning five miles northwest at Steenstraate and curving round to Saint Eloi, some three miles south of Ypres. Shelling had nearly destroyed the historic Cathedral and 500-year-old Cloth Hall of Ypres, but the Germans justified this action by contending that the towers of these structures were used as observation posts.

Tactics used by both sides were largely conditioned by Flanders' topographical features, recognized by the Germans as terrain "not favorable to an attack from east to west." The low-lying land is broken by a semicircle of hills. Mount Kemmel, a 500-foot rise in the ridge southwest of Ypres, was of decided strategic value. If the Germans could capture this position the town would fall. The ridge offered excellent observation and placement of artillery for convergent fire; batteries could be easily screened from defenders on the lower level, while reinforcements and supplies could be brought up in the rear unseen.

A Canadian brigade arrived at the Ypres salient during mid-April, giving the French a badly needed rest. To the Canadians, the French trenchworks left much to be desired. Lengthy stretches of trench had no traverses to provide defense against enfilading fire. And in a lowland area where a high water table prevented digging more than two feet, it was also imperative that parapets be raised by sandbags or soil breastworks four feet or higher. Those that had been built by the French were not broad enough to stop bullets and some trenches even lacked this feeble defense. None had parados for protection against gunfire from the rear.

French morale was also reflected in the sanitary facilities which, declares Canadian official history, were "in a deplorable state and in a very filthy condition, all the little broken down side trenches and shell holes apparently being used as latrines and burial places for bodies. . . . The trenches and ground behind them were littered with dead, buried and unburied, and the numerous shallow graves greatly hampered digging."

Soon the breastworks were raised and widened. Where possible, the Canadians deepened existing trenches, also cutting traverses and new communications trenches. All were interconnected so that men could move to any section without being exposed to enemy fire. A continuous belt of barbed wire guarded the whole system.

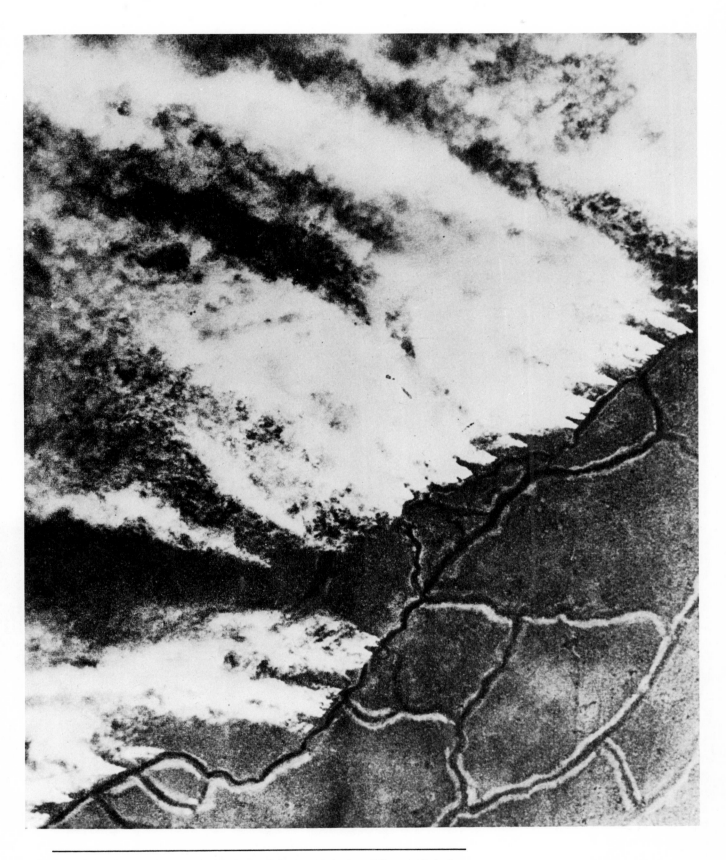

A massive German gas attack, shown in an aerial view. The gas is being
released from cylinders and wafted by the wind to the Allied lines.

The Devastation at Ypres

The tower of Saint Martin's Cathedral.

The high school.

The street leading to the Cloth Hall.

The Cloth Hall.

The ramparts and moat.

A dwelling.

The entrance to the cloister and the
ruins of Saint Michael's Cathedral.

The Cloth Hall and market place.

133

Simultaneously with the Canadian move to defend Ypres, Austro-German armies were concentrating in Galicia "to annihilate the offensive power of the Russians for all time," according to German Chief of Staff Falkenhayn. To divert possible Allied suspicion, he ordered the German forces on the Western Front to engage in various activities combined "with attacks insofar as the modest numbers remaining there permitted." A project of this nature involved no substantial advance, but an excellent opportunity to test new strategems or new weapons. "The battles of Ypres which began on 22nd April," German official history records, "had their origin on the German side solely in the desire to try the new weapon, gas, thoroughly at the front."

April 22, 1915, was a sunny warm Thursday, but far from serene in the Ypres salient. For the previous three days the surrounding land had thundered and quaked under one-ton high-explosive shells fired from the awesome 420-mm. howitzers. German objectives were mostly non-military in Ypres and nearby villages: streets, roads, and bridges had been selected as targets, but the powerful shells also destroyed churches, public buildings, homes, and lives. The area of fire was mainly to the north and east of Ypres. A lull beginning in the late morning ended at 4 P.M., when the French sector north of the town was furiously bombarded, the barrage slowly shifting to the Canadian front line.

Ninety minutes later the shelling ceased. Two French divisions, Algerian Turcos and African Light Infantry, between Langemarck and the Yser Canal, watched a strange greenish-yellow cloud slowly sweeping towards them. Nobody knew what to make of it. And then as it reached them they began choking, gasping in agony; many collapsed, suffocating to death, their eyes, noses and throats burning as though seared with acid. More than 160 tons of chlorine gas had been released from specially placed cylinders in the German trenches. Almost three times heavier than air, the poison gas billowed along the ground on a light northeast wind and rolled down into the trenches. The British troops first learned of the new weapon when they saw screaming survivors clutching their throats as they ran blindly in crazy-quilt patterns. But the gas-choked Canadians, who were not utterly disabled, doggedly saved the front. The gassed French left a four-and-a-half-mile unguarded gap, but the Germans advanced only two miles and paused, waiting for the gas to waft away. Falkenhayn had asserted that it was more essential to begin a gas attack at an early date than to advance any distance through enemy lines.

Late that night the Canadians worked feverishly to fill the gap and haul artillery into position; German flares lit the night, exposing them to fire. Despite traces of remaining chlorine, the Canadians extended their left flank to form a thin line to the French sector. A feat of high heroism was performed by Lance Corporal Frederick Fisher, who inched forward with a machine gun to hold off the enemy. He won the Victoria Cross, Britain's highest award, at the cost of his life. Had the Germans followed through the unprotected gap, they would have bisected the Ypres salient and encircled fifty thousand British and Canadian troops.

That the Germans had intended to use gas was abundantly clear, although the Allies had persistently ignored the warnings. Prisoners taken the previous month by the French mentioned the gas cylinders, but did not know the type of chemical to be used. This information was published in the "Bulletin of the French Tenth Army" in Picardy, March 30, but French commanders took no action. A stronger warning came from a German deserter who appeared on April 13th at the French 11th Division near Langemarck. Two days later the French Fifth Corps' "Summary of Information," distributed through divisions down to battalion level, reported "the prisoner described tubes with asphyxiating gas (that had been) placed in batteries of twenty tubes for every forty meters along the front." He showed his captors a simple respirator issued to operators of the apparatus.

A Belgian spy returning from behind enemy lines, declared that the Germans would attack with gas, but he neither knew the name of the gas nor the date of its use. A German high priority order in Ghent for twenty thousand respirators "to protect the men against the effects of asphyxiating gas," name unknown, was reported in a Belgian Army bulletin. The account also pinpointed the German location

"Turcos," as the *Tirailleurs Algériens,* native Algerian troops, were called. They were among the first soldiers gassed by the Germans along the Western Front.

A German mortar loaded with a gas shell. The explosive charge in shells such as this was kept extremely small. This allowed more space for the gas, but also limited the range. However, as they were used only to lob shells into the enemy trenches, a distance of five miles or less, short range was no handicap, and these weapons were greatly feared.

German prisoners bring Canadian
wounded to a rail line for evacuation.
Although the ground looks fought
over, and the telegraph lines are
down, the railroad tracks still seem to
be in good repair. More evidence of a
fight can be seen by the dent in the
helmet of the soldier bending
over at center.

of attack—precisely where it was launched.

But only one—General Ferry, commanding the 11th Division—believed the danger was real, and conveyed his concern to neighboring British commanders. Ferry also notified his superiors and was visited by his corps commander, accompanied by a liaison officer from French headquarters. Ferry was reprimanded for having warned the British directly, instead of through official channels at Joffre's headquarters. His recommendation that German trenches be shelled to reduce the danger of gas attack was rejected and he was ordered to dismiss this nonsense from his mind. (Later Ferry was removed from his command because he had been correct.)

The final warning came from the Germans themselves in a radio broadcast on April 17, charging that the British, "yesterday, east of Ypres, used shells and bombs with asphyxiating gas." Before resorting to any new atrocity, the German Supreme Command usually imputed their deed to the Allies, to "morally" justify retaliation.

The British made cursory attempts to ferret some evidence of the warnings, but air recon-

naissance over the German trenches revealed nothing; the cylinders were well camouflaged. General Sir Herbert Plumer, the British commander, incredulous that the Germans would act so ungallantly, merely passed the warning to his subordinates "for what it was worth," and dismissed the matter.

A second German gas attack on April 24 was repulsed by the Canadians, who recognized the greenish-yellow vapor drifting slowly in their direction. But because the German Supreme Command doubted the potency of gas, no strategic value was attached to its initial use against entire armies. Instead, it was misused in a small sector where its effect was negligible.

Hastily improvised respirators were issued to the soldiers, but because the compound's chemical composition was not known they were not particularly effective. Meantime, Charles Lucieto, a French spy, was piecing together the enemy's surprise. Disguised as a German traveling salesman, Lucieto had entered the Rhineland to report on German munitions. Krupp's enormous plants at Essen and Mannheim were under the tightest security. At Mannheim the agent observed that no poison gas was being

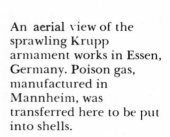

An aerial view of the sprawling Krupp armament works in Essen, Germany. Poison gas, manufactured in Mannheim, was transferred here to be put into shells.

concentrated in cylinders of convenient size for transport to the front, but that railway tank cars were moving away, headed in a northeastern direction.

Lucieto soon learned where they went and why. A glance at a map showed him that the tank cars were rolling toward Essen. The agent became a habitué of local cafés frequented by Krupp's workmen. He was a good listener and generously treated his new acquaintances to rounds of beer, in turn absorbing information from their gossip. Lucieto cultivated the friendship of a lonely old guard at Krupp's plant, who was flattered that he had found a friend in this substantial commercial traveler.

Lucieto's patience was richly rewarded. The guard soon turned to a truly remarkable experiment—poison-gas shells to be fired from a cannon. Feigning a mixture of enthusiasm and doubt, the operative proposed a bet at tempting odds. To win two thousand marks, the plant policeman agreed to furnish convincing proof, and invited him to join in witnessing an actual field test. They chose an inconspicuous position with a clear view of the field. A large motorcade bearing Kaiser Wilhelm and high

government and military officials drew up. Martial airs were played by a military band while an honor guard presented arms.

A large naval cannon and a 3-inch gun were ready for the demonstration; a flock of sheep, browsing on a hill nearly a mile away, was the target. The shell fired from the fieldpiece exploded with a slight thud, entirely different from the standard burst. Within seconds the naval gun fired. Neither shell was aimed at the sheep, but after each burst a dense cloud of greenish-yellow gas rose slowly and drifted toward the flock, covering them like a low-moving fog. After it had blown away all the sheep were dead, and the assemblage departed.

Several days later a sizable fragment of the gas shell was in the Paris laboratory of a prominent chemist, whose analysis should have enabled the Allies to manufacture a gas-proof respirator; and yet the early gas masks were ineffectual. The first was a gauze pad wrapped around chemically treated cotton waste. Another gas mask was the "smoke helmet," a grease-impregnated gray felt hood with a small mica window to see through. Gas readily seeped through the loose stitches and up under

The efficient Germans made use of animals from zoos and circuses in order to save on fuel. This massive log may be used to shore up some fortification or redoubt. However, even in the highly diversified German army, the military specialty of mahout must have been rare.

the bag, with the result that the wearer was more effectively asphyxiated than was the hoodless soldier.

In the Allies' possession was the simple but more effective German respirator given by the deserter, yet they made no use of it in designing their worthless contrivances. The foot soldiers' dread of gas was aggravated by their realization that no effective protection was available. "Gas was a nightmare," reported British poet Robert Graves. "Nobody believes in the efficacy of respirators. . . . Pink army forms marked 'Urgent' were constantly arriving from headquarters to explain how to use these. They were all contradictory. First the respirators were to be kept soaking wet, then they were to be kept dry, then they were to be worn in a satchel, then, again, the satchel was not to be used." By midsummer an improved respirator was developed, but not until November, 1915, did the Allies learn how the enemy made a gas-proof respirator. A trench raid by the Canadian Corps' 7th Battalion bagged twelve German prisoners, whose rubber gas masks were considered a great prize by Canadian intelligence.

The Germans had been disappointed with the trifling effects of gas shells fired at the Russians in January, 1915, and those tested at Essen were a new model. Wind-borne gas attacks were subsequently abandoned: sometimes an aberrant wind would eddy the poisonous cloud back to their own lines. Soon the fixed cylinders were replaced by gas shells which could be lobbed into enemy lines and gave troops no time to dodge the lethal fog. Such a shell had a reduced charge to allow space for the liquified gas, which converted to vapor on bursting.

Shells were designed to be fired from all artillery and mortars, with the reduced charge limiting the range to about five miles. This type of projectile was readily identified by its wobbly spin in flight and soft thud on exploding. Later the Germans used phosgene, a colorless gas three and a half times heavier than air and ten times more deadly than chlorine. In addition to being an asphyxiant, phosgene has a delayed-action effect on the heart, causing total collapse. Both gases evaporate within three to six hours in ventilated areas.

Fighting fire with fire, the Allies proceeded to make their own gas shells, but the Germans maintained the initiative. In July of 1917 they introduced mustard gas, an oily corrosive that blisters the skin causing ulcerated sores and that evaporates only after a prolonged period. Mustard gas terrified the troops. The Allies countered with Lewisite, an equally virulent blistering agent. The Germans also developed a chemical that penetrated respirators, causing the wearers to sneeze violently, retch, and vomit, and forcing them to tear off the gas masks. This maneuver was followed with a carefully timed barrage of other poison gases. At least 125,000 tons of gas were fired at the Allies during the War. In the conflict's last year, fifty percent of German shells were gas filled. Chemical warfare casualties on both sides well exceeded the million mark; one tenth were fatal.

Germany never forgave its deserter who disclosed the impending gas attack. His name was imprudently mentioned in a postwar article by the former commander of the 11th Division. Upon this evidence, the Reich Supreme Court in 1932 ordered his imprisonment for ten years. It is unlikely that he ever regained his freedom; in January, 1933, the Nazis moved into power.

A German 240-mm. cannon. As the Krupp technicians became more proficient, they were able to develop gas shells that could be fired great distances from guns such as this one.

10. The Gallipoli Campaign

Winston Churchill.

10. The Gallipoli Campaign

Britain's venture in Gallipoli was the outcome of slipshod planning and misjudgment. Except for Churchill, who had pressed for the capture of the Dardanelles Strait, this area was a remote consideration to the British War Office. Official interest was stimulated only after Grand Duke Nicholas sent a letter to Lord Kitchener in January, 1915, pleading for repayment of a favor. Barely five months earlier Russia, against all strategic considerations, had complied with an Allied request to attack Germany on the Eastern Front to lessen pressure in the West. Now Russia was in a simultaneous struggle with the Germans in Poland and the Turks in the Caucasus. The Duke hoped for a "demonstration of some kind against the Turks elsewhere, either naval or military."

England's policy toward Turkey was one of lost opportunities. The tottering Ottoman Empire would not have survived a British-Russian onslaught in the first months of the War. The Dardanelles' obsolete defenses were highly vulnerable, and Turkey's two munitions plants on the shore near Constantinople were exposed to point-blank fire from warships. That an Allied armada could easily penetrate the Dardanelles was taken for granted by the Turks. With surprising candor, Turkish official history admits: "Up to February 25 (1915), it would have been possible to effect a landing successfully at any point on the peninsula, and capture of the Straits by land forces would have been relatively easy."

Gallipoli peninsula, the southwest extension of European Turkey, is sixty miles long and from four to thirteen miles wide. An almost barren mountainous strip, Gallipoli had only one dirt road running its length in 1915. The ridges and steep slopes overlooking the beach offered excellent defensive positions, guarding the European side of the Dardanelles Strait, a forty-mile waterway that flows from the Sea of Marmara into the Aegean Sea and ranges in width from 1,400 yards to four miles. Anciently known as the Hellespont, the Dardanelles never freezes; but its two-way currents, rapidly veering winds, and violent storms make navigation treacherous.

Winston Churchill, First Lord of the Admiralty, was the only leading Briton who understood the advantages of forcing the Dardanelles. From the outbreak of war, he had vainly advocated a campaign against Gallipoli. England's last review had been eight years earlier, and the Committee of Imperial Defense had concluded that an army could not win a beachhead against enemy-held positions. Churchill's reasons for capturing the Dardanelles encompassed more than a limited military objective. It was the only route to Russia's Black Sea ports, and would facilitate communications with Britain's eastern ally.

By mid-January, 1915, the British War Office acted on the Grand Duke's request. Churchill

Men of the 2nd Australian Division cluster with boxes of supplies at
the cramped Anzac landing. Some have managed to dig dugouts in the
rugged terrain, but most seem to be simply milling around in confusion.

recommended that the Russians join the Allies in a two-front land and sea offensive, attacking Turkey from the Black Sea. The Russians agreed that this would raise the odds in their favor, but it conflicted with their long-nurtured intention to annex Constantinople and the Dardanelles. That the Allies should share in this victory disquieted the Russians, who declined Churchill's offer. Foreign Minister Sergei Sazonov confessed that "I intensely dislike the thought that the Strait and Constantinople might be taken by our Allies and not by Russian forces . . . I had difficulty in concealing from them how painfully the news affected me."

The British nonetheless resolved to undertake an invasion even without the Russians. Command of the operation was given to Admiral Sir John Fisher, veteran First Sea Lord, who came out of retirement at the age of seventy-four. In early January, 1915, Churchill, with the support of Fisher, cabled Admiral Sackville Carden, commander of the Mediterranean fleet, asking his assessment of a joint British-French strike. Such a project, Carden responded, would open the Dardanelles to the Allies. But the military planners had overlooked one key development—their desultory and meaningless naval attacks on Gallipoli had finally spurred the Turks to strengthen their defenses with German aid and matériel.

A combined British and French naval task force of eighteen English capital ships (including the new *Queen Elizabeth* armed with 15-inch guns), four French battleships, and auxiliary craft steamed to the entrance of the Dardanelles on February 19, 1915. After salvos had silenced the outer forts, raiding parties roamed the area spiking abandoned Turkish cannons. Foul weather delayed the attack five days, then the Allies resumed sporadic bombardment of the remaining forts at the entrance, forcing the Turks to retreat. But as the invaders moved up the Strait, they discovered

that the Turks had strong defensive positions concealed behind the escarpments. An Allied landing on March 3rd was repulsed. As the British planners had neglected to include aircraft for spotting, they could only fire blind on the Turkish positions with at best trifling results.

Nothing was mentioned at the outset, either by Admiral Carden or the Admiralty in London, about subsequent action if the squadron plunged ahead into the Sea of Marmara. Everyone assumed that the mere presence of Allied naval power would drain the Turks of any will to fight.

On March 11, Carden was directed to lead another sea attack but not to sail his heavy ships into the Dardanelles until it was free of mines. A sudden illness forced him to remain ashore and command shifted to his chief aide, John de Robeck, who renewed the offensive on March 18. The Straits had been repeatedly combed and were thought to be mine-free within five miles of the Narrows, Unknown to the British, however, a small Turkish vessel had laid a new line of mines beyond the principal mine field, stringing them where the naval force had been stationed during earlier shelling. All the Allied ships steamed safely past this hazard en route to fire at the forts. With the aid of seaplanes for spotting, Allied shelling silenced most of the shore batteries in the early afternoon.

Minesweepers continued to drag the known danger zone as the French ships withdrew. Suddenly the battleship *Bouvet* shuddered and ripped open as a high pillar of smoke and flame shot up from her deck. Still steaming on, she capsized and slipped to the bottom with her captain and 639 crew members. A few bobbing survivors were rescued. Some observers from a nearby ship thought the *Bouvet* had been hit by a Turkish shell; others believed that it had struck a mine.

Supporting ships moved up, firing at any Turkish position showing a gunflash, and destroyed all batteries by 4 P.M. Then without warning, the British battleships *Irresistible* and *Inflexible* listed sharply and vanished; they were followed by the *Ocean.* Fearing further losses, Admiral de Robeck ordered all surviving ships back to the Aegean. By the time the fleet cleared the Dardanelles, three more British

The British at Gallipoli. Once the troops and supplies had landed, there was very little place to put them.

Cannon

A high-explosive shell frightens mules on the Gallipoli Heights.

Before abandoning heavy guns, the retreating troops usually spiked them. One effective way was to fling a thermite grenade down the muzzle of the gun and the molten metal would weld the breech block to the chamber.

A Turkish cannoneer shuts his ears as his weapon fires. Beside him on a "horse" is the next round ready to be placed in the gun. It looks deceptively small for so enormous a gun.

battleships were limping with large gashes in their hulls caused by exploding mines.

Not until the War's end did the Allies learn that victory had been within their grasp in the first weeks of the attack. Half of the enemy's ammunition was gone and no mines were left. Though the Allies hoped to resume the assault, it was postponed and then replaced with a project to land troops on Gallipoli, with the Navy relegated to a secondary role. No battle plan had been formulated at the War Office in London when General Sir Ian Hamilton, Lord Kitchener's Chief of Staff during the Boer War, was selected to command the invasion forces.

Hamilton had only sketchy instructions and no assistance to develop them into a cohesive campaign. He hurriedly left for the Eastern Mediterranean without his administrative staff, certain only that he was to command an expeditionary force to invade Gallipoli and destroy the enemy. Hamilton's total knowledge of his objective was derived from the 1912 manual of the Turkish army, a faulty map of the combat zone, and tourist guidebooks to Constantinople bought in a last minute rush from local bookshops. When he left London, he had not even selected a landing site on the peninsula.

Since it was not even known whether Gallipoli had water, Hamilton had his men scour the bazaars of Alexandria and Cairo for empty oildrums, kerosene cans, skins, and any other container. As in London, all maps, however inaccurate, and guidebooks were bought in the hope they were better than nothing. Lacking weapons and implements for trench warfare, makeshift military workshops produced mortars, grenades, entrenching tools, and periscopes. Native donkey drivers and their beasts were impressed for transport service.

What this hastily improvised operation lacked in matériel, logistics, and organization was somewhat balanced by the valor of the troops. Some 78,000 men, mostly Australian and New Zealand Army Corps (Anzacs), one

The British beachhead with the grounded *River Clyde* listing slightly offshore. The Allied problem was to claw their way up the hills, at the summits of which waited the Turks.

153

Gallipoli

The grounded *River Clyde,* from which many Allied troops drowned trying to make their way ashore.

A heavily laden troop transport heads ashore under the protection of the guns of the British cruiser *Implacable.*

British liner unloading troops and supplies in Egypt. They were then ferried to the island of Lemnos, the staging area for the invasion.

Special barges transported horses to the already crowded scene.

A breakwater formed of sunken ships provides a convenient, manmade harbor where British troops could be supplied.

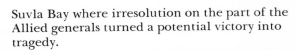

Suvla Bay where irresolution on the part of the Allied generals turned a potential victory into tragedy.

French division, and native Indian troops (Gurkhas) were assembled against the newly formed Turkish Fifth Army of 84,000 men, commanded by the German General Liman von Sanders. Turkey's hereditary enemy, Greece, volunteered three divisions to invade Gallipoli and attack Constantinople from the west, but the Czarist regime objected vigorously. Russia preferred to lose all than chance the remotest possibility of Greece claiming an interest in Turkish territory.

During the forty-eight-day respite following the fleet's withdrawal, General Sanders organized his defenses, stationing Turkish divisions at anticipated landing sites. He was assisted by the Turkish War Minister, Enver Pasha, who commanded a separate army. A lesser figure in the preparations was Mustafa Kemal, known to the postwar world as Kemal Atatürk, the father of modern Turkey. Time was Sander's most precious asset, and British procrastination gave him more than enough.

The staging area for the invading forces was Mudros Harbor on the Greek island of Lemnos, which the Allied flotilla left on April 23. On the advice of Kitchener, Hamilton limited landings to twenty miles on both sides of the peninsula, leaving the selection of beachheads to commanders on the spot. Two days later the Allies landed on four unconnected beaches at Cape Hellas, from which they planned to advance toward the Achi Baba plateau where Turkish gunners had a commanding view of the British fleet. Twelve miles up the western coast on the Gabe Tepe headland, two divisions of the Australian and New Zealand Army Corps also established a beachhead, known as the Anzac Landing.

The consequences of haphazard planning soon emerged. Since Hamilton knew little of Gallipoli, he found it easy to act on Kitchener's suggestion that he grant his commanders a free hand in selecting the time and place of landing. General Sir William Birdwood, commander of the Anzac Corps, believed a night landing would minimize risks from enemy gunfire. But British General Hunter-Weston, commanding the 29th Division, ordered daytime landings to permit the fleet to shell the defenders.

Successful Allied landings were often accidental and occurred at improbable sites. In one case a beachhead was established by the courage of a single man. Troops in the Gulf of Saros were two miles from shore when darkness overtook them. Without hesitation Commander B. C. Freyberg swam the distance with a watertight bag of flares, which he lit in a line along the beach.

General Birdwood's nocturnal landings bewildered his troops who found themselves on untenable beachheads, and precious time was wasted as the confused men sought their bearings. The ancient coal carrier *River Clyde*, converted to a landing craft with huge doors fitted to the hull, was filled with 2,000 soldiers. As the ship neared the shore, surrounded by troop-laden barges, the Turkish guns opened fire. The collier nosed into the sand but the water was too deep for wading. One of the survivors recalled the "water was crystal clear and we could see, lying on the bottom, in perfect formation, the uniformed bodies of the soldiers who had been hit or had fallen while scrambling ashore."

By midmorning of the first day, the beaches were littered with dead and wounded. If the store-bought maps were inaccurate, Birdwood had not improved matters by landing in the dark. His anticipated mile-long beach was less than three quarters of a mile long and about 100 feet wide, blocked by rocky cliffs at both ends. The confined area was a jumble of troops, animals, guns, and supplies. No orderly arrangements would be possible until more land was taken, an impossible ambition during the first days. The total Anzac forces were hemmed into a beach area less than two miles long and four fifths of a mile wide.

Mustafa Kemal was a few miles inland when notified of the landings. Commanding eight battalions and three gun batteries, he hastened to the scarp overlooking the beachhead barely in time to repulse the first Anzacs trudging up the slopes. With no previous battle experience, the Allies literally fought uphill against a foe superior in weapons. Hard pressed by gunfire from above, they found their small spades inadequate to dig amid the hardy scrub roots in the rocky terrain. Cavelike openings were eagerly sought in the steep hills. By nightfall each side had counted 2,000 casualties, and Kemal still held the heights.

Medics descended from the hills carrying an endless line of wounded into the confusion of

Birdwood's beach. Suffering was prolonged when many of these men were moved from ship to ship only to be told that the doctors and their staffs had left for shore with all their equipment and medical supplies.

More than 16,000 Anzacs had landed by April 26, and were thrown together on the lower slopes and ridges. Generals and privates lived in dugouts next to each other, sharing the same emergency rations. Constant shelling by the Turks interrupted, but did not end, new relays of Anzacs from inching up the slopes. Until the end of April, General Sanders withheld attack by his main body, preferring to observe the Allied pattern of deployment. While the Allies attempted to organize their haphazard forces, Sanders proceeded to select positions for his counterattack.

Sanders began his main offensive at the southern beachhead on May 1, but the Turks were quickly routed by Australian forces with the aid of two newly arrived brigades. To relieve his choked beachheads, General Hunter-Weston attempted a breakthrough on May 6, but was stalled by fierce resistance, with much bloodletting on both sides. General Hamilton took command himself but fared no better. Three days of bitter fighting, including repeated bayonet charges, cost the Allies one third of their troops in dead or wounded; and the Turks still held the heights.

As the torrid summer came to Gallipoli in May, malaria and dysentery began to take a mounting toll. One of the most ferocious battles ended in late May, the small combat area filled with mounds of 8,000 Turkish and Allied dead fouling the air with a horrible stench. To prevent an epidemic which would decimate both sides, General Birdwood, at the urging of his medical staff, requested a burial truce with the Turks. Under a white flag, hostilities were suspended for nine hours on May 24, as ministers, doctors, and burial parties joined to eliminate the threat.

Life at the Front. This soldier has hung his shaving mirror on a ruined wall. As there were no underground wells on Gallipoli peninsula, fresh water and wine were imported in enormous quantity.

The Living and the Dead

Turkish dead before the New Zealand lines photographed during the truce, when the antagonists joined together to bury the mounting dead before resuming the carnage.

British artillery in action. The men are wearing flash hoods, which protected the gunners from any flashback caused by powder remaining in the gun after firing. When the breach was opened, the men always had their backs turned because of flashback.

Turkish infantrymen parade in Constantinople. Dallying on the part of the Allies allowed the Turks to bring crack troops to the peninsula, which otherwise could have been taken unopposed.

The brief armistice was almost surrealistic. All participants in the burials wore white armbands and were forbidden to carry field glasses, weapons, or peer into enemy trenches. Besides a cease-fire along the entire front, all trench troops were not to raise their heads above the parapets. Enemy rifles were to be returned without their bolts, a loose agreement that was generously circumvented. Nervousness permeated the front as opposing parties met in the narrow no-man's-land.

Some trenches were only thirty feet apart. Silently the Anzacs and Turks began to dig long, deep trenches or communal graves, but soon exchanged cigarettes and pleasantries in fractured Turkish and English. Both sides furtively probed each other's defenses. While checking the identity of corpses, officers noted carefully the disposition of trenches and security systems. And Kemal was rumored to have donned a sergeant's uniform and worked nine hours with burial parties near Anzac trenches. Before parting many swapped small pocket items.

At midafternoon the last of the dead were gently laid in the burial trenches, when a single shot pierced the silence. For a few uncertain moments the burial parties ceased all action and movement except breathing, dreadfully aware they were between thousands of rifles pointed at them from both sides. No second shot followed and the men turned to finish their task. With handshakes and goodbyes, each side returned to their trenches in the late afternoon. Several minutes later a rifle was fired from somewhere in the Turkish lines, and once again the battlefield was swept by a hurricane of shells and bullets.

While the Allies concentrated on land fighting, enemy naval vessels sent three British battleships to the bottom before the end of May. A Turkish light warship slipped silently down the Dardanelles under the cover of darkness and torpedoed the *Goliath*. Two

An Anzac heads for the coast and medical assistance, lugging a wounded comrade.

weeks afterward a German U-boat sank the *Triumph*. A day later the *Majestic* suffered the same fate. U-boat action in the Mediterranean alarmed the Allies, particularly England. Fearing for the safety of the *Queen Elizabeth*, they ordered her to a British port.

England's position in the Dardanelles improved with the arrival of shallow-draft monitors, mounting 14-inch cannon, able to move about with little danger from mines. British submarines also entered the Strait sailing into the Sea of Marmara and the harbor of Constantinople, where they took a heavy toll in Turkish shipping. A transport filled with 6,000 troops was torpedoed in the harbor itself. Turkish losses included a battleship, a destroyer, 5 gunboats, 44 steamers, 11 transports, and 185 sailing vessels. Britain's price for this destruction was eight of the assigned thirteen submarines.

At the beginning of August, a new major landing was made with two divisions at Suvla Bay in northwestern Gallipoli. It was largely unopposed by the surprised and outnumbered Turks, who retired from the beaches to the heights to await reinforcements. Instead of pressing forward, however, the indecisive British commanders, including Hamilton, squandered priceless time discussing strategy.

By the time the Allies decided to attack, Sanders had had time to transfer two divisions in full strength from Bolayir to Sari Bair Ridge, which the Allies assumed held only the meager force that had retreated the day of the landing. Too late they realized that the odds were against them, but they fought on doggedly for almost five days, then broke off. Existence on the beach became intolerable as snipers and cannoneers on the heights rapidly thinned their ranks. More than 40,000 Allied casualties occurred in August.

In September two British and one French division were transferred to Salonika and General Hamilton was recalled. He was not given another command. But not until Lord Kitchener visited Gallipoli in November did he fully grasp the debacle. He needed no further urging to evacuate the peninsula. Kitchener's brief stay coincided with a sea of troubles that befell the troops. During the summer they had endured intense discomfort from heat, flies, and lack of water.

In November a thunderstorm preceded a twenty-four-hour drenching rain followed by sleet that turned into a blinding blizzard, leaving about two feet of snow on the ground. Those living in Anzac caves and underground galleries had some degree of comfort, but the exposed troops at Suvla Bay suffered agonies. The downpour turned ravines and gullies into roaring cascades, carrying down tons of mud, dead Turks, and pack animals.

Nature did not spare the Turks either. Perhaps 500 men on both sides drowned in their trenches. Others froze to death. More than 5,000 frostbite cases were suffered at Suvla Bay alone. None could recall such a violent tempest. The Allies were totally unprepared for this storm; no extra warm clothing had been stockpiled. Except for Churchill, no one in London or Gallipoli regretted the evacuation, which began on December 19.

High losses, if not disaster, were anticipated during the departure. In October General Hamilton feared that "it would not be wise to reckon on getting out of Gallipoli with less loss than that of half the total force. . . ." Yet his successor, General Charles Monro, supervised the withdrawal and completed it on January 9, 1916, *without a single casualty*. Every brigade down to its lowest echelon was scheduled to leave in accordance with their distance from the four embarking piers. Small groups of six to a dozen men filed down dozens of little gullies, each closed off by the last man, always an officer, who left timed fuses to explode mines in tunnels. Without lights and with no smoking, soldiers trooped in steady cadence at three miles an hour.

Each single line moved uninterruptedly to its appointed jetty, the sound of tramping feet muffled by a road of sandbags. Generals and privates squeezed together in motor barges, each holding 400 men. A careful count was kept to be certain that no one was left behind. The only sound was that of the barges throbbing seaward from memories of defeat. The Turks were so completely deceived that they continued to fire shrapnel and bullets at the empty trenches.

Enemy chagrin at this ruse was articulated by Mustafa Kemal, absent from the peninsula at that time: "Had I been there, and had the British got away without loss, as they did, I would have blown my brains out." But his German allies appreciated the skill of the operation. A dispatch by the military correspondent of the *Vossiche Zeitung* read: "As long as wars last, the evacuation of Suvla and Anzac will stand before the eyes of all strategists as a hitherto unattained masterpiece."

Almost a half million Allied soldiers had been shipped to Gallipoli in 1915, and more than fifty percent became casualties. The expedition included 410,000 British and 79,000 French troops. British casualties amounted to 214,000; and French to 47,000. At least a half million Turks were engaged and 251,000 casualties were sustained, according to their official records, but these are suspect. Other estimates place the figure much higher, but whatever the number, the flower of the Turkish army was crushed, and General Edmund Allenby's risks were reduced in the forthcoming Palestinian Campaign.

Gallipoli tarnished sterling reputations. Prime Minister Herbert Asquith removed Churchill from the Cabinet and Lord Kitchener no longer commanded the unquestioning loyalty of government ministers. His authority was diminished by shifting munitions control from him to a new ministry, headed by Lloyd George. Churchill donned a uniform and served in France until 1917, when he returned to favor and was appointed Britain's Minister of Munitions.

Lord Kitchener (second from right) observes the situation at Gallipoli for himself.

The end of the Dardanelles Campaign: the battleship *Cornwallis* shells the supplies left behind on the beach to see that they do not fall into enemy hands.

11. The Inferno: Verdun

General Erich von Falkenhayn.

11. The Inferno: Verdun

As 1915 drew to a close, the Central Powers looked forward to a promising year. Together with their new Bulgarian ally, Austro-German troops had overwhelmed the Serbian Army in the Balkans, forcing its remnants to seek refuge in Greece. Czar Nicholas' armies were still dazed from their defeat, allowing the shift of nearly half a million German troops to the Western Front, and Germany was now free to wheel her might against strongpoints in France without peril to positions elsewhere.

German Chief of Staff General Falkenhayn drafted a memorandum to the Kaiser on Christmas Eve, 1915, in which he assessed the military alternatives. Britain was singled out as the main enemy but, except for U-boat warfare, was too far off for invasion. "Her real weapons on the continent," he asserted, "are the French, Russian, and Italian armies." Ruling out Russia and Italy, he argued for a concentrated offensive against France which "has almost arrived at the end of her military effort. If her people can be made to understand clearly that in a military sense they have nothing more to hope for, the breaking point would be reached and England's best weapon would be knocked out of her hand."

Falkenhayn did not think a mass breakthrough essential. He planned to "bleed France white" by selecting an emotionally hallowed area "for the retention of which the French would be compelled to throw in every man

they have." Belfort and Verdun were the two places that met his specifications, but he endorsed the latter. Verdun was a somnolent French provincial town of some 14,000 protected by a massive complex of fortifications that bulged into the German lines. Verdun, too, was uncomfortably close (twelve miles) to the principal German railway system, in case the French chose to start an offensive. Falkenhayn also reckoned that Verdun was the northwestern gateway to Paris, about 135 miles away.

Under the code name of operation *Gericht*— meaning "place of execution"—the campaign was scheduled for February 12, 1916. To assure the Kaiser's consent Falkenhayn recommended that the Fifth Army, commanded by the Crown Prince, which had faced Verdun since the Battle of the Marne, be assigned to spearhead the assault. Falkenhayn did not show the original memorandum to the Crown Prince or his Chief of Staff, General Schmidt von Knobelsdorf. Instead they were given a general order for "an offensive in the Meuse area, in the direction of Verdun." The Crown Prince construed this to mean that his objective was the capture of Verdun, which Falkenhayn emphatically did not want. If the fortress succumbed to an onslaught, his grand strategy to "bleed France white" would be thwarted.

Reinforcements were drawn from battle-hardened units of the Wehrmacht. Three army corps were shifted to the Crown Prince's command in January, 1916. The Brandenburg

French soldiers at the foot of the aptly named Dead Man Hill,
a bulwark in the Verdun fortress system. After repeated assaults
and horrendous bloodshed on both sides, it was taken by the Germans
in May, 1916, during the last gasp before their campaign faltered.

III Corps arrived after a brief spell in a rest camp. By mid-February more than thirteen divisions had been deployed to the salients in or around Argonne, Champagne, and Lorraine, a staggering mass of troop power in a sector of about twenty square miles. While the Crown Prince held nominal command, the crucial decisions were made by eighty-year-old Field Marshal Gottlieb von Haeseler and General Knobelsdorf. Nonetheless the central strategy throughout the campaign was forged by General Falkenhayn.

German preparations for the huge offensive began with an awesome concentration of cannon from Russia, the Balkans, and the Krupp works. Lined up around the scene of assault were 542 mine throwers. Combined with additional flanking armament, more than 1,400 cannons were arrayed on a front less than eight miles long! Among these were thirteen earth-shattering 420-mm. siege howitzers.

Especially vicious were the mine throwers, which fired canisters packed with more than 100 pounds of high explosive and assorted scraps of metal. The mines could be seen trundling end over end in a high arc, but this warning was usually too late. The blast destroyed entire stretches of a trench system. Another fearsome weapon was the 130-mm. "whizz bang," that fired 5.2-inch shrapnel shells at the speed of a rifle bullet and cut down the French without warning. Not completely satisfied that these instruments would fulfill their expectations, the Germans also introduced the flame thrower.

The elaborate preparations around Verdun did not go unnoticed, but warnings by French Intelligence officers that an offensive was in the offing were ignored by Joffre who was preoccupied with his coming summer campaign on the Somme. After the fortresses of Liège and Namur had fallen to the Big Berthas, Joffre believed the Verdun fortifications could serve no useful military purpose. More than 4,000 guns were removed from the forts, at least 2,300 of which were large-bore artillery. As late as January, 1916, cannon were detached from the casemates for service elsewhere. Instead of buttressing Verdun until it became France's stoutest stronghold, French Headquarters virtually denuded it.

Conflicting reports of Verdun's invincibility brought an Army Commission to the site in July, 1915. General Auguste Dubail, commanding the Group of Armies East, which encompassed the Verdun sector, assured the parliamentary delegation that the fortress system was adequately protected. Another witness, General Coutanceau, the military governor of Verdun, testified to the contrary, for which he was unceremoniously dismissed.

At the end of 1915, a report found its way to General Gallieni, then Minister of War. Written by Colonel Emile Driant, Deputy for Nancy, and a prominent military analyst, it stressed an alarming need for more guns, manpower, and supplies, including even barbed wire. Another delegation of the Army Commission visited Verdun to investigate. A confirmed report to Gallieni was sent to Joffre for comment. In a rare display of anger, Joffre denounced "soldiers under my command bringing before the Government, by channels other than the hierarchic channel, complaints or protests concerning the execution of my orders . . . calculated to disturb profoundly the spirit of discipline in the Army . . ." Driant died a heroic death in the first hours of Verdun's defense.

The morning of February 21, 1916, was bitingly cold. At 7:15, along a six-mile front, concealed German batteries lobbed shells into the fortress complex at the rate of 100,000 an hour. More than two million shells pocked a triangular area of about 14 miles, demarcated by Verdun and the villages of Brabant and Ornes and obliterated the French forward trenches. After twelve hours of bombardment German search units crept forward in the dark to probe for French resistance.

By the night of February 23, the Germans had little to show for their effort. Despite the numerical superiority of seven to one in artillery and three to one in troops, they had advanced only two miles and taken a mere 3,000 prisoners. The next day they cracked the main French line, took 10,000 prisoners, sixty-five cannons and a large number of machine guns. Meanwhile the massed German guns, many wheel to wheel, belched a continuous rolling barrage ahead of their infantry units, levelling trenches, blasting pillboxes, splintering forests.

French morale was benumbed by the violence of the attack and the sub-zero tempera-

French troops testing flame throwers, a new weapon introduced by the Germans at Verdun and quickly copied by the Allies.

Field Marshal Gottlieb von Haeseler who, at age eighty, helped deploy German forces at Verdun.

Artist James Scott's "On the Hindenburg Line." The Line faced Verdun across the Meuse River.

The Devastation at Verdun

A view of the ruined apse of Verdun's Saint Sauveur Church.

The blasted village of Fleury, which stands between Fort Douaumont and Verdun.

Aerial view of the town, bisected by the Meuse River, showing Notre Dame Cathedral. The road that disappears from the lower left corner is the route to Bar-le-Duc—*La Voie Sacrée*.

A line of trucks moves downhill through the desolation around Verdun.

173

tures. The Zouaves, tough colonials accustomed to the heat of Algeria, became brittle at fifteen degrees below zero. On the morning of February 24, a battalion of Zouaves stiffened into insensibility when the commanding major fell. Command was then assumed by a captain whom the troops ignored as they fled rearward. Morale was "restored" by a section of machine guns fired at their backs.

Alarmed at the deepening crisis, General Noël de Castelnau, Chief of the French General Staff, intervened directly with Joffre to check the peril by appointing General Henri Pétain to command Verdun's defenses. Pétain moved into his new post February 25, the same day Douaumont was captured. The loss of this fort was a demoralizing blow; in the words of Pétain, it was the "anchorage of the entire Verdun defensive system." As with the other forts, Joffre had reduced its garrison to a crew of less than two dozen elderly artillerymen,

who operated one gun turret, and a caretaker.

A Zouave division entrenched in front of Douaumont's glacis—the steeply sloped embankment surrounding the twenty-four-foot-wide dry moat—had broken and fled under the continuous bombardment. Trudging through snow squalls and the pall of battle smoke, a nine-man patrol of Brandenburgers had come upon the abandoned, lowered drawbridge. Others followed until 300 amazed Germans were roaming the fort's galleries. The mighty bastion of Douaumont was captured without a shot fired—yet it had withstood 120,000 German shells.

Summoning all the hyberbole at its command, the German government trumpeted the capture of Fort Douaumont "by assault," an exploit witnessed personally by the Kaiser. Matters became more grotesque when a garbled telephone report misled the Germans to proclaim the fall of Fort Vaux on March 9. (It was

"The Assault," by Henri de Groux. French counterattacks at Verdun began in April and by the end of the year Douaumont and Vaux had been retaken.

not captured until June 7.) An exultant Kaiser awarded Imperial Germany's highest order *Pour le Mérite* to the divisional commander who telephoned the message, and to his subordinate who had not captured Fort Vaux.

Defense is impossible without supplies. The German cannon had cut off all routes except a twenty-foot-wide, secondary road from Verdun to the city of Bar-le-Duc about thirty-five miles southwest. A one-track narrow-gauge railway alongside this road carried supplies for the peacetime garrison, but was now utterly inadequate. Quarries were opened along the road and thousands of Territorials working with gangs of civilians used picks and shovels to widen and pave the surface.

Meanwhile Pétain divided the front into sectors for the distribution of heavy guns, shells and other supplies. Upwards of six thousand trucks could traverse the road every twenty-four hours—an average of one truck every fourteen seconds, inspiring the name *La Voie Sacrée*, the "Sacred Way." More than 500,000 troops and 170,000 draft animals moved to the front along the Sacred Way, a tribute to Pétain's innovation in logistics.

After a lull of several days, the German Fifth Army renewed its attack March 5 at another site, on the western (left) bank of the Meuse. Pétain welcomed this tactical blunder, for that section of the line was held by his freshest and best-supplied troops. Now trapped in a murderous artillery crossfire from flanking gun positions across the Meuse, the Germans were forced to lengthen their lines along the river's east bank.

Terrific loss of life was suffered by both sides in the bloody engagement around *Le Mort Homme*—"the Dead Man," the bluff dominating the west bank. Inundated by high-explosive shells, the earth convulsed, lifting and tossing men, equipment, and debris like chaff. Heat

Water collects in shell craters on Fort Douaumont. The Verdun system was not rebuilt. Instead the Maginot Line was built to guard the new frontier.

from the explosions melted the snow, filling the shell holes with water in which many of the wounded drowned. The blinded and mangled, groping for the safety of holes, toppled on their comrades drenching them with blood.

The most colossal explosion of the War occurred when a French gunner accidentally hit a German arsenal of more than 450,000 large-caliber shells. Unknown to the French, the ammunition had been concealed in Spincourt Forest, but had carelessly been left fused. By early April every German 15- and 16.5-inch cannon in the entire sector had been destroyed by French artillery. General Palat, the French military analyst and historian, asserts this double action was decisive in the ultimate defeat of the invader.

Pétain left Verdun on May 1 to command the Center Army Group, and was replaced by General Robert Nivelle who inculcated a determined offensive attitude among his troops. Later, after the enemy had been stalled at Verdun, Nivelle's slogan "They shall not pass" became the nation's battle cry. Slight but significant German gains continued until the summer, when the Allied Somme offensive caused Falkenhayn to redirect his manpower and matériel. Neither fresh divisions nor large quantities of ammunition were thenceforth sent to Verdun.

Fort Douaumont was recaptured in a massive French counterattack on October 24, with 170,-000 troops, more than 700 pieces of artillery, and 150 aircraft. This victory was a triumph for General Charles Mangin and Nivelle. From then on the Germans were steadily beaten back yard by yard. Fort Vaux was retaken in November. By December 18, the exhausted invaders left Verdun to the French. More than forty million artillery shells, plus countless millions of bullets, had been fired by both armies in the ten-month carnage. When incessant shelling, flame throwers, poison gas, and bayonet-charging infantry attacks could not budge the defenders, German sappers burrowed under French positions, detonating powerful explosive mines that blew cavities ten stories deep.

French casualties totaled more than 550,000 men killed, wounded, prisoners, and missing. Germany lost more than 450,000 men in similar casualties. By mid-summer it became evident to the Kaiser that Falkenhayn's tactics were also bleeding Germany white. His resignation was forced on August 28 with little pretense at face-saving. The previous day Romania joined the Allies, much to the astonishment of Germany, for Falkenhayn had assured all that this country could not enter the conflict until her crops were harvested in mid-September. An inviting opportunity arose to shunt the demoted Falkenhayn to an army command on the Romanian front. Hindenburg succeeded him as Chief of General Staff, with Ludendorff joining him as First Quartermaster General, a position equivalent to his deputy.

The Kaiser appraises the situation with Hindenburg and Ludendorff, who replaced Falkenhayn at the head of the General Staff. All three men have one hand obscured in some way, standard practice in the Kaiser's presence. This was to avoid invidious comparisons between normal arms and the Kaiser's withered left arm, about which he was morbidly sensitive.

12. The Somme

General Sir Douglas Haig.

12. The Somme

The Battle of the Somme (July–November, 1916) originated with Joffre. His purposes were to compel German troop withdrawal from the Russian front, inflict mortal blows on the Germans, and relieve the pressure against Verdun. Since the Somme area offered no strategic objectives Sir Douglas Haig, the British commander, when first told of the campaign, preferred a sector more open to attack, such as Flanders. Although not subject to Joffre's control, it was his policy to defer to the French commander's wishes in France if he sensed no disaster ahead. Haig was soon so completely won over to Joffre's plan that he forgot the Somme sector was chosen without tactical consideration, and heralded this front as the gateway to victory.

In January, 1916, the British system of voluntary enlistment was replaced by conscription. Further reinforcements were being drawn from Canada, Australia, New Zealand, South Africa, and India. Haig proposed the campaign be postponed until these reserves gave the Allies a substantial edge. He also waited the arrival of more guns, ammunition, and a new secret weapon—a machine-gun destroyer dubbed a "tank" for security reasons. But Joffre would hear none of this. In his diary of May 26, Haig wrote: "The moment I mentioned August 15, Joffre at once got very excited and shouted that 'The French Army would cease to exist if we did nothing till then.' " The assault date was set at July 1.

Joffre's original plan provided two French armies and one British to attack on a sixty-mile front. But French participation at the Somme sharply decreased as their forces were minced at Verdun. In the final lineup the French portion narrowed to eight miles on a twenty-four-mile front. Joffre's initial allocation of forty divisions was reduced to sixteen, but only five were present on the day of attack. The burden of the campaign was to be borne by the British from the outset. Their initial share increased to an army and a corps totaling twenty-one divisions. A reserve of eight divisions, five of them cavalry, was held in the rear.

The Somme River had been relatively quiet since 1914. If this motivated Joffre, he overlooked the German preparations to strengthen their position in both directions along the river. In the compact chalk soil, they had constructed an elaborate underground network of partitioned galleries to a depth of forty feet. These fortifications included facilities for kitchens, laundries, first-aid stations, and huge reserves of ammunition. Electric lighting—then a rare luxury among civilians—was provided by diesel generators. Even the heaviest bombardment would not penetrate this subterranean complex.

The Somme sector offered its best advantages to the defenders. Entrances and exits were concealed in village dwellings and neighboring woods, whereas the open trench lines on the opposing hillsides were clearly defined in the

An elderly couple survey the wreckage of
their former home, reduced by shellfire.

chalky soil. The Germans also enjoyed an unobstructed view of the Allies up to a range of 5,000 yards. The defensive fortifications rising one above another forced Allied attackers to claw their way up from one level to the next while exposed to fire. The German strongholds in the chalk hills were also honeycombed with ferro-concrete heavy-gun emplacements, transverse communications trenches, and defensive bunkers.

The British assigned an army of civilian conscripts for the Somme offensive, half-trained soldiers without combat experience who could not understand the cynicism of the veterans. The youths fancied themselves sweeping over the top and hurtling on to Berlin. Many of them perished in the first day's charge.

The elaborate preparations being made for the offensive did not escape the Germans. Prince Rupprecht noted in his diary the mounting evidence which included intelligence reports from Madrid and The Hague citing loose and indiscreet remarks by Allied military attachés. Any doubts vanished when French troops moved to forward positions. The Germans almost surmised the exact day of the assault and braced themselves for it.

Beginning June 24, the Allies subjected the German lines to a thunderous artillery barrage. During the six-day bombardment more shells—one and a half million—were fired than had been made in England during the first eleven months of the war. It was a stupendous spectacle. Many Allied soldiers left their trenches those summer evenings just to witness the starlike explosions on enemy positions.

An overrun German trench, including the characteristic "potato masher" hand grenades (lower right) and below them pieces of tubing attached to cylinders buried in the ground. The cylinders held poison gas. The tubes, of flexible lead piping, were led out of the trenches and aimed at the enemy's lines. The cylinder valves were then opened, releasing the gas into the air to be blown toward their target.

The best and worst men were at the Somme. Among those who were to become better known were Bernard Montgomery and Archibald Wavell; poets Edmund Blunden, Robert Graves, John Masefield, and Siegfried Sassoon. Waiting expectantly in the German trenches was Corporal Adolf Hitler, " . . . not ashamed to acknowledge that I was carried away by the enthusiasm . . . and that I sank down upon my knees and thanked Heaven out of the fullness of my heart for the honor of having been permitted to live in such a time."

Later Masefield would recall those moments in his book *The Old Front Line:* "Almost in every part of this old front our men had to go up hill to attack . . . . The enemy had the lookout posts, with the fine views over France, and the sense of domination. Our men were down below, with no view of anything but of stronghold after stronghold, just up above, being made stronger daily."

During the last days of the barrage, rains turned the trenches into mud wallows. German gunfire forced the British to keep below the parapets, aggravating their discomfort. At 7:30 A.M. on July 1, 1916, officers blew their whistles and troops began to leave the trenches. A scorching sun dried the men, leaving their uniforms and equipment caked with mud. They were in trouble from the outset. Each soldier had a sixty-six-pound load which included two sandbags, 220 rounds of ammunition, a rifle, two bombs, and other items, a weight greater than that carried in full marching order. Many were laden with additional gear such as field-telephone equipment, picks, shovels, and boxes holding carrier pigeons. Not surprisingly, very few of them were able to shoot accurately.

Haig kept a running chronicle of events. A half hour after the assault whistles blew, he was pleased to record that all reports were " . . . most satisfactory. Our troops had everywhere crossed the enemy's front trenches." Actually, at that moment, his troops were falling by the thousands under German fire, well before reaching the front trench line. The Germans had accurately zeroed in by map coordinates every square yard of no-man's-land, which by sunset was strewn with more than 60,000 dead and wounded Englishmen. No previous battle in history records such astounding loss in one

day. General Marie Fayolle's French troops fared better than the English. Their artillery assault was well paced, but they were too few in numbers to cut an opening in the German lines.

Despite crippling losses, the British dug in and were strengthened by the arrival of Anzacs and Canadians. Individual deeds of heroism were many, but some were outstanding. In early September Canadian Corporal Leo Clarke was cleaning part of a captured 500-yard German trench system south of the Cambrai road. Most of his comrades were dead or wounded. While in the trench Clarke met a German party of twenty soldiers led by two officers. After twice emptying his revolver, the corporal fired the rounds of two abandoned Mauser rifles, killing one officer, who thrust a bayonet into Clarke's leg. At least sixteen more Germans were killed or wounded before the rest fled. The Canadian fired at the remaining five, killing four. The fifth and sole survivor was taken prisoner. Clarke was awarded the Victoria Cross, but he died in action before the news reached him.

Tanks First Used

The high casualty rate in earlier campaigns caused by German automatic fire spurred the Allies to develop a "machine-gun destroyer," that could pass over trenches and flatten barbed-wire obstacles. On September 15, 1916, the British introduced their secret weapon— the tank. It was the most revolutionary weapon of the War, far more significant than siege howitzers or poison gas. The principal originator was Colonel Ernest Swinton, a writer whose prewar articles envisioned a self-propelled machine moving on a continuous belt similar to the American caterpillar tractor.

But Lord Kitchener, British Secretary for War, rejected the tank as "a pretty mechanical toy but of very limited value." Without Churchill's intervention, the plans might never have left the drawing board. On his own initiative, Churchill, then First Lord of the Admiralty, illegally siphoned funds for the Director of Naval Construction to create a working model.

In time the Germans learned to counter tanks with flame throwers, as here they incinerate a British tank. In the first attacks they were taken too much by surprise for such measures, and even later they were often too terrified by the oncoming, rumbling monsters to resist.

A French 270-mm. mortar draws a crowd as it bellows forth smoke after firing a round. The presence of so many onlookers suggests that the weapon was a new one— at least to this part of the front.

To deceive spies, the vehicle, which resembled a water carrier, was called a tank.

The forty-nine tanks manufactured by August, 1916, were still in the experimental stage, and their crews largely untrained, when Haig ordered them into action against the advice of Swinton and others who had designed and made them. Even pleas by Prime Minister Asquith and Lloyd George, now Minister of War, failed to dissuade him. Only eighteen of the forty-nine tanks reached the field of action. Six of them, assigned to the Canadians, broke down before or during battle. About ten tanks rumbled toward the frightened Germans. The crew of one captured a village. Another took a trench with more than 300 prisoners.

Haig's decision to "expose this tremendous secret to the enemy upon such a petty scale . . . shocked" him, Churchill reported. By the premature use of the tanks before they were mechanically perfected, adequate in numbers, and with properly trained crews, Haig, in the words of the British historian, B. H. Liddell Hart, ". . . not only endangered its future usefulness, but threw away the chance of surprising the enemy while he was unprepared with any countermeasures. The consequence was to prolong the hardships and toll of the war."

Shortly before the tanks arrived, Lloyd George visited Haig and Joffre. The sight of thousands of horses moved him to suggest that

Canadian troops at the Somme climb from their trenches amid shellfire. This was the second wave of assault, as shown by the stretcherbearer (center) wearing his Red Cross armband, going out to look for casualties. The extreme youth of the soldier at far left underscores one of all wars' greatest horrors—the toll it takes of a nation's young manhood; France was bled so white that on the eve of World War II, when asked where were the men needed to come to her defense, a statesman replied: "They sleep in the Fields of Glory."

cavalry charges against massed automatic gunfire was murder, whereupon the commanders condescendingly told him that civilian knowledge of military matters was at best trifling. But Haig had some capacity to learn. On September 16, he shifted three of the five cavalry divisions well to the rear, behind the city of Albert. The other two were kept forward—just in case.

Fighting at the Somme was a series of engagements that subsequently degenerated into localized savage assaults. By November, 1916, both sides were too debilitated to continue. British losses alone—in killed, wounded, prisoners, and missing—amounted to 420,000. Similar French casualties were 204,000, while the Germans' totaled 670,000. "The Army had been fought to a standstill and was now utterly worn out," confessed Ludendorff in his memoirs.

Allied gains were picayune for the cost—a thirty-mile strip only seven miles at its widest, lacking any worthwhile position for attack against strategic objectives. Joffre's military career ended with the Somme. In a government shake-up, the new premier, Aristide Briand, decided that Joffre was dispensable. Haig not only weathered the political tempests, he was even promoted to Field Marshal. As an indirect outcome of the Somme offensive, however, Lloyd George replaced Herbert Asquith as prime minister.

A group of Anzacs leave for the front. Their sly cheerfulness combined with the odd bump under the coat of the man with his coat over his shoulder lead to the suspicion that they're getting away with something, probably a dog. Although pets were against regulations, they were popular at the front and the men often smuggled them into the trenches. They were a valued ally in the ceaseless war against the rats that infested the battle zone.

A Canadian makes repairs in a farrier's trench well behind the lines. The depth and width was sufficient to make it a shelter for animals as well as men. ▶

13. Sea Warfare

Admiral Sir John Jellicoe.

13. Sea Warfare

At the outbreak of hostilities, a stroke of chance and the good judgment of Winston Churchill enabled the British fleet to hedge most of the German navy in the harbors of Kiel and Wilhelmshaven. The Royal Navy had been engaged in annual exercises when Archduke Francis Ferdinand was assassinated. Anticipating trouble, Churchill had ordered the fleet to continue on full war footing. This measure ultimately enabled the British Expeditionary Force to be ferried safely to northern France.

Aware that German sea power could not cope with the Royal Navy in open combat, the Berlin Admiralty resorted to sinking Allied shipping by surface raiders and U-boats (submarines—in German, *Unterseeboote*). England countered with search-and-destroy measures, simultaneously deploying the Grand Fleet in a blockade of Germany. Sea warfare consisted mainly of isolated, limited engagements—some in distant oceans—leaving the British in control of the sea lanes. But U-boats became a growing menace, and were not effectively countered until 1917, when groups of ships were convoyed by swift American destroyers armed with depth charges.

Disaster at Falkland

Admiral Graf Maximilian von Spee's Asian Squadron was Germany's most powerful na-

val arm away from home waters in August, 1914. His armored cruisers *Gneisenau* and *Scharnhorst*, and two light cruisers *Emden* and *Nürnberg* were moored at Tsingtau on the Shantung peninsula, Germany's only Far Eastern colony. Spee knew that his ships would never reach Germany if he went by the shortest route—the British dominated Suez Canal. By steaming easterly along the Pacific and the South Atlantic, his chances of safety increased. The *Emden*, at the request of its captain, set out as a lone raider to destroy maritime commerce in the Indian Ocean.

Spee did not confine his homeward journey to passive sailing. He stopped at Christmas Island and the Marquesas, severed English transoceanic cables at Fanning Island, and shelled Tahiti. But he was unable to drop anchor at German Samoa, for it was held by New Zealand troops. The Squadron reached Easter Island on October 1 to rendezvous with the cruisers *Dresden* and *Leipzig*. Within a week the warships met colliers at the Juan Fernández Islands, about 500 miles west of Chile, then set course for the South Atlantic.

Spee's route and destination were suspected by the British, who sent Vice Admiral Sir Christopher Craddock to attack the squadron. His force, an outdated battleship, two armored cruisers, and a light cruiser, confronted the Germans on November 1, off the Chilean coastal city Coronel. The battleship, with a top speed of fifteen knots, was too slow for the

The naval section of the Krupp works at Essen, where the giant gun turrets were manufactured and assembled. Of greater importance, Krupp's experts supplied shells with delayed-action fuses—with devastating effect on British ships.

An Australian destroyer creates a massive bow wave as it slices its way through the water.

The German light cruiser *Dresden*, the only ship to escape destruction at the Falkland Islands. She was later sunk at Juan Fernández.

action. Without the support of her 12-inch cannons, Craddock recklessly rushed toward the enemy. In a short and furious battle, the *Good Hope* and *Monmouth* were sent to the bottom with all men including the admiral. Only the light cruiser *Glasgow* escaped.

The horrified Admiralty in London mobilized thirty warships, including nine French and Japanese, to cruise the ocean lanes that might be entered by Spee. The units were deployed so that the German squadron would be outmatched by any group encountered. Admiral Frederick Sturdee, assigned to lead the attacking forces, steamed toward the eastern coast of South America. At the same time, the battle-cruiser *Australia*, armed with 12-inch guns, was racing up from its South Seas patrol. Its armament and speed together would enable it alone to destroy Spee's squadron.

Meanwhile, Spee and his men were guests of honor at a victory celebration given by the German colony at Valparaiso, and attended by Chilean officials. His three remaining ships then rounded Cape Horn into the South Atlantic, and headed toward Port Stanley in the Falkland Islands where he planned to seize supplies and demolish the radio tower. By coincidence, Sturdee's squadron was in port December 8 when a deck officer on the *Nürnberg*, peering through his telescope, saw the unmistakable tripod masts of the battle-cruisers.

The Germans veered sharply and fled with the faster British ships in pursuit, the fine visibility and calm seas offering excellent battle conditions. Three hours of pounding with 12-inch shells were necessary to sink the *Scharnhorst;* the *Gneisenau* followed her two hours later. The poor armor-piercing capability of British shells—bursting on impact instead of first penetrating the hull—necessitated an enormous expenditure of ammunition.

The faster *Nürnberg* and *Leipzig* were overtaken later in the evening and capsized under repeated salvos. Along with four warships and two colliers, the Imperial German Navy lost 2,300 sailors—including Admiral Spee and his two sons. Only the Speedy *Dresden* escaped, shrouded in darkness and rain. Four months later she was traced to the favorite German ship haunt in the Juan Fernández Islands and destroyed.

The End of a Raider

Australian seamen in lifeboats remove survivors from the beached *Emden*.

The *Emden* in her prime.

A conception of the end of the *Emden:* "The *Emden* Beached and Done For," by Australian artist Arthur Burgess.

HMS *Sydney* racing through heavy seas. After the destruction of the *Emden* there was no further need for her in the Pacific and she was sent to the North Sea.

Karl von Müller, commander of the *Emden*.

The Raider Emden

For three months the *Emden* marauded the South Pacific. Captain Karl von Müller's 3,500-ton raider was fast and mounted ten 4.2-inch guns. Müller planned not only to sink cargo vessels and cut trade with India to a starvation level, but to spread the word among Asians that Teutonic benevolence was preferable to British and French imperialism. In the first two weeks of its campaign, the *Emden* captured thirty merchantmen in the Bay of Bengal. Müller disguised his three-stack ship with a false fourth funnel.

Although the *Emden* left a wake of ruin that became a nightmare to the Allies, Müller and his crew of 361 comported themselves with civility, treating captured crews within the letter of international law. But the raider's days were running out. Her last mission was to blow up the radio tower and port installations on Cocos Island, about 500 miles southwest of Java. Local operators, suspicious of the vessel's crude dummy stack, sent an alarm "strange ship off entrance" before the *Emden's* radio operator could jam it. A landing party then demolished the tower and transmitting apparatus. Unaware that the message had been sent, Müller waited for a collier to coal his ship.

About fifty miles away a large Anzac convoy received the signal in the morning of November 9, 1914, and the light Australian cruiser *Sydney* immediately raced to the scene. Müller mistook the smoke on the horizon to be that of the collier, and realized too late that it was an enemy that outmatched the *Emden*. Besides a weight advantage of 2,000 tons, the *Sydney* was three knots faster and mounted eight 6-inch guns. Shortly after the firing commenced the *Emden* became a blazing pyre. To save the survivors, Müller drove the wreckage on a reef. For his treatment of prisoners, the captured captain and his officers were permitted to keep their swords.

Battle of Dogger Bank

In the first month of war, the sunken German light cruiser *Magdeburg* provided a windfall to the Allies. While probing the interior of this vessel at the bottom of the Baltic Sea, a Russian diver chanced upon a lead-weighted case containing the secret German signal code and squared charts of the North Sea. A copy was given to the British, who thereby were able to decode all the secret radio communications of the German Navy. Later the Germans altered the code, but not enough to mislead the Royal Navy, which meanwhile had developed directional radio receivers to locate the positions of enemy warships.

Besides establishing dominance in distant oceans, the British were determined to control the North Sea. At the end of August, 1914, Vice Admiral Sir David Beatty organized a raid against German warships patrolling the approaches to Helgoland, a heavily fortified island guarding the chief German naval base about forty miles eastward. Beatty's fast battle-cruisers, reinforced by several light cruisers and destroyers, swooped out of a fog, sinking three German light cruisers and a destroyer. The British squadron then withdrew before German warships from Wilhelmshaven could get under way. This sortie was splendid for British morale.

The Germans kept themselves in trim by irregular hit-and-run raids on Scottish and English coastal areas. Their targets were usually civilian, never the well-defended British naval ports. In December, 1914, the Germans shelled two Yorkshire ports at nearly point-blank range, killing at least 500 civilians. Then they proceeded to test British North Sea defenses. Under a moonless sky on the night of January 23, 1915, Vice Admiral Franz von Hipper's squadron of four battle-cruisers, four light cruisers, and nineteen destroyers slipped out of Wilhelmshaven. His targets were British naval patrols and fishing vessels on the Dogger Bank, a wide shoal of the North Sea midway between England and Denmark, celebrated for its codfish.

By radio intercepts the British learned of this foray, and a fleet steamed out to meet the marauders. Early next morning, some 190 miles west of Helgoland, five battle-cruisers and four light cruisers from Rosyth on the Firth of Forth combined with three additional light

The German fleet in Kiel harbor.

Dogger Bank

Admiral Sir David Beatty.

German seamen scramble for safety along the sides of the capsizing *Blücher* as some of their shipmates scatter into the water. The *Blücher* was sunk by Beatty's forces at Dogger Bank.

cruisers and thirty destroyers from units stationed at Harwich. Under Beatty's command the squadron set course to meet the German raiders. Admiral Sir John Jellicoe, commander in chief of the Grand Fleet, had sailed from Scapa Flow to link forces with Beatty, but arrived too late for the battle.

Acting as advance scout for Hipper, the German light cruiser *Kolberg* steamed up from the southeast, and shortly after 7 A.M. caught sight of the British light cruiser *Arethusa*. The exchange of gunfire attracted the attention of Beatty and Hipper, who met for the first time. They would meet again at Jutland in the greatest naval contest of all time. Taken aback at such unexpected force, Hipper reversed course and steamed at full speed for the safety of Wilhelmshaven. In the following five-hour running battle, the slightly faster British ships gradually reduced the distance. Plunging ahead at twenty-eight knots, Beatty's flagship *Lion* narrowed the range on the *Blücher*, Hipper's slowest battle-cruiser, firing the first salvo at 8:52 A.M. Soon most of the opposing vessels were in full combat. Sensing a sure kill, the British kept their guns on the *Blücher*. In little more than an hour, the ship was convulsed with internal explosions, but refused to sink.

Gunners on the battle-cruiser *Derfflinger* fired dozens of 11- and 12-inch armor-piercing shells into Beatty's flagship, forcing the *Lion* to lag astern at fifteen knots while other British ships chased the fleeing enemy. No longer hindered by the *Blücher*, Hipper made the most of his chance to speed homeward. Unable to pursue from the crippled *Lion*, Beatty appointed Admiral Moore, commanding the *New Zealand*, to lead the chase, and signalled by flag, "attack the enemy's rear." Cautious to the point of timidity, Moore misread Beatty's order and concentrated bombardment on the *Blücher*, already too damaged to offer any resistance.

Beatty quickly signalled again, "keep closer to the enemy," whereupon Moore moved his squadron closer to the hapless *Blücher*. Now ablaze fore and aft, a few of her small guns firing erratically, the *Blücher* slowly capsized at 12:15 P.M. As Hipper's ships vanished over the southeastern horizon, Beatty transferred his flag to the fast destroyer *Attack* and overtook his squadron, where he again shifted his flag to the battle-cruiser *Princess Royal*. At 12:30 P.M. a message from the Admiralty warned him the entire High Seas Fleet had steamed out to escort Hipper's group into Jade Bay. While Beatty was sailing back to England, Jellicoe and the Grand Fleet arrived at the scene and helped tow the battered *Lion* to Rosyth for repairs.

That Dogger Bank did not end in a more decisive British victory was largely due to the bumbling Admiral Moore, who was forthwith removed. German losses were one sunken battle-cruiser, two others damaged, and 954 seaman killed. British casualties included two damaged ships and fifteen dead. The German Admiralty was most disturbed by the British foreknowledge of its naval movements. For the next eighteen months the High Seas Fleet was kept in harbor, and emphasis was placed on U-boats.

German warships at anchor in Kiel.

The German fleet passes in review. These ships show two stacks to the three of the larger *Emden*.

H.M.S. Vindictive

On the night of May 9–10, 1918, the outdated heavy cruiser *Vindictive* steamed into Ostend harbor on the Belgian coast under heavy artillery fire. At the entrance to the anchorage, a major base for German submarines, the ship was grounded and scuttled by its crew who escaped on two fast motor launches. Although the waterway was partly blocked, U-boats continued to operate from the base with only some inconvenience. Shown is the battered ship and its daring crew after a previous unsuccessful raid.

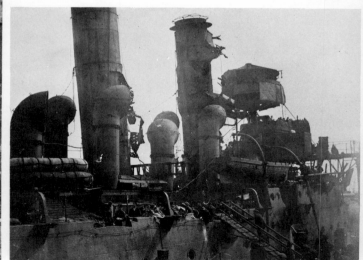

14. Battle of Jutland

British cruiser.

14. Battle of Jutland

In January, 1916, the aggressive Admiral Reinhard Scheer was appointed commander in chief of the German High Seas Fleet. He had long fretted at England's "hunger blockade" of Germany and his frustration intensified when the Kaiser decelerated the U-boat blockade under threat of American intervention. Despite his militance, Scheer avoided all-out battle with the stronger British Navy. Instead, he began a series of hit-and-run raids along English coastal areas intended to draw British warships in pursuit, and these he would attack, provided the odds were with him.

Britain had thirty-seven battleships and battle-cruisers of the Dreadnought class against Germany's twenty-three capital ships and an even greater advantage in cannon power—168 guns in 13.5- and 15-inch caliber and 104 12-inch guns against 176 German cannons of 12-inch bore. The British also had thirty-four heavy and light cruisers against eleven German, and eighty destroyers to sixty-three.

Scheer sent small groups of cruisers against English coastal cities, and foggy weather deterred British pursuit. By May 30, he had worked out a scheme to draw the Royal Navy into a trap. His bait was a squadron of light cruisers and destroyers under Admiral Franz von Hipper that was to cruise up the Norwegian coast. The British, he reasoned, would not send their entire fleet to intercept a limited foray. Trailing fifty miles behind would be Scheer commanding the High Seas Fleet in

full strength. If the British struck, Hipper was to offer token resistance then turn tail, leading the pursuers into range of Scheer's armada.

German sailing plans were known to the British the previous day, but Scheer's purpose remained a mystery. A radio station at Wilhelmshaven continued to broadcast with the call letters of Scheer's flagship, *Friedrich der Grosse*, to make the British Admiralty think that the main High Seas Fleet was still in port. Toward the end of May, British naval decoders intercepted a rash of radio messages indicating unusual naval activity. Further suspicion was aroused when U-boat packs were seen off the Scottish coast. Sensing extraordinary action, Admiral John Jellicoe and Vice Admiral David Beatty hit on what was virtually the same scheme. Scheer was to be misled into an attack against apparently weaker British units which, after a brief exchange of fire, would retreat toward the main Grand Fleet lurking beyond the horizon.

Before daybreak of May 31, Hipper's flagship, the 26,000-ton *Lützow* led the decoy squadron up the Danish coast to the Skagerrak, the eighty-mile-wide arm of the North Sea separating Denmark from Norway. Scheer chose this route so that the numerous British spies along the coastal areas could report the German units. To pinpoint his position further, Hipper's radio transmitters chattered incessantly. Indeed the Germans disclosed more than they intended. Radio-direction-

An early zeppelin flies over the German High Seas Fleet as it steams
along in cruising formation. These three or four columns sailing together
like a checker-board kept the fleet compact, yet able to deploy quickly
in case of battle.

finding stations on the British east coast identified the 28,000-ton *Bayern* as the major radio-communications unit of the German Navy.

On the night of May 30, the Grand Fleet steamed eastward in divergent directions to meet again some fifty miles west of the Norwegian coast. Beatty's decoy group consisted of four battleships and six battle-cruisers, while Hipper's squadron comprised five battle-cruisers. Both had light destroyer scouts.

A seaplane carrier, the old converted Cunarder *Campania*, on which a forty-yard flight deck had been installed, was scheduled to sail with Beatty's group, but an error prevented the carrier's captain from receiving his orders until ninety minutes after Beatty's departure. Jellicoe first learned of the *Campania's* absence at midnight, when it sailed alone into the darkness; and not until 2 A.M. did he know that it had left Scapa Flow. Mindful that the carrier was in submarine-infested waters without escort, Jellicoe ordered her back to port. The resultant lack of air reconnaissance played a fateful role in the Battle of Jutland.

Admiral Beatty's course brought him approximately in line with Jellicoe, but some seventy miles farther south. Shortly after 2 P.M. of May 31, Beatty turned northward to rendezvous with the main fleet at the Skaggerak in the late afternoon. At that moment, Hipper's flotilla was thirty-five miles east, steaming northward on a parallel course, while Scheer's main fleet was trailing at a distance of fifty miles. The two German admirals were unaware of Beatty's presence.

A few minutes after Beatty's ships swung to the north, a lookout on the *Galatea*, a light cruiser on the eastern flank, caught sight of a Danish tramp steamer *N.J. Fjord* in the distance, puffing an unusual amount of steam. Cutting out of formation, the *Galatea* went to investigate. Simultaneously the *Elbing*, one of Hipper's light cruisers screening his western

---

In what was most likely the first air-sea battle in history, the zeppelin *L-43* tried to bomb HMS *Sydney* in the North Sea. The bombs fell too erratically to hit the ship and the altitude of the zeppelin kept her out of antiaircraft range. When all its bombs were gone, the zeppelin left with no damage inflicted by either side. The scene was painted by Charles Bryant.

flank, saw the same steamer and wheeled toward it. Spotting each other at almost the same time, the two vessels flashed warnings to their respective fleets, "Enemy in sight!"

Had the aircraft carrier been with Beatty's squadron this encounter, favorable to the Germans, could have been avoided, for the antagonists would most likely have met farther north, within range of Jellicoe's main might. The *Galatea* and *Elbing* raced toward each other, exchanged salvos at 2:52 P.M. and broke off action. Only a dud landed on the British vessel, and a seaman's hands were seared when he picked up the shell to throw it overboard. Before nightfall 265 warships—149 British and 116 German—and about 100,000 men would join in a titanic conflict over more than 400 square miles of ocean.

Beatty directed all ships to "assume complete readiness for action in every respect" then snapped an imprudent order. His six battle-cruisers were to steam ahead at their top speed of twenty-five knots, while his four slower but more powerful battleships were left behind. Intent on engaging the five enemy battle-cruisers, including Hipper's *Lützow*, Beatty sacrificed his numerical edge of nearly two to one.

Upon being sighted by the British, Hipper turned southeast in accordance with Scheer's plan, toward the waiting main High Seas Fleet. Beatty's squadron followed and Hipper opened fire at 21,000 yards. The German admiral's chief concern was the longer range of the British 13.5-inch and 15-inch batteries against his 11- and 12-inch guns, but in the brief exchange, German gunnery easily bested the British. Beatty's flagship *Lion*, and the *Tiger* were hit repeatedly.

Nearly every German salvo struck its target, or straddled so closely that the blast buckled British hull plates. At 4 P.M. a projectile pierced the *Lion's* turret amidships and exploded. Only the turret commander, Royal Marine Major F. J. Harvey, survived the blast long enough to save the ship. The explosion broke open the turret gun's breechblock, igniting the powder bags. His legs blown off, the dying Harvey called through the voice tube an order to flood the magazine. For his valor, Major Harvey was awarded the Victoria Cross posthumously.

The British suffered a stunning blow in the loss of the *Queen Mary*, a 26,350-ton battle-cruiser mounting 13.5-inch cannons. A salvo of German armor-piercing shells penetrated her nine-inch-thick steel plates and, according to an eyewitness, caused a "small cloud of what looked like coal dust . . . from where she was hit, but nothing more until several moments later, when a terrific yellow flame with a heavy and dense mass of black smoke showed ahead, and the *Queen Mary* herself was no longer visible." Only 9 out of her 1,275-man crew survived.

A few minutes later the *Indefatigable* was struck by two missiles from the evenly matched 21,000-ton *Von der Tann*. Thirty seconds later, with no visible evidence of smoke or fire, the ship exploded with a deafening roar carrying a crew of 1,017 to their watery death. As with the *Queen Mary*, a magazine had exploded. Men on nearby friendly vessels watched aghast as "all sorts of stuff was blown high into the air, a 50-foot steam picket boat . . . being blown up about 200 feet."

His hat rakishly cocked, Beatty slowly paced the bridge of the *Lion*, surveying the seascape. Flames soared skyward from stricken ships. Shells plunging into the water exploded as though they had struck steel, sending up hundred-foot geysers. Dead fish floated on the surface as far as the eye could see. Bobbing in their midst were struggling men, mangled bodies, and the debris of destroyed ships. Two of his craft were sunk, and the rest damaged except for the *New Zealand*.

Beatty resolved to continue the skirmish, confident the four dreadnoughts would soon join him. Suddenly, German shells struck the *Princess Royal*, enveloping her in smoke and flame. Turning to his flag officer, the admiral, with a trace of annoyance, commented: "Chatfield, there seems to be something wrong with our bloody ships today. Turn two points to port," which was toward the enemy.

Shortly Beatty was rejoined by Admiral Evan-Thomas' squadron of battleships—*Barham, Malaya, Valiant,* and *Warspite*. Scheer's scheme to waylay Beatty was now foiled. Instead of setting course to trap the British squadron between Hipper's battle-cruisers and his main fleet, the German admiral was compelled to expose his hand to save Hipper from certain destruction.

A light cruiser, two miles from the *Lion*

On the Sea

French Flotilla Sinking German Ship Zeuta, *16 August 1914*
by A. von Romberg. Captured German War
Painting, Office of the Secretary of Defense.

The Battleship Posen *in
Night Action* by Adolf Bock.
Captured German War Painting,
Office of the
Secretary of Defense.

Minesweepers, Halifax by Arthur Lismer,
Canadian, 1885-1969.
The National Gallery of Canada,
Ottawa, The Canadian War
Memorials Collection.

Surfaced U-Boat Shelling Freighter by Adolf Bock.
Captured German War Painting, Office of the Secretary of Defense.

*Admiral Rheinhard Scheer, Commander of the
German High Seas Fleet* by Arnold Busch. Captured German War Painting,
Office of the Secretary of Defense.

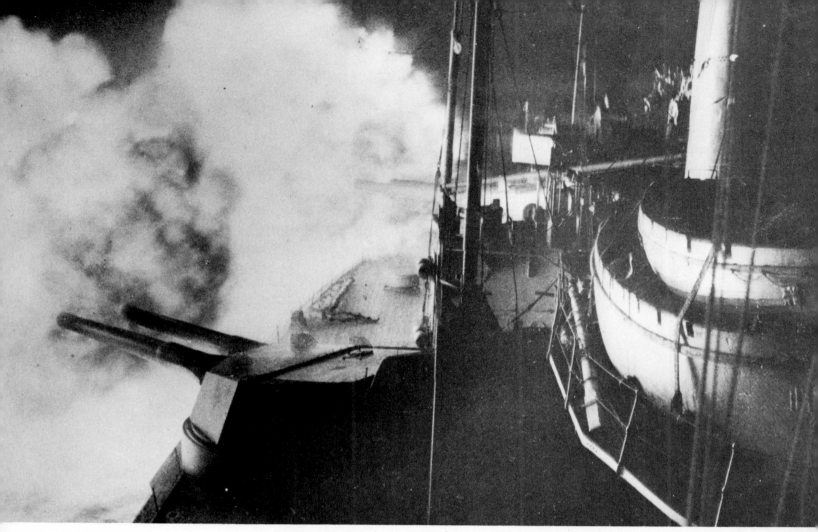

The flash of the great guns lights up the deck of the *Hercules*, firing at night.

Only the bow of a stricken ship shows above water as the fleet in the background proceeds at Jutland. Because of the vast distances involved, the haze, and the tremendous amount of dense coal smoke emitted by both fleets, few informative photographs of the Battle of Jutland exist.

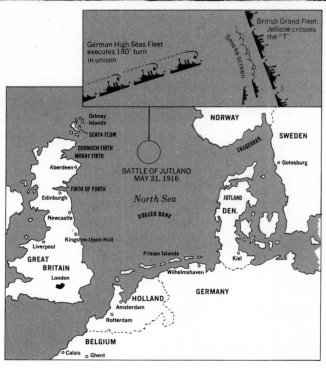

Map shows location of the Battle of Jutland in the North Sea. The German ships are shown reversing their direction to escape the fury of Jellicoe's massed guns.

sighted Scheer's armada at 4 P.M., and promptly notified Jellicoe and Beatty. Beatty held his course until the German main fleet loomed on the horizon, then turned 180 degrees and raced northward seeking the protection of Jellicoe's cannon. Evan-Thomas failed to see the flag signal to turn, and his battleships became the target of enemy gunfire and sustained damage and casualties before eluding the Germans. The *Barham* and *Malaya* were hit several times, and the *Warspite's* steering gear was temporarily disabled. The British also inflicted punishment; every gun on the *Von der Tann* was twisted into useless wreckage, and the *Lützow* was barely able to proceed under her own steam.

At 5:30 P.M. German advance destroyers saw several British light vessels steaming toward them from the northeast. These were scouts attached to a group of three battle-cruisers under Rear Admiral Horace Hood sent by Jellicoe to strengthen Beatty's squadron. In a

The Grand Fleet steams off to sea.

214

brief action, the German light cruiser *Wies-baden* was pounded and sunk with most of her crew. Two destroyers, the German *V-48* and the British *Shark*, also were lost.

Two aging British cruisers, the 14,600-ton *Defence* and her sister ship *Warrior* engaged Hipper's battle-cruiser at 6,000 yards. Within four minutes the *Defence* was blown up and her crew of 908 men lost; *Warrior* sank the next day while being towed to a Scottish port. The German score thus far was three bat-

tleships, two battle-cruisers, and three destroyers against only one light cruiser and two destroyers.

The two armadas were now plunging toward each other, but only the British knew it. Jellicoe was in constant communication with the Admiralty in London where decoding experts—the captured German naval code books before them—intercepted messages between Scheer, Hipper, and the Admiralty in Berlin. Aided by radio-direction finders and the Ger-

Strength at Sea

Iron Duke,
Admiral Jellicoe's flagship.

The *Deutschland*, belted by thinner armor, was already obsolete at Jutland.

The battle cruiser *von Moltke*, which became Hipper's flagship at Jutland after the loss of the *Lützow*.

British warships steaming at sea.

man Navy's squared chart of the North Sea, British technicians determined the changing positions of the High Seas Fleet. By 5:45 P.M. Jellicoe was notified where the enemy had been an hour and a quarter earlier.

The British fleet was steaming south in a formation of six parallel rows of four battleships. Each column was 2,000 yards apart, with 500 yards between each ship. This formation was undesirable for battle, as only a small number of guns could be fired forward; maximum firepower is possible only when the ships are broadside in a line, allowing each one to aim its fore and aft batteries simultaneously.

To deploy the battleships in a single broadside line would take four minutes, but this action presupposes the enemy is directly ahead and his exact distance is known. If he approaches the left or right flank, a substitute maneuver is used to allow the fleet to form a single line broadside to the attacking force. Jellicoe could not decide on his maneuver until he knew Scheer's course and position.

At 6 P.M. Jellicoe's *Iron Duke* and Beatty's *Lion* were in sight of each other. "Where is the enemy's battle fleet?" the commander in chief signalled, but received no answer; Beatty had lost Scheer's forces. Ten minutes later the question was repeated and four minutes elapsed before Beatty replied by blinker: "Have sighted the enemy's battle fleet bearing S.S.W." The enemy was moving directly toward the right flank of the Grand Fleet. Jellicoe briefly studied the compass, then ordered a deployment to port. Within seconds his left column raced ahead followed in smooth succession by the other five until the twenty-four dreadnoughts formed a single battle line 15,000 yards long, moving southeast.

Until this maneuver was completed, Scheer had not known the Grand Fleet was in the area. His light scouting vessels had scarcely signalled him when the northeastern horizon became a flashing panorama of white and orange fire followed by a hail of huge explosive shells. Jellicoe was performing the strategic maneuver of crossing the "T," in which Scheer's row of ships, one behind the other, were drastically handicapped in firepower while the British Grand Fleet could bombard them with all guns flaming.

The Royal Navy was shooting under favor-able conditions. Except for stabbing flashes from gun muzzles, Jellicoe's ships were obscured by the dusky eastern sky and the dense coal smoke wafting eastward from the German stacks. Within ten minutes Scheer's forward ships received at least a dozen crippling hits. Fires were raging in the *König*, and the *Lützow's* bow was almost under water; she later sank. *Von der Tann's* superstructure collapsed, her cannons hanging askew over a deck littered with dead and dying men.

Scheer wasted no time. At 6:36 P.M. he issued the classic naval order *Gefechtskehrtwendung nach Steuerbord* at which the battle formation swung to starboard and reversed course, each vessel turning 180 degrees in unison, then vanished into the mist. Before escaping the Germans administered a blow. Though the *Derfflinger* had been hit several times, she fired a parting salvo at Hood's flagship *Invincible*. A thunderous explosion broke the 17,250-ton vessel in half. Bow and stern each pointed 100 feet skyward then both halves sank with the entire 1,026-man crew.

After the Germans retreated, Jellicoe, afraid that his ships might suffer damage from mines (none were carried by the Germans) dropped astern or torpedoes fired from destroyers, ordered his fleet to reverse course. The antagonists disappeared from each other's view. In the brief lull that ensued Jellicoe re-formed his fleet into six columns and altered course southeast, intending to set his ships as a barrier between the High Seas Fleet and Germany. Shifting course slightly again brought Jellicoe in a shallow crescent between Scheer and his home base. Time was running out; the sky was darkening and the mist getting denser.

At 7 P.M. the German ships were seen approaching from the west. Scheer had decided to cross behind the British in his homeward dash, but he miscalculated and blundered again into Jellicoe's armada. This time his "T" was capped more menacingly than before. Once more conditions favored Jellicoe's forces. Scheer's fleet was silhouetted against the still-light western sky while the British were but murky forms to German target spotters.

Four minutes after the Germans were detected, Jellicoe altered his course slightly to narrow the range, and opened fire at 9,000 yards. The next fifteen minutes were a deafening inferno of blasting cannon and exploding shells. Ships emerged from the mist like phantoms, fired a salvo or two, then disappeared again. The forward German ships were blanketed with concentrated fire. Scheer was unable to see his enemy except for muzzle flashes.

To divert British attention from his main units, Scheer ordered a smokescreen through which German destroyers launched torpedoes, all of which missed. Next Scheer directed his battle-cruisers to "charge the enemy; make straight for him!" Behind this protective screen the rest of the High Seas Fleet once again reversed course. As the last ships were speeding away from the British, the cruisers, too, broke off action and rejoined their fleet. The badly damaged *Lützow* was left to sink while Hipper transferred to the *Moltke*. At his side, serving as his Chief of Staff, was Erich Raeder, who was to be commander in chief of the German Navy in World War II.

Hipper's already battered vessels were further damaged. Large amounts of water rushed into gaping holes. All his battle-cruisers shipped 1,000 tons or more of seawater; the *Seydlitz* kept going with 5,000 tons of water sloshing dangerously below decks. (That these craft were repaired and returned to service in three months is a tribute to the skill of their designers.) Aboard the *Derfflinger* more than 150 men lay dead, her main turrets in shambles. The surviving crew stumbled about in gas masks against the deadly fumes from the fires below.

Fearful of torpedoes, Jellicoe turned in the opposite direction from the westward-fleeing Germans. The distance widened until 8 P.M. when the British admiral felt secure enough to turn after the Germans, but darkness diminished his remaining chance of victory. At 8:25 P.M. Beatty's fast battle-cruisers came within range of several German units to the west, and opened fire. The Germans replied with several salvos, but both sides soon lost sight of each other.

In the night Jellicoe was reluctant to resume the battle. His longer gun range and numerical superiority offered no advantage against small ships sneaking into torpedo range. A further hazard lay in the danger of his ships accidentally colliding or firing at each other in the dark. He knew that Scheer's homeward course would be one of three channels through German minefields. By patrolling the routes between Scheer and the German coast until morning, he planned to conclude the battle in daylight.

The British armada re-formed in three parallel columns, with destroyers deployed 9,000 yards astern to guard against torpedoes. Any warship within sight of this flotilla would be tabbed an enemy. At 9:17 P.M. the formation cruised southward with Beatty's squadron in the van. A minelayer sailed to block Horn Reef Channel off the Danish coast, one of Scheer's three possible escape routes. In the early hours of the night the two enemy fleets sailed on a roughly parallel course six miles apart, each unaware of the other. Scheer was anxious to avoid another battle or be driven farther away from the German coast. Determined to slash through the British picket line if necessary, he set course for Horn Reef Channel at 9:10.

The last episode of the battle began at 11:30, when the spearhead of the German fleet, sailing eastward toward Horn Reef, encountered the British rearguard of destroyers. There followed a pandemonium of collisions on both sides, frenzied skirmishes under the glare of starshells, searchlights, and blazing ships. A few minutes after midnight, the British cruiser *Black Prince* moved toward the dim outlines of heavy ships, apparently in the belief they were friendly. Captain Bonham signalled the secret challenge for the day. The reply came swiftly. Powerful light beams gripped the cruiser as four enemy battleships fired broadsides, turning her into a huge fireball. In an explosion that rocked the night, the *Black Prince* disappeared with 37 officers and 825 men.

A British destroyer torpedoed the obsolete *Pommern*, the only German capital ship lost in the battle. Hipper's light cruiser *Elbing* sank in an accidental collision with the battleship *Posen*. The English destroyer *Spitfire* rammed the German battleship *Nassau*. Some men survived only by luck. Captain Wintour of the British destroyer *Tipperary*, which later sank, bent over; an enemy projectile whizzed across the top of his head, taking his cap and leaving a skin-deep groove in his scalp.

Scheer's fleet disengaged itself and continued course for Horn Reef, arriving at 3:30 A.M. Two

British battleships watched it from a distance of less than three miles, but failed to notify Jellicoe. A dispatch from the Admiralty informed him the High Seas Fleet might head toward Horn Reef, but was hazy in details. London also neglected to inform him that Scheer had requested aircraft to reconnoiter Horn Reef—clear evidence of his plans. At daybreak Jellicoe had resumed his search for stragglers but found none. At 4:15 the Admiralty reported that Scheer was about to reach the safety of Horn Reef. After a final sweep for British survivors, the disappointed Jellicoe set course for Scapa Flow.

The Battle of Jutland had ended, and each side hotly disputed the other's claim to victory. By material standards, the Germans suffered less damage and fewer casualties. British losses amounted to three battle-cruisers, three light cruisers, and eight destroyers with six other ships severely damaged and 6,945 casualties; the Germans lost one outdated battleship, one battle-cruiser, four light cruisers, and five destroyers. Four other vessels were heavily damaged and there were 3,058 casualties. In actual weight, the British lost 115,025 tons and the Germans, 61,180 tons.

German technical proficiency clearly exceeded that of the British; their armor-piercing projectiles with delayed-action fuses penetrated English hulls and exploded with devastating effect. British shells often burst on impact without boring holes through enemy plates. The upper decks of German craft afforded better protection in long-range dueling and torpedoes exploding against their reinforced sides were less crippling. Moreover German signalling techniques, range-finding, and night-fighting equipment outclassed those of the Grand Fleet.

In the critically important system of protection against fire, the Germans excelled by a wide margin. Shell explosions in German gun turrets caused no further damage; well-shielded vertical passageways prevented fire from descending to the magazine. At least three British battle-cruisers were blown up when shells bursting in their gun turrets ignited a chain of charges down to the gunpowder deck. No German ship was lost through such deficiency. That English naval architects had concentrated on speed and large-bore cannon, and neglected other essential improvements, became evident in the battle.

In his report to the Kaiser, Scheer remarked that the Imperial German Navy could "inflict substantial damage on the enemy, but . . . even the most favorable issue of a battle on the high seas will not force England to make peace . . . . The disadvantages of our geographical position, compared with that of the Island Empire . . . cannot be compensated for by our fleet. . . ." Unrestricted submarine war, he concluded, was imperative "even at the risk of war with America." Contrary to British claims, the High Seas Fleet was *not* bottled up in harbor. Scheer led three sorties against Allied shipping —in August and October 1916, and in April 1918. The British inability to destroy the German Navy dashed all hope of opening the Baltic Sea to Russia, perhaps hastening the downfall of the Czarist government.

No less a person than Beatty himself voiced consternation at the Royal Navy's defects, which he should have known long before Jutland. A month before he succeeded Jellicoe in November, 1916, Beatty gloomily confessed that the Grand Fleet could offer little aid if Germany were to attack Denmark. At the beginning of 1918 Beatty told a conference at the Admiralty that "the German battle-cruiser squadron must now be considered definitely superior to our own." The new armor-piercing projectiles ordered after Jutland, he added, would not be available to the Grand Fleet until that summer.

Turning to the effective use of naval power, the Admiral asserted that the "correct strategy of the Grand Fleet is no longer to endeavor to bring the enemy to action at any cost, but rather to contain him in his bases until the . . . situation becomes more favorable to us."

A destroyer pioneers in shooting a torpedo from an amidships tube.

15. Submarine Warfare

Captain Turner of the *Lusitania*.

15. Submarine Warfare

Germany was the first belligerent to recognize the potential of submarines. Naval officials originally saw these boats as scouting units and defensive craft to guard harbors against attack from the sea. During the first weeks of the War they were used to machine-gun English fishing trawlers in the North Sea, but this ended when British vessels also mounted machine guns, or were escorted by armed patrol boats. At the War's outset, Britain had thirty-six submarines, all limited to shore patrol. Germany had twenty-eight, but only ten were capable of cruising as far as 2,000 miles.

The War was not quite two months old when the submarine showed what it could do. The *U-9* was commanded by thirty-two-year old Otto Weddigen, on his first tour of duty. At daybreak on September 22, 1914, his log noted 200 uneventful miles. Lolling six feet beneath the surface off the Dutch coast, Weddigen decided to take a last look through the periscope before returning to Wilhelmshaven. Shadowy outlines soon formed the identifiable shapes of three armored British cruisers. At 6:30 A.M., about twelve feet under water, Weddigen loosed a torpedo as the *Aboukir* passed into his line of fire. Her captain mistook the explosion for a mine, and signalled the other two vessels to move closer for survivors. But the ship sank too fast even for lifeboats to be lowered.

As the *Cressy* lowered boats, the *U-9* fired another torpedo. Without shifting position, Weddigen sent a third torpedo into the *Hogue*, which was firing wildly in various directions. Only the *Cressy* still hovered half afloat. The U-boat captain surfaced to finish her off. Only then did the survivors realize what had happened. More than 1,600 lives were lost.

The Lusitania Is Torpedoed

No German act so outraged American public opinion as the sinking of the *Lusitania*. Among the 1,198 victims were 291 women and 94 infants and children. On Saturday, May 1, 1915, the giant liner backed from her Hudson River berth and sailed for Liverpool. On that day the German submarine *U-20* slipped out of Emden to prey on Allied shipping. Waters surrounding the British Isles had been proclaimed a war zone by the German government; *all* vessels, enemy or neutral, would be sent to the bottom.

Cunard had proudly hailed the *Lusitania* as "the fastest and largest steamer now in Atlantic service." Her maximum speed of twenty-five knots was more than twice the speed of any submarine. Mindful of this advantage, the British Admiralty, in a confidential memorandum to ship captains on April 16, 1915, stressed:

"Fast steamers can considerably reduce the chance of successful surprise submarine attack

Celebrities and socialites in hansom cabs and private carriages cluster
at the dock to see the *Lusitania* off on her maiden voyage from Liverpool
to New York in 1907.

by zigzagging. This course is invariably adopted by warships when cruising in an area known to be infested with submarines. The underwater speed of a submarine is very low, and it is exceedingly difficult for her to get into position to deliver an attack unless she can preserve and predict the course of the ship attacked."

Despite this warning, the Cunard Company's directors ordered the *Lusitania* to proceed at three-quarter speed to save coal and labor. For some reason, Captain William Turner also neglected to follow a zigzag course in what were clearly dangerous waters.

On May 7, Walther Schweiger, commanding the *U-20*, surfaced some twelve miles off Old Head of Kinsale on Ireland's southeastern coast, having taken a toll of two British steamers and one sailing ship. The *U-20* was returning to base when the lookout sighted a steamship. Submerged to forty-four feet, the *U-20* moved ahead at full speed to reach striking position ahead of the liner.

An hour later the submarine was within a half mile of the 785-foot liner and Schweiger fired a torpedo. Most of the *Lusitania's* passengers had finished lunch and were on deck gazing at the coast of Ireland. In horror they watched the long, white streak of foam in the torpedo's wake. Eighteen minutes after the torpedo struck, the "Queen of the Atlantic" disappeared beneath the waves. Schweiger recorded her agony:

"Scored starboard hit right behind gangway, and observed an exceptionally strong explosion that caused a huge cloud of smoke to gush high above the smokestack. Most likely, a second explosion (boiler, coal, powder?) accompanied that of our torpedo. Superstructure and bridge above point of impact were blown to bits. A fire broke out. The ship came to a halt at once, listing heavily to starboard and her bow sinking rapidly. It seemed as though she would capsize any minute. There was great confusion aboard. A number of lifeboats were lowered apparently by people who had lost their heads. The tackles were released so unequally that every now and then, a boat full of people would hit the water stern or bow first and sink at once."

Germany defended the torpedo attack, charging the *Lusitania* was a warship carrying explosives and munitions. (The ship's manifest listed a mere 4,200 cases of small-arms cartridges and 1,271 cases of unloaded shrapnel shells.) News of the disaster, acclaimed throughout Germany as a great triumph, was typified in the *Kolnische Volkszeitung:* "With joyful pride we behold this latest deed of our navy." A *Lusitania* medal was issued to memorialize the event.

Anti-German prejudice raced quickly throughout traditionally tolerant England. Crowds broke windows of German-owned stores, destroying their contents while police watched in amusement. Persons of German birth were expelled from the London Royal Exchange and exchanges in other sections of the country. Combing through the 19,000 enemy aliens already registered, the government interned all German males between the ages of seventeen and forty-five.

In a scathing note to Berlin, President Woodrow Wilson denounced the sinking as a violation of international law and a crime against humanity. Nor would the United States "omit any word or act," he emphasized, in defending the right of neutrals to travel on nonmilitary matters anywhere they pleased. Never before had a neutral country so angrily challenged a belligerent without drawing the sword.

Wilson's warning sobered only the German Foreign Office, which feared America's military potential. But the admirals scoffed, certain they could handily trounce the United States on the high seas. To prepare a reply to Wilson, the Foreign Office requested all information on the *Lusitania* incident from the Admiralty, which didn't even bother to acknowledge the request. The admirals' influence on the Kaiser would lead to a resumption of unrestricted U-boat warfare that would ultimately turn the tide against Germany.

Q-Ships

As the German campaign against Allied commerce reached a crisis level, the desperate British Admiralty entertained and rejected countless ideas. An unsung hero provided a solution. Germany's unrestricted submarine warfare was directed at armed ships, which

The submarine "pens" at Zeebrugge, Belgium, were heavily reinforced shelters to shield submarines from air or sea attack while they were in port.

The Austro-Hungarian *U-20* in the Adriatic. Italy was wooed by the Allies partly in the hope her fleet would bottle up that of the Dual Monarchy, leaving the Mediterranean free for Allied shipping.

The captain and crew of the *U-9* were heroes to the Germans after sinking the British cruisers *Aboukir*, *Cressy*, and *Hogue* early one September morning in 1914.

French troops interrupted on their trip
from Marseilles to land at Gallipoli take to
the lifeboats as their torpedoed ship
settles to the bottom.

Submarines lurking below the surface of
the water could only be spotted from the
air. However, bombing techniques and
equipment were not sufficiently advanced
for planes to pose a serious threat except
as spotters for surface vessels armed with
depth charges.

An explosion rocks the stricken freighter *Stromboli* as the now-surfaced submarine inspects its kill.

were sunk without warning. Unarmed merchantmen, however, particularly sailing vessels, were not sent to the bottom until crews took to the lifeboats. Enemy boarding parties then ransacked the ship for booty before it was sunk by gunfire, to economize on torpedoes. The Q-ship, or decoy, was devised to counteract this practice.

Sighting an old tramp freighter lumbering slowly along a trade route, the German commander surfaced his raider and halted the tramp by firing a shot across its bow. A previously rehearsed "panic party" of officers and crew rushed to the lifeboats. Sometimes the masquerade included a seaman in captain's garb rushing about holding high a brilliantly hued (stuffed) parrot in a cage, a spectacle that always amused the Germans.

Meanwhile, concealed 12-pound guns were aimed at the U-boat which was closing in for a looting party. When the raider was in range, the camouflaged walls surrounding the guns fell away on hinges and the Royal Navy's White Ensign was hauled up the mast. Before the U-boat could fire her deck gun or crash dive, she became a target of deadly cannon fire. This was effective only so long as the submarines were sunk and no report of the episode reached Berlin.

Jules Silber was one of Germany's most ingenious wartime spies. He had lived away from his native land long enough to speak flawless English, and was fully accepted as a Canadian. Silber's linguistic gifts made him welcome in the British postal censorship where, without any previous training as a spy, his abundant common sense enabled him to avoid suspicion.

One day Silber opened an envelope and stumbled on an outstanding piece of intelligence. The sender wrote that her brother, a naval officer, was stationed at an important base near home. He was working on a secret project that would end the U-boat menace. Silber, sensing a high-priority secret, went to the port where the writer lived and visited her in his official capacity as a government censor to warn her against disclosing secret information in her correspondence. The woman pleaded with Silber not to take any step that would jeopardize her brother's career. During their conversation the censor extracted the details.

Q-ships—each was identified by a secret Q number—were tramp freighters, sailing ships, and fishing trawlers patched up and made seaworthy. Manned by naval crews wearing the nondescript clothing of merchant seamen, the decoy ships were armed with concealed guns and torpedo tubes. Silber sent the information on to Berlin.

Soon U-boat commanders abandoned gallantry. Torpedoes struck without warning. Crews did without the pleasures of Scotch whisky and British tobacco. To remain afloat in unequal battle, the decoy ships were made buoyant with lumber and cork. Upon firing a torpedo at a tramp steamer, the enemy raider observed the damage before he surfaced to sink the vessel by shelling.

It was a critical moment for the Q-ship's captain, who was ordered to hold fire until the submarine moved into range. Any suspicious gesture would send the U-boat into a crash dive, followed by another torpedo that might finish the decoy. The "panic party" of officers and crew jostled each other into lifeboats, lowered away and rowed desperately from the crippled vessel. Such maneuver sometimes emboldened the raider to surface. At which moment the gunners would act.

The decoy ship *Q-5* was zigzagging along the trade route to Liverpool when an unannounced torpedo punched a gaping hole in its hull. Severely burned men in the engine room held their posts until rushing seawater forced them on deck, where they lay concealed, despite agonizing injuries. For nearly a half hour the gun crews stood in deepening water while the *Q-5* was sinking slowly; no man made a false move.

The still-submerged *U-83* moved slowly toward its quarry, and surfaced at point-blank range satisfied that no danger threatened. Scarcely had the captain emerged from the conning tower when the first shot decapitated him. Punctured by more than three dozen shells, the U-boat sank quickly. Only after the marauder was sent to the bottom did the awash *Q-5* send for aid. A nearby destroyer and sloop arrived and the destroyer towed the half-submerged victor to port.

More than 180 decoy ships in varying design and size were equipped to grapple with the

U-boats. Not fully convinced of their capability, the British Admiralty initially tested them on a piecemeal basis. By the time they were fully accepted the Germans knew the secret. Still, Q-ships sank eleven U-boats and damaged at least sixty from July, 1915, to November, 1918.

About 200 German submarines were sunk during the War, and the British claim credit for 145 of them. To achieve this score, the Royal Navy mobilized more than 5,000 auxiliary vessels, hundreds of miles of steel nets, and perhaps a million depth charges, mines, bombs, guns, and shells.

೧೧೦೧೦೧೦೧೦೧೦

A destroyer running down a submarine, as painted by an unidentified artist. Allied commanders were eager to employ this tactic on the principle that even if the destroyer were damaged or sunk, it was still worth far less than the shipping that an active submarine could destroy.

16. War
in the Air

Field Marshal von Haeseler and
(right) Count von Zeppelin.

16. War in the Air

Air Power Flaps Its Wings

In August, 1914, the warring general staffs saw only a limited role for the airplane. French interest in aviation was kept alive only by a handful of civilian sportsmen. Neither Joffre nor Foch had the remotest confidence in flying, which the latter had dismissed a few years earlier as "all very well for sport but for the army it is useless." English military authorities were equally doubtful of the plane's power as a weapon.

By all military considerations Germany should have been well ahead in air power. For years the Germans had budgeted their resources for the conflict. Yet even the German High Command thought of the plane just as an observation outpost, and consigned the air force to an insignificant role in the signal corps. By 1911 Germany had two small but thriving aircraft firms that manufactured the Albatros and Aviatik, powered by the excellent Daimler and Mercedes watercooled engines, and at least fourteen private flying schools.

Europe entered the war with a maximum of 375 serviceable combat planes. Germany had 180 suitable for observation duty, plus 300 training aircraft and 13 zeppelins. France could muster only 130 and England 65 planes. Not designed for military service, nor armed, all were built of wood and wire, the wings and fuselage covered with doped fabric. There were more aviators than aircraft, but even so fewer than 100 men in uniform knew how to fly. Aviation officers who offered assistance to ground forces were repeatedly rebuffed. Reconnaisance was the function of cavalrymen, who grumbled that their horses became terrified by the noise of the engines of low-flying aircraft.

Without a tradition of their own, the embryo air forces had to improvise and develop their techniques. Aerial observation was an unknown skill. Most observers were artillery and cavalry officer volunteers, but the aviators were usually enlisted men and all were quite unfamiliar with the form and shape of marching troops, gun installations, ammunition dumps, and the like as viewed against the dark contours of earth. Spotting enemy concentrations or movements was further complicated by aircraft design. Often the observer's downward view from the biplane was blocked by the lower wing. His forward view was cut off by the engine, exhaust pipe, and radiator. Other viewing angles were blurred by a cage of struts and wires which secured the wings to each other.

Not surprisingly, aerial reports in the first weeks of the War were almost consistently inaccurate, which weighed heavily against the fledgling air force in the eyes of already skeptical commanders. German observers were no better than French or English. During the week of August 7, a British Expeditionary Force of 100,000 troops arrived in France, then moved northeastward for twelve days before they were

Airmen were less restricted than ground troops in keeping pets. The jaunty Lafayette Escadrille adopted such exotic mascots as lion cubs, of which they had two—Whiskey and Soda. This one is Soda.

seen by General Kluck's units. Despite daily sorties over the area by German planes, not one air observer had seen the British army. (In time air spotters became so proficient that troops were forced to move at night.)

Life was pleasant for airborne soldiers in 1914. Flights over hostile territory were gay interludes as enemy pilots waved airily to each other. Neither side had capacity for much else. Planes were unarmed but the pilots wore side arms, mostly to indicate that they were in military service. Every aviator enjoyed the full-time service of a mechanic and a personal batman. All were quartered at least twenty miles behind the lines. German pilots were especially well treated. Stationed in occupied France, they selected whichever château or well-stocked inn struck their fancy. For all the pampering, pilots on flight were exposed much more to inconvenience than danger in 1914. Since motor oil coagulated to the consistency of grease in cold weather, non-congealing castor oil was substituted as an engine lubricant and the fumes belched directly from the engine into the aviator's face. An hour of such inhalation had the same effect on human plumbing as several tablespoons of the cathartic.

The Royal Flying Corps, consisting of thirty-seven obsolete sporting planes, flew across the English Channel and landed near Amiens on August 13, 1914. Two weeks later the R.F.C. downed its first enemy plane in a manner similar to cowboys hemming in a runaway steer. Flight Lieutenant H. D. Harvey-Kelly, accompanied by two planes of his squadron, was flying high on routine patrol when he noticed a German plane in flight several thousand feet below. Alerting his two pilots, Harvey-Kelly dived toward his quarry.

Afraid that the wild Englishman would crash into him, the German nosed earthward. As he levelled off, a glance warned that Harvey-Kelly was above and behind. The two other British pilots quickly grasped the tactic and flanked the German, forcing him to land. Before his plane rolled to a stop, the terrified pilot jumped out and disappeared into a wooded area. After burning the plane, the Britons flew back to base and shared the maneuver with their comrades. The R.F.C. repeated this tactic against other enemy planes until machine guns were installed on aircraft.

Bricks, Darts and Pistols

One day in September, 1914, a pilot decided that war was a grim game, drew his pistol, and fired at a passing enemy plane instead of waving. Shortly thereafter, French observers in two-seater planes began toting rifles, but strong winds and the bone-shaking engine vibration drastically impaired their accuracy. Other observers carried bricks to fling at a German propeller—even at the pilot. Some were armed with containers of *fléchettes*, pencil-sized steel arrows, to drop on enemy aviators. By all accounts, these were more successfully used in dart games.

Small bombs and hand grenades were tried with limited success. Bomb sights were unknown, and pilots or observers held the missile over the side, aiming by eye. No account was taken of speed or windage. A check by the R.F.C. showed dismaying results—of 141 bombing raids made on railroad depots to paralyze troop movements, only 3 were successful.

Parachutes were used by balloon observers, but not by aviators or their observers. Cockpits were too small to allow parachutes, and no one thought of designing a plane with enough room for them. If a damaged plane could not be glided safely to the ground, the pilot usually died in the wreckage. To protect themselves against bullets from lower flying enemy planes or ground troops, airmen sat on cast iron stove lids.

With the increasing exchange of rifle and pistol fire, some Allied pilots began to mount machine guns. As no one had yet devised a means of firing bullets through a whirling propeller, machine guns were installed on the upper wing of biplanes, or carried at the front of the pusher-type planes which had the propellers in the rear. Often the heavy weight of a Lewis machine gun kept an Allied plane from gaining the altitude that an unarmed plane was capable of. German pilots soon learned to ignore Allied planes on which machine guns were not visible, and to keep ahead of and above those showing signs of weapons.

Sometime in February, 1915, four German two-seater observation planes returning to their base noticed a single-seater French plane flying in their direction. Since it was without an aerial observer and had no visible weapon, the eight Germans eyed it only with curiosity as it came closer. To their astonishment spurts of yellow flame suddenly came through the propeller. The first round killed one German pilot and his plane spun downward to crash in flames.

Maneuvering slightly, the French plane fired another burst into a second German plane. Bullets ruptured its fuel line, spraying gas on the hot engine, and most of the flimsy craft had burned before the wreckage hit the ground. The survivors had seen enough. Turning tail, they sped back to base where their story was greeted with skepticism. Whoever heard of bullets being fired through a spinning propeller! Simple mathematics told them it was impossible, for all machine guns discharged bullets at the rate of 600 a minute. By all standards, such a stream of lead could not pass through a two-bladed propeller whirling 1,200 times a minute.

In the ensuing weeks other German planes were shot down by bullets whizzing through a French propeller. No matter how many German planes were in formation, the sight of a French plane flying in their direction sent all scurrying back to the base. But after several weeks, the fortunes of war smiled on the Germans. While on patrol over the front lines, a French single-seater plane lost altitude when its engine sputtered and died. The pilot became confused and glided to earth behind enemy lines. Before he could burn his plane German soldiers pounced on him.

He was Roland Garros, famed as a prewar barnstorming pilot. His was the plane armed with a Hotchkiss gun—invented by an American—mounted in front of the cockpit, and aimed directly toward the wooden propeller. The blades facing the gun's muzzle were protected by wedgeshaped steel plates, deflecting those bullets that struck the propeller. This contrivance was almost as hazardous to the pilot as to his enemies, for richocheting bullets might have smashed into the engine or the pilot. Until his involuntary landing, Garros had shot down six German planes by this novel technique.

Garros' little Morane plane had been forced down by a clogged gas line. It was cleaned and flown to Berlin for inspection by General Staff officers and a young civilian Dutchman, who had hurriedly left his airplane plant at Schwerin in northern Germany. He was given a Parabellum air-cooled machine gun, the standard infantry weapon, and told to duplicate the French pilot's feat in forty-eight hours. Anthony Fokker was recognized as the finest airplane designer in Europe at that time, but he had never handled, much less fired, a machine gun. Yet within the prescribed time Fokker and his mechanics developed the synchronized machine gun that was able to fire through the propeller arc without hitting the blades. His invention incorporated a system of cams that allowed the weapon to fire only when the propeller was not aligned with the gun. Neither Fokker nor his assistants had ever attended an engineering school. Every problem was solved by high mechanical intelligence.

A Dutch national, Fokker had early exhibited a remarkable aptitude for advancing the capability of the new flying machine. In 1910, at the age of twenty, he built and flew the fastest and sturdiest monoplane in existence. He first offered the aircraft to the Dutch army, only to encounter cold indifference; he then turned to France, England, and Russia. As in Holland, military authorities paid more attention to Fokker's youth and lack of technical education than to the inherent worth of his plane. Only the Germans recognized his ability and provided him with production facilities on their soil.

Beginning in 1915, both sides were producing new and improved planes designed exclusively for military use. It was a process of action and reaction in which each innovation was countered by a defensive or offensive development to neutralize the new advantage, be it a faster, higher flying plane or new armament. Six months after the Fokker E-1 monoplane appeared with its synchronized machine gun, the Germans lost their tactical superiority in the same manner that the French had. To prevent the Allies from learning the secret of Fokker's gun, German pilots had been forbidden to fly even *near* the front lines. But an aviator lost his direction in a fog and landed in Allied territory. Like Garros he was captured before he had time to burn his plane.

A few weeks later French and English planes were equipped with the American-invented Lewis air-cooled machine gun synchronized to fire through a spinning propeller. Later the Germans temporarily regained their advantage, when the Fokker E-111 was armed with twin Spandau machine guns. Germany's lead in aircraft was mostly due to Fokker who designed nearly sixty different types between 1914 and 1918. Belatedly the British recognized his abilities, and sent him a written offer of $10 million if he went to England and designed aircraft for the R.F.C., but Fokker did not learn of this until the War was over. German intelligence intercepted the offer and understandably withheld it.

If aerial warfare initially left the generals unimpressed it quickly gripped the imagination

A German observer jumps from his balloon. Since balloons were shot down with great regularity, observers were provided with parachutes — the only airmen to be so equipped. As for the others, the infantrymen would eye them without envy, saying, "It's a long way down and you only fall once."

◀ Because air power was an untried force in 1914 its proponents tried just about anything they could think of in the hope that something would work. Here, in what appears to be a desperate attempt to counter Fokker's synchronized machine gun, the French have installed a gun above the propeller of a Morane-Saulnier monoplane. It is difficult to see how they expected the pilot to fly the plane and man the gun at the same time.

of the public. Air power at that time could not tip the scales of victory, but it had a morale value unforeseen by the military. The German High Command first recognized that aerial heroes diverted the civilian populace. Aerial deeds were prominently reported, and press campaigns encouraged civilian correspondence with German aces.

Oswald Boelcke and Max Immelmann were the first to attract public attention, followed by the less-well-known Eduard von Schleich, nicknamed "The Black Knight" for painting his Albatros biplane black after the combat death of a close friend. He survived the War with thirty-five aerial victories and became a Luftwaffe general in World War II. Both Boelcke with forty kills and Immelmann with fifteen perished in combat.

Aces and Heroes of the Air

Charles Nungesser;
French; 45 victories.

Raymond Collishaw (standing);
British; 60 victories.

James T. McCudden;
British; 57 victories.

Manfred von Richthofen;
German; 80 victories.

Hermann Goering (center);
German; 22 victories.

Georges Guynemer;
French; 54 victories.

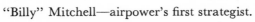

"Billy" Mitchell—airpower's first strategist.

Ernst Udet;
German; 62 victories.

Raoul Lufbery;
American; 17 victories.

Donald MacLaren;
British; 54 victories.

241

The Allies also produced their quota of heroes. France acclaimed René Fonck, seventy-five enemy planes; Georges Guynemer, fifty-four; Charles Nungesser, forty-five; and lesser aces. But English and Canadian heroes did not become so well known, for their names were soft-pedaled with typical British reticence. Only later did the English public and the world learn the names of their great aerial fighters: Edward Mannock, seventy-three victories, the Canadians William Bishop, seventy-two, and Raymond Collishaw, sixty, and a host of others.

As the conflict dragged into 1916, the war-weary people on both sides became fired with the exploits of this new breed of hero. In 1916 greater newspaper coverage was given to dogfights by Americans serving in the Lafayette Escadrille than to the crucial battles of Verdun and the Somme, which if lost would have turned the tide against the Allies. After the United States became a belligerent the saga of ex-automobile racer Captain Eddie Rickenbacker (twenty-six victories) would be told and retold in many embellished versions.

Belief in America's industrial might heartened the French and British, who eagerly watched the skies expecting them to darken behind a gigantic umbrella of planes from the West. When America declared war, however, her air power amounted to a mere 109 planes, about evenly divided between the Navy and the Signal Corps of the Army. Every one was designed for training purposes and none could survive even brief combat.

Aerial chivalry began and ended with World War I. Initially aviators accepted their allies and enemies alike as members of a noble knighthood. The pilot's unwritten code was exemplified by Max Immelmann when a British flier he had wounded crash-landed. Landing nearby, Immelmann took his adversary from the wreckage and tended his wounds. The Briton, a Lieutenant Reid, was brought to Immelmann's headquarters where he was treated more as a guest than a prisoner. For two days Reid and his captor dined and drank fine French wines. After the festivities, the Englishman was confined to comfortable quarters in a prison camp reserved for captured airmen. When Immelmann was killed in 1916, Germany went into mourning.

Not all pilots shared Immelmann's gallantry. Baron Manfred von Richthofen, Germany's greatest air hero, had two passions—slaying men and animals—as revealed in his diary. Called the "Red Baron," from the crimson color of his Albatros biplane, Richthofen took frequent leaves to shoot stag and boar in German forests. He also destroyed eighty Allied aircraft, killing eighty-seven men, the highest score of any airman in the War. After each victory, he ordered an engraved sterling cup, inscribed with the date and type of plane gunned down.

Shot down in April, 1918, the twenty-six-year-old Red Baron was given an impressive funeral by the British. His coffin was escorted by six captains (Richthofen's rank) and a cortège of pilots and he was given a farewell salute by an honorary firing squad. A photograph of his flower-decked grave and a message reporting his death were dropped behind German lines by a British pilot.

Credit for gunning down the Red Baron is claimed by two of the Allies. The Royal Air Force credits Roy Brown, a Canadian, but according to Australian official history Richthofen met his end by ground fire from the 53rd Battery, Fifth Australian Division.

No performance ever drew the attention of more spectators than combat pilots high above the mud-churned battlefields of France and Belgium, according to Raymond Collishaw, the fourth-ranking Allied ace, who went on to become Air Vice Marshal of the Royal Canadian Air Force in World War II.

Describing aerial antagonists as "waltzing partners," dodging each other's bullets, Collishaw recalls, "The theatre was in the clouds as fighter pilots on both sides played to audiences of infantrymen cheering them on from the trenches below. The waltz started when one plane would get on the tail of another. The two aircraft would fly in ever-smaller circles until finally one could bring his guns to bear on the other, then the dance ended. The enemy pilot would stick with it and refuse to break off even though the gap was closing, fascinated like a goat by a snake, until he was shot down."

The most widely known maneuver devised in World War I is the so-called Immelmann turn. Flying in a steep climb apparently to form a loop, the pilot at the peak would make a half

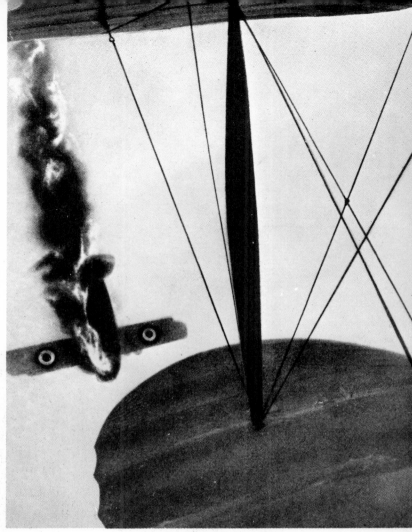

Aerial combat. All of these photographs are
composites. Very little air combat photography was
taken in World War I due in part to the slow
film available.

In the Air

*Destruction of German submarine in the
North Sea by French Hydroaeroplane* by Henri Farré.
Courtesy, Air Force Art Collection.

*Observer on Wing Firing
Rifle at Attacking German
Aeroplane* by Henri Farré.
Courtesy, Air
Force Art Collection.

Victory of Guynemer
by Henri Farré. Courtesy,
Air Force
Art Collection.

*Hydroaeroplane in Distress
Attacked by Enemy Machine*
by Henri Farré.
Courtesy, Air Force
Art Collection.

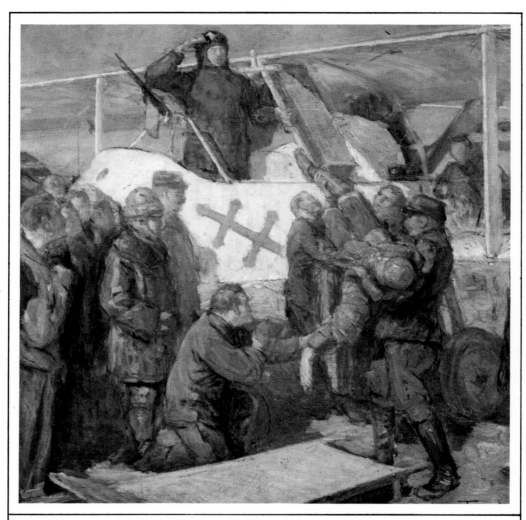

Death of Captain Féquant. Plateau of Malzeville
by Henri Farré.
Courtesy, Air Force Art Collection.

Air Warfare

A German pilot demonstrates how to drop a bomb. The first recorded use of bombs in aerial combat came in 1911 in the Tripolitanian War. They were dropped by Italian pilots on Arab troops fighting on the side of the Turks.

The first successful takeoff of a plane from a ship came in 1918 when French Lieutenant Georges Guierre flew his Hanriot HD-1 from a platform on the battleship *Paris* at sea off Toulon.

Antiaircraft gunners on the alert. Ground fire was not particularly effective and some pilots maintained that the inability of gunners to identify aircraft made them more of a threat to their own planes than to the enemy.

The German single-seater Albatros biplane was one of the best flying machines in the War.

A zeppelin, cruising. The gun platform mounted on the top in addition to gondolas along the sides gave some protection against pursuit planes.

roll and, levelled out, speed off in a direction opposite to that expected. In biographical dictionaries, encyclopedias, and some military history books, this maneuver has been credited to Immelmann. But a number of surviving fighter pilots declare Immelmann never executed it.

Among these voices is that of Collishaw. "The Royal Flying Corps pilots," he writes, "always understood that Immelmann did not invent the maneuver attributed to him, instead it was devised in 1916 by the famous R.F.C. stunt merchant Armstrong of No. 60 Squadron. The Immelmann turn at the outset did not

consist of a rapidly climbing turn followed by a half roll at the top of a loop. At first it consisted of a rapid climb with full rudder applied so that when the aircraft stalled at the top of the turn, it fell over towards the earth to regain flying speed, and in doing so the plane made an about turn.

"The so-called Immelmann turn developed in 1918 was again thought to have been devised by Armstrong of the R.F.C. The 1918 version consisted of a half roll at the top of the loop. The object was to rapidly alter course. It was the maneuverability and flexibility of the Sopwith Camel that permitted this maneuver when under assault, and it was designed to turn the tables on an antagonist who . . . would then find himself at a disadvantage.

"The 1918 pilots, particularly the Americans in the Camel squadrons, became confused between the act and function of the 1916 so-called Immelmann turn and the 1918 half roll at the top of the loop, and so they called the 1918 maneuver the 'Immelmann Turn.' "

Collishaw continues, "the 1916 Fokker Eindekker (Immelmann's plane) was structurally too weak to withstand the maneuver of the half roll at the top of the loop. What is more certain, however, was that the Fokker monoplane was fitted with an engine of insufficient power to perform the act.

"As a matter of interest one can say that the half roll at top of the loop was not the sort of thing a practical war fighter pilot would indulge in to upset the gun aim of an adversary. The first warning usually reached the attacked pilot from the noise and impact of the hostile bullets. The assailed pilot would instantly take violent avoiding action—often this resulted in momentary loss of control, but it effectively offset the hostile pilot's aim. When under assault from the rear it would manifestly be silly to calmly put the nose of the aircraft down to gain the requisite speed needed to execute a loop and a half roll. The hostile pilot would simply depress the nose of his aircraft and easily follow his target until it turned upward to commence the loop. What was needed when under fire was instantaneous and rapid avoiding action."

Zeppelins Over London

German zeppelins began to raid English areas in January, 1915, but only with desultory results. Their function was to fly over and drop bombs on major British cities in an attempt to compel the government to withdraw troops and weapons from France to defend England. London was first bombed on the night of May 31 by the *LZ-38*, commanded by Captain Linnarz. Searchlights could not spot the ship, which was at a great height. The German bombs left seven dead and thirty in-

jured and damaged some residential and commercial buildings. Linnarz proved to be a man of his word. During a previous attack, in which he had been unable to reach the capital, the raider had dropped a card warning: "You English. We have come and we will come again. Kill or cure. German."

The period was called "the Great Zeppelin Scare." However this *schrechlichkeit* (literally "frightfulness") so counted on by the Germans failed in 1915 for the same reason it did twenty-five years later: the British as a people are not inclined to panic. Furthermore, whatever capacity the zeppelins had to inflict damage was offset by their inherent disadvantages: Zeppelins were able to operate only in the most favorable weather. Moreover the German High Command believed that their zeppelins, which could soar higher than airplanes, were beyond attack by British fighters. In truth, these "super-weapons" were quite defenseless. Pursuit planes might not reach the altitude of rigid airships, but they could easily riddle them with incendiary bullets before the big ships could soar to safety. A spark reaching the highly flammable hydrogen gas would turn an airship into an inferno, melting even the aluminum framework.

The big ships were also unable to maintain stability against high winds. Eleven zeppelins set course for England on the night of October 20; three never returned. Strong winds were their undoing. One dropped its bomb load with ineffectual results and was blown across to France, where it was shot down by antiaircraft fire. Another, after dropping one bomb on Piccadilly Circus, was also blown out of control and crashed in southern France. Gusts buffeted the third over a French forest, shearing off the forward gondola with its crew. Then she bolted high into the air and was last seen out of control over the Mediterranean Sea.

Initial defenses against zeppelins revealed the lack of attention given to them by British authorities. The original antiaircraft weapons were rifles and machine guns aimed upward, and no one believed a plane armed with the latter could destroy the flying leviathans. Tactics evolved by trial and error. Attempts were made to fly above the zeppelins and drop small bombs, but these often rolled off.

British Intelligence never tried in prewar

The *L-39*, shot down by antiaircraft fire by the French near the village of Compiègne.

Zeppelins

The *L-20* after it ran out of fuel and crashed off the coast of Norway in May of 1916.

Captain Heinrich Mathy, commander of the *L-31*, shot down over Potter's Bar, a suburb of London.

Pilothouse of the *L-49*.

The *L-49* was the only zeppelin to be captured intact. It was forced down by the French near the resort town of Bourbonne-les-Bains.

years to learn how zeppelins were constructed. For some time after London was bombed the British, for no logical reason, believed each zeppelin was rendered fireproof by a thick layer of inert gas, perhaps nitrogen, between an outer and inner skin. They were further perplexed when their earliest bombing attempts failed to explode the airships. Later on, when attacking planes were armed with 16-pound, prong-tipped incendiary bombs, the results were different. At the same time someone invented the incendiary bullet, and many zeppelins that reached England never returned home. One by one they were sent down as flaming pyres.

The first zeppelin shot down was sighted over Essex by Lieutenant Leefe Robinson, whose two machine guns were loaded with explosive and incendiary bullets. While the airship was riding underneath thick clouds viewing its target area, Robinson flew above and along its length with both triggers pressed back. In flames the invader plummeted earthward. For this deed Robinson won the Victoria Cross. Before the week ended, the score rose when the *L-32* was shot down in a similar manner by Lieutenant F. Sowery. A third, the *L-33*, was the target of simultaneous fire from a plane and ground antiaircraft batteries. Miraculously it did not burn and landed with minimal damage.

Deciding that the best defense was an offensive, British air chiefs sent planes to destroy zeppelins at their home bases, one of which was located in Evere, Belgium. Lieutenants J. P. Wilson and J. S. Mills, flying Farman planes, reached the zeppelin base just before dawn and circled the area waiting for enough light to bomb the hangars. Assuming they were friendly planes, the ground troops did not fire at them. Both pilots were at 2,000 feet when the first light outlined the long sheds. Aiming by eye, Wilson dropped three 65-pound high-explosive bombs into the center of a structure. Then Mills zeroed in but was diverted by antiaircraft fire. Rising to 5,000 feet, he flew directly over the column of smoke that billowed up from his partner's strike, and released four 20-pound bombs. A blinding flash lit the land and the stricken zeppelin in the shed collapsed in a shapeless mass of metal. The stricken airship was the *L-38*, the same ship whose com-

mander had left his calling card in England some weeks before.

While Wilson and Mills were blowing up the *L-38*, another pilot, Lieutenant Reginald Warneford, was on a mission to destroy a second zeppelin base in Belgium. As he approached Ostend at midnight on June 7, Warneford blinked in astonishment. A zeppelin slowly cruised ahead. The new *L-37* was undergoing a night test, and a group of engineers and designers from the zeppelin plant were aboard to oversee technical details. The 521-foot-long airship, made buoyant by eighteen ballonets inflated with 953,000 cubic feet of hydrogen, was operated by a crew of twenty-eight. Machine gunners, stationed in each engine gondola, held Warneford off and some bullets pierced nonvital parts of his plane.

Half an hour later he sneaked "behind but well above the Zeppelin," Warneford later wrote in his log. "Height then 14,000 feet and switched off my engine to descend on top of him. When close above . . . at 7,000 feet I dropped my bombs (six twenty-pound incendiaries), and whilst releasing the last, there was an explosion which lifted my machine and turned it over." The blazing airship crashed into a convent near Ghent killing two nuns. All but one of the zeppelin's crew perished.

Forced to land behind enemy lines, Warneford decided not to burn his plane when no Germans appeared. An inspection showed the engine had only a broken gas line. Quickly he improvised a union with the ferrule of his cigarette holder. Cranking an engine by turning the propeller was not easy for one person as the engine had no idling speed—only on and off. Great agility was needed for a lone pilot to leap into the cockpit before the plane roared off, but Warneford managed to do it and returned home safely. A grateful England awarded him the Victoria Cross. Ten days later, however, he died when flung from the cockpit of a new Farman biplane; seat belts were still a rarity.

One of the last zeppelins to bomb London was the *L-31* commanded by Captain-lieutenant Heinrich Mathy, the Germans' most feared raider. Lieutenant W. J. Tempest was at an altitude of 14,500 feet when he recognized the airship fifteen miles away, trapped in the glare of a dozen powerful searchlights. To reach his target, Tempest had to fly through "a veritable inferno of bursting shells." He was only five miles away when the mechanical fuel pump supplying air pressure in the gas tank stopped operating. The pilot switched to the emergency hand pump, a task that demanded tremendous effort at 15,000 feet. (At that time airmen had no oxygen system to sustain them in rarified altitudes.)

By sheer determination, the pilot continued pumping until he was within range, but the zeppelin had just jettisoned her bomb load and was soaring rapidly. With his remaining strength Tempest "gave a tremendous pump at my petrol tank and dived straight at her, firing a burst . . . as I came in. I let her have another burst as I passed under her and then banked my machine over, sat under her tail, and flying along underneath her pumped lead into her for all I was worth. As I was firing, I noticed her begin to go red inside like an enormous Chinese lantern. I had set her afire. She shot up about 200 feet, paused and came roaring down straight on to me before I had time to get out of the way. I nosedived for all I was worth, with the Zeppelin tearing after me." Tempest "managed to corkscrew out of the way as she shot past me, roaring like a furnace." Then he levelled the plane and watched as the *L-31* hit the ground in a forest of sparks.

By October, 1916, the German High Command recognized that zeppelin warfare was ineffective. Only fifty-one raids were made during eighteen months in which 196 tons of bombs were dropped, killing 557 persons and injuring fewer than 1,360—hardly worth such an enormous expenditure in a period of critical shortages in men and matériel. An estimated eighty airships were lost to Allied gunfire and turbulent elements. Long before the law of diminishing returns became operative against zeppelin raids, Berlin strategists were working on plans for a heavier-than-air bomber.

London was Germany's preferred bombing target. Aside from being the Empire's political and cultural seat, it was the vital center for the armed forces. By June, 1917, the Germans had enough new bombers to resume bombing raids. The Gotha plane was immense for its time, being designed to carry a pilot and two gunners, one of whom doubled as a bombardier. Its wing span was nearly seventy-eight feet, and the

A Gotha bomber shot down by ground fire in 1918.

fuselage forty-one feet long. Powered by two 260-horsepower engines, it could carry a half-ton bomb load at 12,000 feet.

Flying in a diamond formation, fourteen bombers left their base at Ghent, Belgium, for the 175-mile trip to London. Under a bright midday sun, they released their loads, killing and wounding nearly 600 persons. Some ninety-five pursuit planes raced skyward, but free of their loads the Gothas rapidly gained height and speed and escaped. Once again, however, the grand strategy would backfire. The attempts to compel withdrawal of British forces on the continent to defend London eventually resulted in near disaster for the German air forces.

Plane losses mounted with successive raids, and finally forced the Germans to stop all daylight bombing. Improved pursuit fighters and more powerful antiaircraft guns held the Gothas so high that bombing reverted to its primitive period of hit or miss. The British in turn built four large bombers, the Handley Page 0/100, to retaliate. Their plans and con-

struction were zealously kept secret; but the first plane, flown to France in January, 1917, landed intact on a German airfield. The pilot had made a navigational error.

By the Armistice more than fifty plane raids had been made on England; seventy-three tons of bombs had been dropped, killing almost 860 persons and wounding 2,060. Although the British to some extent depleted their strength in France to beat off the invaders, Germany scarcely profited. The English became more determined to fight to the end, and recognized the need for an Air Ministry. Until then the air forces were in two separate parts, directed by an Air Board that lacked executive authority. Field Marshal Sir Douglas Haig opposed a separate unit, fearing that "an Air Ministry . . . would assume control with . . . theories not in accordance with practical experience." Aircraft played no major role in World War I; however it introduced a decisive third dimension in subsequent conflicts.

Like almost all the innovations introduced into World War I, close support of troops by aircraft was started by the Germans. Its most spectacular use came in 1918, however, when ''Billy'' Mitchell filled the sky with 1500 planes to give aid to the infantry attacking the Saint Mihiel salient.

253

17. Nivelle's Offensive

General Robert Nivelle.

17. Nivelle's Offensive

Prelude to Mutiny

No other Western general staff surpassed the French in scorn and distrust of its troops. Prior to the outbreak of hostilities, French military leaders had estimated that some fifteen percent of the reservists would refuse conscription. Actually the number was little more than one percent, and recruiting offices were mobbed by more than 350,000 volunteers. The high command was further astonished when 3,000 deserters from the peacetime army voluntarily returned to their units.

In a country that had been divided by political rivalries, even the murder of Jean Jaurès, the highly popular leader of the French Socialist Party, caused no civil disorder. Breaking with the German and Austrian sections of the Socialist International, Jaurès had publicly urged his followers to join in a "holy war for our beloved France . . ." Jaurès was shot by a demented youth on July 31, 1914, less than twenty-four hours before mobilization. Under different circumstances his assassination might have triggered nationwide strikes and rioting, but with the War so close things had changed. Never since its inception in 1871 had the Republic been so united.

President Raymond Poincaré appeared before the Chamber of Deputies on August 4 with his war message. Deputies who had been his critics and rivals joined in standing while the President delivered his martial speech. Fre-

quently interrupted by cheers and applause, he exhorted all Frenchmen to unite in a "Sacred Union" irrespective of political views and to "join together as brothers in a common patriotic faith."

Long suspicious of the military clique, French politicians now did an about-face and entrusted their nation's fate to the generals. Under a law dating from 1878, the President declared that a "state of siege" was warranted by "imminent peril caused by a foreign war or armed aggression." Although the legal decree amounted to a proclamation of martial law throughout France and Algeria, the Chamber of Deputies ratified it without debate.

It soon became clear that the general staff was unfit to be entrusted with this power. Of all the forces on the Western Front, the French suffered the most calamitous defeats, brought on by the incompetence of their generals.

During the autumn of 1916, talk of peace began to spread on both sides. Many leading figures in Germany conceded that total victory was impossible, and cautiously inquired how to end the conflict on tolerable terms. Even General Ludendorff no longer boasted of a decisive outcome. On the Allied side, Haig assured final victory in 1917. General Robertson was annoyed that anyone should doubt it. Joffre guaranteed the Germans would be worn down by attrition, and he expected the British to bear the brunt of the war.

But Joffre's reputation was now flawed. His

Raymond Poincaré, President of the Republic, addressing the Assembly. At his right is Aristide Briand, War Minister in 1914, Premier in 1915.

At right, Poincaré wears the ornately brocaded jacket accorded only to the "Immortals," the forty members of the *Académie française*, to which Poincaré had been elected in 1909.

blunders had been too costly for France and his influence was diminishing rapidly. In the first ten months of 1916, more than 861,000 French troops had been killed, wounded, missing, or taken prisoner. In the French Chamber, deputies denounced Joffre for the mounting casualties and his indifference to them. Secret sessions were held by the Chamber and Senate in early 1916 to discuss the military reverses. Reflecting the mood of the populace, the angry legislators were prepared to topple the highest political and military figures if necessary, and with his own career at stake, Premier Aristide Briand won a vote of confidence only on condition that Joffre be dismissed.

Toward the end of October, when the battle of Verdun seemed lost, General Robert Nivelle, the local commander, had ordered a surprise assault. Caught unprepared, the Germans had retreated leaving all they had captured earlier. It was a highly auspicious moment for Nivelle. Yearning for a hero, the French acclaimed him the architect of victory. He impressed Briand as a suitable replacement for Joffre, who was "promoted" to Marshal of France, then sent to pasture. Nivelle boasted that he had the key to victory but he declined to reveal his strategy. Briand did not press him. With the retirement of Joffre, enough had been accomplished for the time being.

General Robert Nivelle, sixty years old when he was appointed commander in chief of the French Army, was born into a family with a long military tradition. He had attended the cavalry school at Saumur, but later chose the artillery, in which he excelled. At the start of the War, Nivelle had held the rank of lieutenant colonel. Promoted to colonel, he had turned his knowledge of large-bore guns to good use during the Battle of the Marne. As the French infantry ahead of him collapsed, he propelled his artillery through their broken lines and fired point-blank at General von Kluck's forces.

A French-built heavy field artillery piece. The Skoda and Krupp works were the best-known makers of munitions, but French industry also produced some fine armaments. France's best known firm was that of Schneider at Le Creusot.

259

Prior to the Somme offensive in April, 1916, Joffre had become dissatisfied with Pétain's strategy at Verdun. His solution was to promote Pétain to lead the Group Armies of the Center and replace him with Nivelle. Soon the artillery expert began to halt the German advance. The celebrated slogan "They Shall not Pass," which captured the imagination in all Allied nations, was coined by Nivelle, although it is often attributed to Pétain. Concentrating his strategy on driving back the Germans, Nivelle contrived a plan with General Charles Mangin, his chief aide. They intended to regain Fort Douaumont, seized by the Germans during the initial attacks against Verdun.

More than 500 cannons were placed on a rise overlooking Douaumont. Three refreshed infantry divisions and three battalions of battle-tested African troops, who had been intensively trained in an area simulating the terrain surrounding Douaumont, were transported in full strength. Divided into assault units, each was provided with its target and drilled until all men could locate their objectives in the black of night. Previous tactics were jettisoned. These troops now ignored their flanks, which needed no protection in darkness. They had only to follow closely behind a rapidly advancing artillery barrage, then strike.

When all was ready, a mountainous barrage of explosives were hurled for almost a week against the Fort. Suddenly, at 2 P.M., October 22, 1916, the gunfire changed to a rolling barrage, such as precedes advancing troops. Whereupon 630 camouflaged German heavy guns began a violent bombardment.

But no troops appeared. The French cannonade had been a diversionary tactic to draw German fire, exposing their gunsites. Pinpointing their targets, French gunners rained destruction on the enemy. Two days later more than half of the German batteries had been blown to bits. Now using trench mortars, French assault troops, aided by compasses, dashed forward just before daybreak. No opposition was offered. Within two hours the French tricolor waved over Fort Douaumont. It was the first substantial victory since August, 1914, and cost relatively few lives. Nivelle's strategy forced the Germans, within several weeks, back to the line from which they had first attacked Verdun many months earlier.

As he traveled to Chantilly on December 12, 1916, to assume supreme command of the French Army, Nivelle exuded confidence. Electrified by his "Verdun method," few disputed his grand announcement: "The experience has been conclusive. Our method has been tried out. I can assure you that victory is certain."

Unlike Joffre and Pétain, Nivelle was articulate, which enabled him to persuade many politicians to his point of view. Abel Ferry, a youthful and critical member of the Parliamentary Army Commission, wrote of Nivelle: "Good impression; clear eyes which look you in the face, neat and precise thoughts, no bluff in his speech, good sense dominates everything."

Both President Poincaré and Prime Minister Lloyd George, despite their distrust of the military, were also captivated by Nivelle's manner. He even charmed the Prime Minister into subordinating Field Marshal Douglas Haig to his command, and into endorsing the catastrophic offensive he contrived in 1917.

Nivelle presided over a complex, triple-headed command. He was flanked on one side by Colonel D'Alenson; on the other by his chief aide, General Charles Mangin. The former was depicted by an observer as "immensely tall and bony, with a cavernous face and arresting eyes. . . . Always badly dressed, with untidy hair and beard, he walked about the corridors with his hand in the belt of his breeches, seeing no one, lost in thought, with the air of a melancholy Quixote. . . ."

Meeting D'Alenson for the first time was a startling experience. His intense eyes glittered, his pronounced cheekbones and deeply sloping forehead were covered by taut yellowish skin. He was dying of tuberculosis, but only he knew it. General Nivelle fell completely under his influence. D'Alenson was driven by a burning conviction that he was destined to save France.

"Victory must be won before I die," he intoned, "and I have but a short time to live." More than anyone, D'Alenson masterminded the ruinous 1917 campaign on the Chemin des Dames, which left the French Army in shambles and led to mutinies that rocked the nation. A logical mind would have rejected D'Alenson's plan, but Nivelle's facade concealed a skein of impulsive passions.

General Mangin, Nivelle's other aide, was the most hard-bitten commander in the French

Army. His troops nicknamed him the "Eater of Men" and "the Butcher." He was disdainful of life, even his own. Commanding the 5th Division of Nivelle's III Corps, Mangin at the age of forty-nine lived only for war. Beginning in his youth, he had spent much of his life as a soldier in the French overseas colonies "pacifying" restless natives.

From the time he returned to France to lead a brigade against the Germans, Mangin almost invariably slept in a desert tent. Claiming staunch admiration for his African troops, he would order them into a hurricane of machine-gun fire without a twinge of remorse. He was the archetype of a professional warrior. His leathery face and neck were tanned and creased by the Sahara sun and wind. A wide, thin-lipped mouth resembled a knife slash. Walking with a rapid, jerky gait, Mangin adopted Napoleon's habit of standing with hands behind his back, head thrust forward, glowering at those around him.

Before the Battle of Verdun, Mangin had been rehabilitated by Nivelle after his ruthlessly pressed black Territorials had broken and fled. The two then intertwined their careers until Nivelle's star was eclipsed. Sharing his superior's fall and disgrace in 1917, Mangin was undoubtedly sincere in requesting that he be permitted to continue fighting as a simple soldier, but his request was turned down.

Shortly after New Year's Day in 1917, Prime Minister Lloyd George, Premier Aristide Briand, and a group of high Italian political figures met in Rome to discuss the disappointing progress of the War. That no generals were present reflected their lack of confidence in their military leaders. About the only definite agreement reached was a refusal to endorse the mass bloodletting favored by the generals to win even a small area. They also conceded that a renewed German-Austrian offensive would force the Italians out of the War. Some kind of

Franco-British campaign was necessary to save their southern ally, but none of the leaders could come up with a workable plan.

General Nivelle visited Lloyd George on January 15 to present his plans for a radically new offensive involving speed and concentrated assault, similar to that so successfully demonstrated at Verdun. British civilian leaders were impressed by this dapper general. That he was a Protestant whose mother was British formed another bond. There would be no lurking Anglophobia to abrade relations.

The Prime Minister and his associates were intrigued by Nivelle's plan. They knew of his strategy to recapture Fort Douaumont, and endorsed his intention to apply the same methods on a vast scale. Some members of the British general staff, however, were less im-

General Charles Mangin.

pressed. They were not sure that a single, successful attack against a solitary fortress like Douaumont could be repeated effectively against an extended front, such as the main German trench system.

Nivelle won the day. Convinced that he had daring imagination, Lloyd George told his own generals if they had a better plan he would listen. He warned them the government would not sanction another Somme, which had been the only plan submitted months before by Haig and Joffre. Haig and his troops in France were ordered to "conform to the views" of the French commander in chief to "carry out the orders of all that relates to the conduct of operations." Thus Haig was subordinated to Nivelle.

The coldest winter in the memory of many settled over western Europe. It was a rare day when the temperature rose to 10° above zero. Frozen limbs and bodies were common. Compelled to exist in such agony, the troops soon took on a rebellious mood.

Through the Intelligence Bureau and Postal Control, which inspected and censored mail from the soldiers in the trenches, Nivelle was informed that "the man in the ranks is no longer aware why he is fighting. He is completely ignorant of anything happening outside his own sector. He has lost both faith and enthusiasm. He compares his life with that of a convict. He carries out his duties mechanically. He may become the victim of the greatest discouragement, display the worst weaknesses."

Temporarily distracted by these rumblings, Nivelle wrote from the luxury of his château to Minister of War Lyautey: "I have the honor to inform you that I have reported the following pacifist intrigues to the Minister of Interior (M. Malvy). Faced with this grave threat to the morale of the troops, I am persuaded that serious measures must be taken. I should be obliged if you would get in touch with M. Malvy in order to decide on measures for

---

Snow covers a trench system during a cold spell. Never known for their comfort, the trenches look particularly bleak under these circumstances.

putting an end to these intrigues immediately. . . .

"For more than a year, there have been pamphlets . . . getting into the hands of troops. Their distribution has now reached epidemic proportions. In a two-week period now we are catching up with more than we ever seized during a three-month period in 1916. . . . They furnish doubts as to the justice of the cause for which the soldiers are fighting . . . affirm the impossibility of victory. . . . Others are full of the most dangerous information and the worst kind of advice. . . . These scurrilous publications undermine the spirit of the soldiers, unnerve and dishearten them. . . . Some soldiers keep up a regular correspondence with individuals suspected of running the propaganda. . . ."

Urged on by D'Alenson, Nivelle increased the tempo of preparation for the offensive. The French army was divided into groups: The Group Armies of the North led by General Franchet d'Esperey; the Group Armies of the Center under General Pétain; and the assault force, the Group Armies of Reserve commanded by General Micheler. A fourth group, the Group Armies of the East, was led by General Castelnau.

Nivelle subjected his army group generals to a continual barrage of directives for the campaign. His mood was explicit: "I insist that the stamp of *violence*, of *brutality*, and of *rapidity* must characterize your offensive; and, in particular, that the first step, which is the *rupture*, must in one blow capture the enemy positions and all the zone occupied by his artillery" (Nivelle's italics).

Nivelle's plan included a double-pronged assault by French and British forces against an enormous, exposed German bulge. During the Battle of the Somme, the Allies had dented the German line, which curved east and west along the Aisne River. This salient was still open to attack by the British from the north and the French from the south.

The overall plan entailed a British lunge several days before the French, to draw German defenders north. The southern, exposed German flank would then be stormed by the French, who were expected to come crashing through, ripping a seventy-mile opening in the German trench system which would be flooded by the Aisne, ending in decisive victory.

Nivelle's plan was not without merit. The German salient was thinly manned and vulnerable; the defending troops had been severely bled in the Somme battle during the summer of 1916. But success would be impossible if the Germans were warned in advance.

Divisions were shifted south of the German salient to receive training in the Verdun method. New tanks were brought in to be combined with rolling barrages. Lightning speed was Nivelle's basis for victory; to grind over German gun emplacements before they could be used against the attacking French.

Commanders were requested to estimate the rate of advance of their troops following the rolling barrage. Substituting optimism for judgment, impossible speed rates were fixed. General Mangin boasted his men could race forward at more than thirty yards a minute, and continue this pace for at least several miles. Nivelle set this jog-trot as the standard. Officers who doubted that heavily laden troops could maintain such speed were silenced.

Troops were trained to attack in steadily advancing relays, fresh units moving ahead of the exhausted one. Light 37-mm. field guns, easily handled by two soldiers, were distributed by the thousands; they were intended to silence machine guns. The central slogan, "Keep Moving," was endlessly drilled into the men, who were expected to have penetrated through the rearmost German positions seven hours after the attack began. The logistics were staggering. Mountains of supplies were brought forward, airfields were constructed, and huge gun emplacements were lined up as far as the eye could see.

Clearly, one of the great contests lay ahead. Even the air bristled with excitement. Crack Senegalese troops were brought in to spearhead attacks against strong points. Some thirty-five battalions were drawn from various tribes in French West Africa.

Others who entered this odd kaleidoscope included several Russian brigades, sent to rein-

---

Aerial view of a trench system showing how each line was connected by zigzag traverses to the one behind. The tank traps were deep trenches twelve or more feet wide and the entire system was protected by barbed-wire entanglements.

TANK TRAPS

NO MAN'S LAND

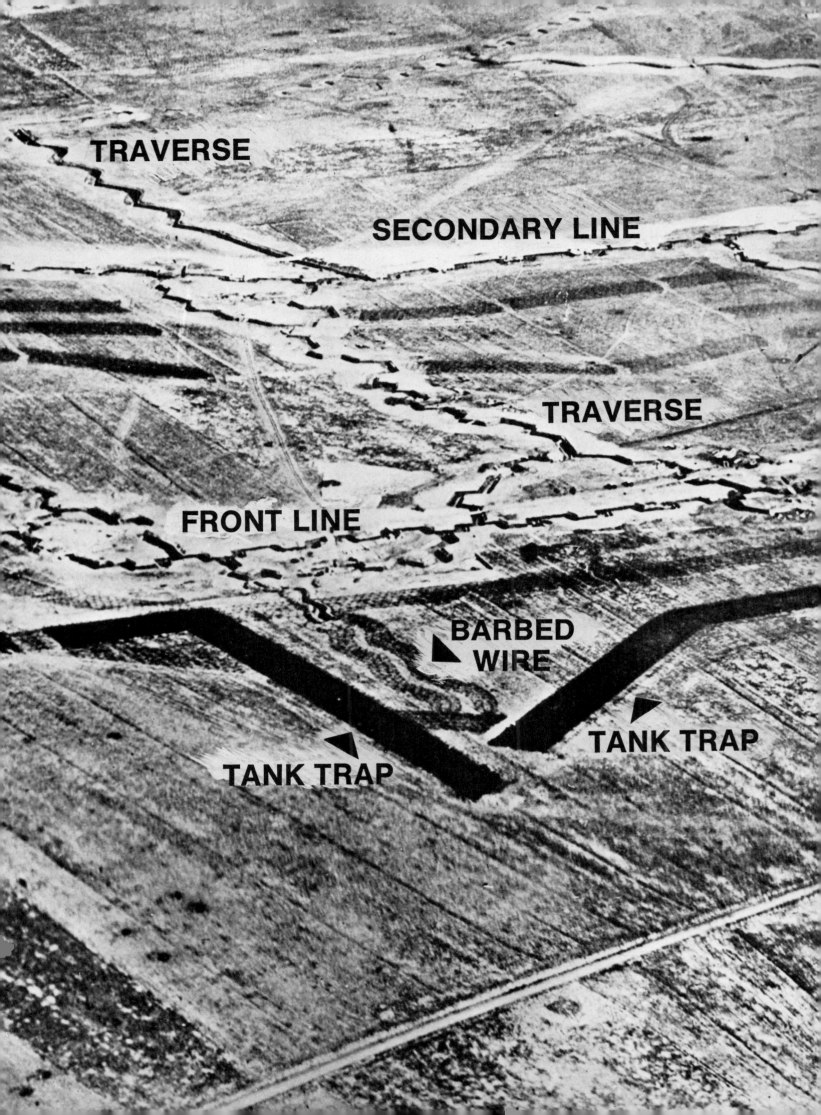

German grenadier with "potato masher" grenades and heavy wire cutters. The grenade cluster on the ground was used to destroy trench sections.

Dum-dum bullets, so called because they were first tested by the British at their arsenal in Dumdum, India. By blunting the top and making a slit just above the case, the bullets would be able to inflict greater and more serious wounds. They were outlawed by the Geneva Convention; this photograph was released by the Germans as a protest against what they considered to be war atrocities committed by the French.

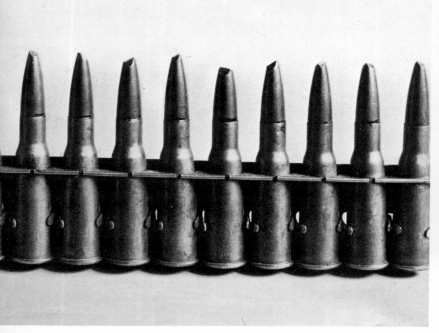

The mechanization of the War is attested to by this mobile motorcycle machine gun, shown in front of an armory in New York City.

The Weapons of War

German staff car with wire-cutting device. Both sides strung wire across roads at throat level, hoping to decapitate a passing enemy.

Under the eyes of their German captors, British prisoners strip their dead of valuables.

French officers inspect a mobile shield captured from the Germans. Hiding behind the shield a man would extend his wire cutters through the hole in the center to clear a path for assault troops through barbed-wire entanglements.

French grenadiers. The grenade was fixed to the rifle barrel and fired by a blank cartridge.

force the badly depleted French Army, and almost to a man infected with a revolutionary mood. Their French officers wore Russian uniforms, on the quaint assumption that this would encourage obedience.

At Verdun the troops had been spurred to enthusiastic sacrifice by a quiet but full explanation of the attack plan. This time, Nivelle, fearing that otherwise his troops might defect, ordered a publicity campaign worthy of a Hollywood press agent. Battle plans outlining strategy and objectives were sent to the ranks. Soldiers were given propaganda speeches by their officers, leading them to expect decisive victory.

Inevitably, the Germans received the information, too. Two critical documents were captured in routine trench raids, showing the exact boundaries of the assault between Reims and Soissons. Crown Prince Wilhelm noted this good fortune: "A brilliant advance carried out in the sector of the 3rd Army, south of Ripon, on March 3rd by the 51st Reserve Division brought us, in addition to considerable booty, into possession of the French Army Order. . . .

"It had been drawn up by Nivelle on December 16, 1916. This memorandum contained matter of extraordinary value. It made clear this time there would be no question of a limited attack, but a breakthrough offensive on a grand scale was contemplated. . . . The memorandum brought important disclosures above all as to the particular nature of the surprise which the attack had in view. This was based on the fact alleged to have been observed on our side, that our defensive artillery . . . made only a weak reply to the artillery preparation which preceded the attack. . . . We ventured to hope that the surprise might in this way be most effectively met, and the sting taken out of the first attack, which experience had shown to be the strongest. . . ."

Facing each other on the Western Front were 180 Allied divisions against 150 German. Aware that they could not withstand a double-pronged assault against their exposed bulge, the Germans withdrew. Their front line was now straight, obviating the hazard of a two-sided thrust. Moreover, additional troops became available to reinforce the flat front.

Gunners don their gas masks as they prepare to unlimber their massive mortar.

So immersed was Nivelle in his scheme that it never occurred to him that his adversary would voluntarily relinquish a seventy-mile-wide bulge. He also ignored the possibility of the enemy's capturing his maps, plans, and orders. And he made no attempt to gather intelligence of German operations.

Beginning in the dark morning hours of February 9, the Germans proceeded to retreat from the salient. Under "Operation Alberich," named for the malevolent dwarf in the Nibelung saga, a methodical schedule of devastation was begun. Resigned to ceding their hard-won territory, the Germans were determined to leave it a wasteland.

Not a building was left standing. Thousands of farmhouses and homes were demolished, fruit trees chopped down, bridges and railheads dynamited, and reservoirs and wells poisoned. The earth was scorched with Germanic thoroughness, as all troops retreated to the Hindenburg Line. This immensely strong defensive position extended south from Arras to a corrugation of hills commanding a view of the Aisne River, where the Group Armies of Reserve were.

Here the German defensive line curled westward along the ridge called Chemin des Dames. It was a natural strongpoint to which supplies could be brought unobserved by the Allies. No previous defense system in the history of warfare was more impregnable than the Hindenburg Line.

Nightly scenes of villages disappearing in flames were the first evidence that the Germans intended to abandon their salient. Nivelle was notified of the enemy's withdrawal as front-line commanders recommended an immediate attack against the weakened lines. But Nivelle and his staff regarded these reports as bordering on sedition. An order issued by the French general staff prohibited the repetition of such "insubordinate rumors." If Nivelle were to assess the enemy's retirement realistically, he would be forced to junk the complex strategy evolved over past months.

Systematically retreating in stages, the German troops withdrew beginning every midnight. At 4 A.M. the mass of men had abandoned their line of trenches, leaving behind a small machine-gun guard to rake any advanc-

ing troops. At daybreak they too retreated. By March 19, the salient was empty of Germans. The evacuation had been completed without loss.

As French troops shuffled into the fire-blackened bulge, all about them the land was uninhabitable and dangerous. The territory was studded with booby traps. Demolished roads and bridges had to be reconstructed before soldiers and equipment could advance. Starving civilians required food and shelter. More rats than humans prowled the land, devouring the dead horses and other livestock killed by the Germans.

Reoccupation of the bulge won Nivelle the acclaim of his countrymen. At parties and social gatherings, civilians congratulated each other for the nation's fortune in having such an outstanding strategist as commander in chief. The front line soldiers, however, sensed that they were marching toward something less than victory. Finding no bulge at which to strike, Nivelle announced the campaign would proceed according to plan, but the main blow would be against the Chemin des Dames at the southern tip of the Hindenburg Line.

Nivelle considered the withdrawal a picayune matter, requiring only a few tactical alterations. In the meantime, he was about to encounter another problem on the home front. Premier Briand's government was replaced on March 19, by that of Alexandre Ribot, an eighty-year-old politician. Ribot made an excellent appointment in his new Minister of War, Paul Painlevé, who was cut from a different cloth than his predecessors.

Since he was responsible for the overall management of the War, Painlevé insisted on commensurate authority, unlike previous war ministers who never questioned general staff decisions. Minister Painlevé was different, too, in other respects. In his youth, he had won renown as a mathematician. Now at fifty-three, this undersized scholar with a high-pitched

---

French troops inspecting a trench to ensure that no live enemies remain.

voice proceeded to examine Nivelle's master plan. Unlike many politicians, Painlevé was naturally frank. Perhaps his international acclaim as a mathematical genius had left him without further personal ambition other than to serve France.

Painlevé was scarcely settled in office when he met with Nivelle to learn his plans. Following brief amenities, the outspoken Painlevé flatly declared that if he had held his ministry at the time Joffre was sacked, his choice would have been Pétain as commander in chief. Whereupon, he turned to military matters. He told Nivelle that he was disquieted to learn that his battle plans, including the precise date for the offensive, April 8, were discussed in salons, cafés, and elsewhere throughout Paris.

Aside from the possibility of the enemy's learning the details and exact date, the minister naturally assumed that the plan had been cancelled following the Germans' retreat. Further, Czar Nicholas had abdicated on March 15, leaving Russia ready to sue for peace, and thereby freeing many German divisions to buttress the Western Front. Painlevé blinked in astonishment as Nivelle affirmed the offensive would vary only slightly.

Because the salient no longer existed, Nivelle explained, French guns and troops would punch a hole in the German front, then fan out behind the bewildered enemy destroying his trench system. Losses to the French would be trifling, Nivelle continued, since the Hindenburg Line could not withstand the hammer blows of the French siege guns.

"I do not fear numbers," Nivelle said. "The greater the numbers the greater the victory." Painlevé was puzzled. As Nivelle unreeled his plan, it sounded like a repeat performance of Joffre's two-year ruinous generalship on the Western Front.

Seized by a sense of disaster, Painlevé began to scrutinize Nivelle's plan. He allowed rumors of his intention to circulate. Soon various commanders approached him with doubts. Painlevé heard that since the German retreat from the salient, Nivelle's entire strategy was in need of revision. Time and again the minister was told that Russia's imminent collapse would enable many powerful German divisions to strengthen the already heavily fortified Hindenburg Line.

America's increasingly antagonistic attitude toward Germany was cited as a pivotal reason for abandoning Nivelle's plan. France need not bleed alone, but should wait until the United States entered the War. Reinforced, the Allies could pulverize the German army. Painlevé's dismay deepened when he heard that his predecessor, Minister of War Louis Lyautey, had scoffed at Nivelle's plan as one that might have been imagined by "the army of the Grand Duchess of Gérolstein," referring to a popular farcical opera. But Lyautey had not confronted Nivelle with his doubts.

If further proof were needed, it was furnished by Charles de Freycinet, an esteemed French political figure. On March 25, he placed before Painlevé a memorandum written by a high-ranking officer attached to the Group Armies of Reserve. Allegedly representing the collective views of all senior staff officers, the report declared that the Germans were fully prepared for the French offensive. If the Germans repelled the attack, "the best corps in the Army, the 1st, 20th, 2nd Colonial, the 32nd, and more besides, will be decimated."

Desperately trying to resolve the problem, Painlevé made an unusual move. Three of Nivelle's top army commanders were invited to present their views separately. General Micheler, who was interviewed March 28, openly disapproved of the offensive. Next came General Pétain. He, too, saw no victory in Nivelle's plan. The third commander, Franchet d'Esperey, was equally pessimistic.

With only days left, Painlevé decided that an appeal to reason might dissuade Nivelle, and invited him to a dinner at the War Ministry on April 3. Other guests included Premier Ribot and André Maginot, Minister of Colonies. Tactfully explaining to Nivelle all the facts militating against his plan, Painlevé emphasized the tremendous advantage of waiting until the United States entered the War.

Nivelle repeated the reasons for his decision to attack. The German withdrawal entailed only minor variations in the French plans. Any contrary view was the product of ignorance. Nivelle reassured his listeners that the drive would end the War in weeks.

Although America was only three days from declaring war, Nivelle discounted its effectiveness as an ally. Any military aid supplied by the United States, he insisted, would not be forthcoming for at least another year. Returning to the German defenses, Nivelle exuded confidence. The Hindenburg Line, he said, would collapse under the first onslaught.

The commander paused momentarily, then walking to an enormous wall map of the Western Front, pointer in hand, he swept a wide arc. All this, he announced grandly, will be ours within days. Nivelle had assessed his listeners well. He was talking to leaders who hungered for even a morsel of victory. For almost three years France had known only defeat, dishonor, and despair.

Minister Painlevé took Nivelle's hand and said: "General, if your offensive resulted only in giving us back this vast territory and all it contains, the government and the nation would consider it a great victory and owe you an immense debt of gratitude." With a smile Nivelle responded: "That would be nothing; a poor little tactical victory. It is not for so meager a result that I have accumulated on the Aisne 1,200,000 soldiers, 5,000 guns and 500,-000 horses. The game would not be worth the candle."

A French heavy tank. The bulbous gun port on the side allowed the tankmen to defend themselves against a flank attack.

But the German defense system was now battle ready, based on a fundamentally new strategy. The conventional series of trenches, a mile or more in depth, had been replaced with thousands of concrete pillboxes bristling with machine guns. A foray against any nest would draw fire from the surrounding ones. Behind this was a complex arrangement consisting of many thousands of dugouts, in addition to natural caverns, which would shelter troops during the heaviest bombardments. When the barrage ceased, defenders would rush forward to repel any French troops that might have passed through the machine-gun nests. Described as "elastic defense" by the Germans, it was devised to thwart Nivelle's campaign quickly and completely.

Nivelle was due for another jolt. His original plan assumed that his forty-four French divisions would greatly outnumber the enemy's nine divisions. But enough German manpower had been tapped from the Russian and other fronts to assemble forty-three full-strength divisions along the Hindenburg Line. When told of this new ratio, Nivelle dismissed the information as irrelevant.

Only one more wrinkle had to be ironed out before Nivelle's plan could be put into operation. Painlevé arranged a final conference with Nivelle. Many commanders, and even civilians, sent him memoranda indicating the folly of proceeding with the offensive. Present this time was President Poincaré.

In midmorning, April 6, ten days before the big guns would roar, the group convened in the President's private railway car at Compiègne, close to general headquarters which had recently been shifted to prepare for the offensive. To encourage candor, no minutes were taken. Only the highest political and military figures attended. Aware of the meeting's purpose, Nivelle was now icily polite.

Poincaré began by noting that France, already poor in manpower, should avoid this calculated risk; for if the venture failed the nation might suffer grievous losses. The President was respectful, affording Nivelle an opportunity to abandon the plan but still retain his power and prestige. War Minister Painlevé spoke in a similar vein.

After all had expressed concurring views, Nivelle replied. Distant and aloof, he made no

French Territorials. The Senegalese formed one of the French Army's most effective units.

effort to meet their objections. "I will not, under any pretext," he declared, "get involved in another Battle of the Somme." Predicting the offensive would rout pacifism in France, he proceeded to make promises which even he must have known could not be fulfilled. To assuage the fear of losing manpower, the general promised that if his offensive was not successful in forty-eight hours, he would end the battle and withdraw all troops.

Nivelle spoke to a silent and unconvinced audience. His army group commanders were asked to express their opinions. Under the cold stare of their commander in chief, they understandably did not express their true thoughts, with the exception of Pétain. Without hesitation, he answered: "We have not the means to carry it out. . . . Even if it were to succeed, we could not exploit it. Have we 500,000 fresh troops to make such an advance? No. Then it is impossible."

Nivelle cut Pétain short: "Since I am in agreement neither with the government nor with my own subordinates," he remarked, "the only course open to me is to resign." It was an unexpected turn. Their government already shaky, the ministers knew that they could not satisfactorily explain the resignation of the commander in chief at such a crucial moment in the War. Nivelle's departure would be followed by a demand for a new cabinet.

Interested in preserving national harmony and their own positions, the ministers rationalized that even if Nivelle were only a mite successful, the risk would be self-liquidating. Even if the worst occurred, Nivelle had promised he would call off the offensive if it was not successful within forty-eight hours.

As darkness descended on April 15, the evening of the offensive, a cold, wind-swept rain began turning to sleet and the temperature dropped rapidly. Trudging toward their positions, ankle-deep in mud, coats heavy with

Indochinese troops with their distinctive sloping helmets, modeled after the sampan hats worn by the farmers in the rice paddies.

water, the men were slowly drained of energy. On reaching their assault stations, they huddled under pelting sleet while company commanders read Nivelle's order of the day: "The hour has come! Courage and Confidence! Long live France!"

Behind the enemy lines, Prince Rupprecht of Bavaria, commander of the German forces, read the Kaiser's message to his soldiers: "Your armies are undergoing heavy artillery bombardment. The great French infantry attack is hourly awaited. All Germany is expectantly watching her brave sons. Greet them for me. My thoughts are with them."

During the night-long French artillery barrage, tens of thousands of troops moved forward. Despite bone-chilling rain and sleet, a new sense of power permeated the ranks, the men awed by the gigantic display of armed might. Earlier in the day, blue uniforms literally extended to the horizon on either side. Morale had not been so high since August, 1914.

As assault whistles blew before daybreak, troops clambered up trench ladders "over the top." Reserve battalions scraped forward, expecting a clean kill. But as they sloshed onward in the mud, a sense of despair began to overwhelm them. Despite the huge number of French cannon, they were inadequate to shell the entire area. The German barbed wire entanglements were strung with cowbells that clanked as French soldiers stumbled against them in the blackness.

Where French explosive shells had blown away barbed wire, Germans sent blazing yellow flares over the scene. Under this umbrella of light, attacking troops were cut down by artillery and machine-gun fire. The creeping barrage, based on Mangin's calculations, moved faster than the soldiers could advance. Caught without artillery protection, the French soldiers paid dearly.

Unable to bypass the strongpoints and attack the rear German positions, the French soldiers flattened themselves in mud-filled shell holes. Explosive shells and machine-gun bullets darted at them. By 7 A.M. Nivelle's timetable was in shambles. French battalions had been scheduled to move into assault trenches every fifteen minutes. As the troops staggered and crawled back, those in the trenches behind them were unable to move forward and the follow-up men fell upon them in a jumbled mass.

In their headquarters, members of the general staff, ignorant of the impasse, assumed some troublesome machine-gun nests were responsible for the delays, but that these soon would be silenced. Mangin issued another order to hasten progress. His Sixth Army, assigned a frontal onslaught, was commanded ". . . not to allow the enemy to establish a continuous line of machine guns. You must take advantage of the gaps and pass through the islands of resistance."

Few gaps were left, and they were passages to eternity for many thousands of Frenchmen. At midday sleet and snow fell thickly, ending visual communication and air observation. Battery crews lost sight of their forward troops. Artillery commanders, acting on garbled reports, assumed the men had not yet left the trenches. Drawing their barrages back to starting positions, they hurled tons of shells onto the advancing French troops.

This was the first battle in which the French used tanks on a large scale. Called "Schneiders," after the armament factory which manufactured them, most of the 200 tanks were bogged in the mud and became easy targets for artillery. At 2:30 P.M. the Germans counterattacked in force. By nightfall the French had advanced 600 yards instead of the six miles Nivelle had projected. Only the courage of the French troops prevented the Germans from driving them farther back. No less a foe than Crown Prince Wilhelm saluted the "personal valor of the French poilu."

The brave Senegalese failed their French comrades for the first time. Freezing sleet was their undoing. Unable to hold rifles in their frost-bitten hands, they stumbled forward until their officers were killed. Then they turned about, hurrying toward the rear.

Most tragic was the utter collapse of the traditionally inefficient French Medical Service. Preparations had been made for 15,000 wounded; but the casualties the first day amounted to 90,000. One hospital had only four thermometers for 3,500 beds. Lack of even the most rudimentary medical facilities prevented care for the wounded, who were left lying in the mud.

Communiqués from Nivelle's headquarters were fabricated to deceive the nation. Forty-eight hours came and went, forcing Nivelle to break another promise. He was no more able to withdraw his troops than was King Canute to hold back the sea. As the situation worsened, no amount of deception could conceal the truth.

Nivelle's farthest advance was made on April 17, when his troops seized Fort Malmaison, a gain of two-and-one-half miles. Actually the Germans withdrew from this salient to regroup. For the next two weeks Germans and Frenchmen fought furiously on an almost stationary front. Reports of the slaughter at Chemin des Dames spread through the ranks, becoming wildly exaggerated. Isolated cries, "Down with the War!" and "Down with the bungling generals!" were heard more frequently. Troops on leave waved red flags and sang revolutionary songs.

Even officers began to protest Nivelle's strategy. War Minister Painlevé's worst suspicions were confirmed when he toured the Aisne sector. He heard firsthand accounts from officers who complained: "This is regression. We haven't learned a thing. We are sticking to the methods of 1915. Of course, we'll get citations and decorations but we don't care. We'd rather throw them at the heads of our leaders. It's not the honors that we're interested in, but a wiser policy, more sparing of human lives!"

Eventually even Nivelle realized that his offensive was a colossal misadventure. In this moment of crisis, Nivelle revealed himself. Seeking scapegoats, he insinuated to Painlevé and other ministers that the debacle was Mangin's fault but his attempts to shift responsibility were coldly rejected.

Apparently overcome by hysteria, Nivelle traveled to Dormans, General Alfred Micheler's headquarters, where he stormed into the conference room shrieking accusations at his subordinate in the presence of the latter's staff. But Micheler was not one to suffer abuse in silence. Ignoring rank, he turned on his commander in chief. "You wish to make me responsible for your mistake," he bellowed, "me, who never ceased to warn you of it. Do you know what such an action is called?" he demanded. "Well, it is called cowardice!" Nivelle shrank under his subordinate's tongue-lashing, staggered to his car as if drunk, and drove off.

French official history lists casualties during Nivelle's offensive at 96,000, which is highly improbable. General Richard Thoumin, a French military historian, reports French casualties at 180,000. Thoumin served as a front-line officer during the war. Entirely sympathetic to his colleagues and caste, he had no reason to manufacture this figure and discredit them. Others place French losses at more than 200,000, and the Germans, who dealt more blows than they received, admitted 160,000 casualties.

In twenty-one months of war, French casualties had amounted to more than 3,000,000. The French troops were courageous and prepared for battle-imposed hardships, but they would no longer be driven to slaughter. Denied all legal means to seek redress, the troops exploded in revolt. For the next two months, the French Army was in a state of paralysis.

Pétain Restores Morale

The mutiny began on April 29, 1917. The air was heavy with sullen moods, but officers pretended not to notice. The company commander refrained from scolding his slovenly men who, wearing five-day beards, pointedly passed him without saluting. Ordered to the front, troops took advantage of the confusion and trekked rearward. Drunken soldiers sauntered past their officers staring at them in exaggerated disdain. Others rampaged about drinking wine from looted stores, shouting "Down with the War!" Revolts spread even to such privileged units as the 60th Chasseur Battalion. Formed of special fighters, one battalion was attached to each infantry division.

Military leaders deluded the government—but not for long—by misnaming mutiny as acts of "collective indiscipline." The location of whole divisions was unknown to general headquarters. A military police unit, sent to arrest roving mutineers, demonstrated more bravery than judgment. With a mad bellow, the mob tore away their weapons, pummeled them senseless and left them hanging by their feet from lampposts.

During the darkest days only two reliable divisions stood between Paris and the Germans, who had no inkling of the chaos that convulsed the French. Fearful that the Germans might glean vital information from prisoners, the French high command continually shifted their front-line troops. None of the soldiers who were captured even hinted at the mutiny. The poilus had revolted against incompetent leadership—but they were not traitors.

Disobedience usually surfaced when a unit, after fierce fighting, was allowed only a brief rest then ordered back to the front. No enmity was shown toward junior officers—lieutenants and captains—who merely transmitted orders and suffered the agonies of trench warfare like themselves. But the troops were openly hostile to staff officers, denouncing them as "drinkers of blood."

On the same day that the mutiny surfaced, a frightened government concluded, that if France was to survive, Nivelle must go. Without fanfare or ceremony, General Henri Philippe Pétain was appointed Chief of the General Staff and "technical adviser to the government," with an office in the War Ministry. To the

The fast, efficient French 75's symbolize the armament that General Pétain (above) depended upon until American forces could come in.

nation at large, this announcement meant little or nothing, but Nivelle and his staff saw the handwriting on the wall.

After Nivelle's campaign turned to a holocaust he was bluntly told to resign for the good of France. Determined not to make matters easy for the government, he insisted upon public dismissal. The Minister of War equivocated until May 15, then he officially named Pétain commander in chief. It was a dazzling rise for the sixty-year-old professional soldier who had begun the War as an inconspicuous colonel not far from retirement.

Pétain promptly dismissed his predecessor's staff, replacing them with artillerymen who shared his view that battles are won by liberal use of large-bore guns and economizing on manpower. Until he took command, artillery was secondary to infantry assault. Most gunnery schools had been discontinued to release their cadres for the April offensive. Now an artillery research center was established, where coordination between gunnery and infantry was taught as an integral part of military science.

Turning his attention to the Army's inner crisis, Pétain dealt with a major source of discontent—leave for the soldiers. At no time before the War did the army concern itself with the matter of leave. The school-of-attack leadership had believed that a lightning victory would release the men in months, if not weeks. As trench warfare stagnated, soldiers were theoretically allowed one week of furlough for every four months at the front. But mounting casualties led to a manpower shortage which the army sought to overcome by curtailing leaves; and these were cancelled for all troops three or more months preceding an offensive. Furloughs were considered a privilege, not a right, and given grudgingly. Many men spent eighteen months at the front without one.

Soldiers on a seven-day leave never knew how much of their leave time would be used just to make the trip home. Weighed down by pack and rifle, they plodded miles to the nearest rail line and waited hours or days for a train. Except for the respite from enemy fire, conditions were similar to the front. Without provisions for even elementary comforts, the men lounged and slept in the cold, sleet, or rain. The stations had no facilities for sleeping or washing. Food was hard to obtain—wartime inflationary prices placed most victuals beyond the soldier's pay.

Pétain ordered his commanders to "insure seven days of leave every four months to everyone. . . . The leave schedule is to be made up with the greatest care . . . and posted for inspection by those concerned." Additional orders followed. Adequate truck transportation was to be provided for furloughed troops from the base to railroad stations. Increased train schedules reduced their waiting time. Facilities exclusively for soldiers were installed at stations—low-cost meals, barbershops, washrooms, free medical service, and bunks.

The sources of discontent were systematically removed until the Army's fighting qualities—except for troop strength—had been restored. Pétain predicated his strategy on manpower from the United States, now an ally. "We must wait for the Americans," he told his subordinates. Under his command the French Army was guided by the slogan, "Lavish with steel, stingy with blood."

Probably no French commander understood the temper of the troops better than Pétain. He visited nearly ninety divisions, hearing complaints and eliminating their causes. He would reproach the most senior divisional officer if a justified complaint had been ignored. The Medical Service was completely reorganized, and unit commanders were held personally responsible for their efficient operation. Order and morale were restored by the end of June.

Until recent years, one of the most closely guarded French secrets was this mutinous episode of 1917. Aside from one brief chapter in French official history, the army wrapped the affair in silence. Pétain seldom mentioned the incident and left no memoirs. Historian Richard Watt suggests ". . . there were at least 100,000 men in active mutiny, and probably many more."

Official reports list 412 mutineers condemned of whom 23 were shot—incredible in relation to the number of troops involved. How many were executed with or without a court-martial remains unknown. Other rebels were banished to Devil's Island and penal battalions in Africa, to return to France in 1924, granted amnesty by their government.

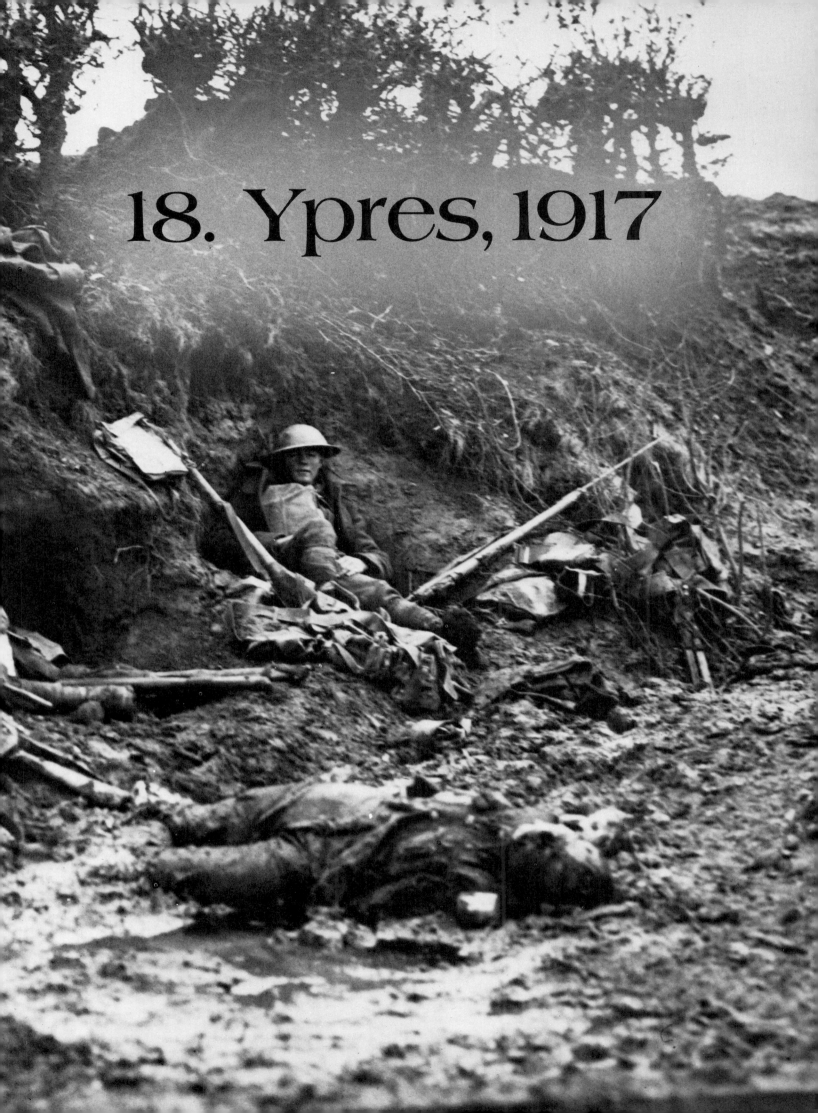

18. Ypres, 1917

General Sir Hubert Plumer.

18. Ypres, 1917

Sir Douglas Haig was never wholly convinced that machine guns and tanks had relegated cavalry charges to the history books, and as if to proclaim this view, throughout the War his shining boots always wore spurs. His 1917 plans for a campaign against the enemy in the Ypres sector of Flanders revived a cherished dream—a crashing breakthrough that would afford him "opportunities for the employment of cavalry in masses," in a sweep to the Belgian coast where the U-boat bases at Ostend and Zeebrugge would be captured.

The Flemish fields had been reclaimed from primal swamps after centuries of toil. But bombardment in earlier battles had wrecked the complex drainage and dike system, then subsequent rains and shelling had churned the district round Ypres into a sea of ooze, pocked with murky, stagnant ponds, reeking from the refuse and offal of living men, corpses, and carcasses. Reports by the Belgians to the General Headquarters emphasized that the terrain was unsuitable for military operations. Horses and artillery would sink in the sludge if they were not caught in time. But Haig was more impressed by a dry map of the area.

In this sector the Germans were entrenched along an eight-mile natural elevation extending between the villages of Passchendaele and Messines. Each half of the ridge bears the name of its nearest village. Prime Minister Lloyd George and the British cabinet had become wary of Haig's selection of battle sites of little

strategic value to the Germans, and fraught with peril for the British. But supported by, among others, the First Sea Lord, Jellicoe, who was concerned with the submarine threat from Channel ports, Haig won the day.

Since 1914, the Ypres salient had been held by the British Second Army, commanded by the resourceful Sir Hubert Plumer. He had contrived a project literally to disintegrate the Messines half of the ridge mass, which hemmed in the English southeastern flank of the salient, by tunneling under it and blowing it up. Welsh miners and other troops labored for two years at the most prodigious sapping operation in military history.

Under the glare of naked light bulbs, thousands of men swung picks and heaved shovels to dig shafts down to 125 feet, while water pumps chugged continuously. A series of nineteen tunnels, some nearly one half mile long, were bored, in addition to five miles of galleries. This excavation was crammed with one million pounds of ammonal, a high explosive, placed under critical enemy positions.

It had also occurred to the Germans that by undermining the British position with explosives they might end the impasse, but their tunneling operations began much later and never caught up with Plumer's miners. In some places they reached a depth of sixty feet. English monitors, aided by microphones, listened apprehensively as German burrowers worked toward them—at one time a German

British troops "mopping up" in a German trench after the lines had been overrun. A thorough search of each bunker was necessary to ensure that no one remained concealed, able to jump out and shoot the attackers from the rear.

cross-cut ended less than two feet from a British tunnel. Over each shaft the British placed signs that read "Deep Well," but the Germans were not deceived.

Surface preparations for an assault could be clearly observed, and captured British prisoners talked—some even revealing the assault date, June 7, to be preceded by a seven-day bombardment. But none mentioned the sapping project and all denied such venture when questioned. The suspicious Germans sent raiding parties to fetch clay brought up from the excavations and the specimens left no doubt about the depth of British digging. Yet no attempt was made to evacuate Messines Ridge for the Germans discounted the possibility that British explosives buried so deep could cause more than a tremor.

On the night of June 6, Plumer commented approvingly on the job, adding: "Gentlemen, I don't know whether we shall make history tomorrow, but we shall certainly change geography."

Zero hour was 3:10 A.M. A half hour before, all British guns ceased fire while troops waited in the trenches with fixed bayonets. Several minutes before 3, German green and yellow flares lit the night, signalling for artillery fire. After a brief flurry of shells over British lines, the front again fell silent. At zero hour, the plungers of battery cases were rammed down, simultaneously detonating all nineteen mines. As clay and mud blew high into the air, shock waves reverberated across the Channel and were even felt in London by the Prime Minister at 10 Downing Street. Craters up to 300 feet in diameter and nearly 100 feet deep were blown in the German lines, killing or mangling more than 20,000 Germans. As the first streaks of dawn illuminated the pillars of smoke and dust, nine divisions—including one Anzac—charged with unsheathed bayonets. The initial advance met no resistance, but behind the front line opposition grew progressively strong-

A German battalion marches through an unidentified French village. The officer at the right of the first rank of horsemen is Erwin Rommel, the famed "Desert Fox" of the African campaigns in World War II.

284

April, 1917. A Canadian unit keeps watch at the bitterly contested Vimy Ridge, south of Ypres.

er. At the end of a full day's fighting, 7,300 German prisoners had been taken, but after several days Plumer's losses reached 25,000 with no additional gain of territory.

Haig wanted the action completed before the torrential August rains mired the Ypres salient. His plans included the capture of the ridge and then an advance to the Channel ports. General Plumer had executed the first phase of the campaign, but his lack of progress against stiffening resistance prompted Haig to bring up General Hubert Gough and his Fifth Army, presumably to share equal command with Plumer, but actually to direct the assault.

Not only were Gough and his staff unfamiliar with the terrain around Ypres, but the Fifth Army was a loosely gathered force with raw troops scattered throughout its divisions. In the ensuing realignment of forces, with Plumer's Second Army shifted to the right and the left position held by the Fifth Army, the bulk of Gough's supplies arrived either too late or were dumped in the wrong staging area.

Opposing Gough was the German Fourth Army, commanded by General Sixt von Arnim and his able chief of staff, Colonel Fritz von Lossberg. Unknown to the British, the Germans were applying their new strategy of elastic

defense, originated by Lossberg. Under this plan the enemy was to be allowed to advance somewhat, but only at a cost of enormous casualties.

The Fourth Army's defenses encompassed six lines of entrenchments buttressed by machine-gun lunettes faced with concrete and arranged in diamondlike formation. For the conventional trench system was substantially abandoned, replaced by a series of reinforced concrete pillboxes each of which could withstand even an 8-inch shell—although a direct hit usually brought death by concussion to the occupants.

The forward positions were manned only lightly, but resistance would get increasingly more rugged as attacking troops came into rear areas. Gough was also unaware of the Germans' new weapon—mustard gas fired in shells. Even Prince Rupprecht was optimistic, writing in his diary: "My mind is quite at rest concerning the attack, for we have never disposed of such strong reserves, so well trained for their part as on the front attacked."

To make their defenses even more formidable, the Germans had also flooded the land so that three sides of each pillbox were surrounded by water. Footpaths extended from

A gutted, ruined tank stands sentinel on a peak
overlooking the total destruction around Ypres.

the rear of each one to allow defenders a quick retreat, whereas attackers were forced to inch forward, jumping from one water hole to another until close enough to fling a grenade into the narrow hole through which the machine gun fired. In future battles the Allies would use the same defense.

Lloyd George, sceptical of Haig's campaign plan, organized a new War Committee of cabinet members, prominent civilians, and military figures with the aim of limiting Haig's powers. He failed when both General Jan Christiaan Smuts and Lord Curzon supported Haig. Lloyd George once again chose not to risk his shaky coalition government on the issue.

On the field more than 3,300 British cannon faced 1,500 German guns. On July 22 the British began an intensive ten-day bombardment in which more than 1,500,000 shells were fired. Seasonal rains began falling on July 30, turning the battleground into a vast swamp. The tanks assigned to overrun the German defenses bogged down helplessly and their armor plates were too thin to withstand the shelling from the massed German artillery. Only nineteen of the forty-eight vehicles allocated for the offensive were able to crawl into

action, and of these seventeen were quickly destroyed. Even so, Gough's infantry advanced several thousand yards on a fifteen-mile front. Then a counterattack forced their retreat almost back to the starting line. On the first day British casualties amounted to 32,000.

Haig's headquarters continually sent back deceptive dispatches such as "We have broken the German line on the entire front of attack," but eventually Gough had to admit that his forces were hopelessly mired. Haig then ordered General Plumer and his Second Army to salvage whatever they could, but it was too late. The campaign was drawn out through the fall until November 20, when subzero weather and icy ground gave an excuse to break off.

Haig's grandiose plan to smash through to the English Channel ended with a few square miles of worthless swampland including the devastated village of Passchendaele. Lloyd George, Haig's old adversary, wrote in bitter recollection that the battle "with the Somme and Verdun, will always rank as the most grim, futile, and bloody fight ever waged in the history of war," and added that it was the result of "stubborn and narrow egotism, unsurpassed among the records of disaster."

19. Collapse
of Russia

Czar Nicholas II.

19. Collapse of Russia

Russia's last major offensive was launched on June 4, 1916, under the generalship of Aleksei Brusilov, her most able commander. The Austrians, furious with Italy for switching to the Allies, had pounced in a surprise attack on the Italians in the Trentino and sent them reeling down the plains of Lombardy. Facing certain disaster, the King of Italy implored the Czar in a telegram to save his regime. Nicholas II ordered an eastern campaign against the Austro-Hungarian armies.

Brusilov struck without warning along a 200-mile front. By omitting a preparatory cannon barrage, he caught the enemy completely by surprise. Russian forces numbering 510,000 men consisted of forty infantry and ten cavalry divisions and 1,770 artillery pieces. This strength was roughly equal to the enemy's, but the Austrian defenses collapsed as the Russians smashed toward their objectives—the crucial railroad hub of Kovel and Lemberg (Lvov), the industrial capital of Galicia. Stunned by the unexpected assault, the Austro-Hungarian Fourth and Seventh armies, an uneasy amalgam of multi-nationals, broke ranks and fled.

Brusilov's success astonished his chiefs at General Headquarters. None had had any faith in his offensive, and no preparations had been made to provide him with reserves or matériel. When their offensive lost its momentum at the end of June, the weary Russians had already rounded up more than 200,000 prisoners and

their advance units were within sight of the Carpathian passes. Had he been reinforced with manpower and supplies, Brusilov might well have toppled the disintegrating Dual Monarchy then and there.

Although Hindenburg desperately needed all the reserves he had at Verdun and the Somme, he promptly transferred fifteen divisions to forestall an Austrian debacle. Russian General Headquarters also sent belated aid to Brusilov, but it came by painfully slow horse-drawn wagons over rutted dirt roads, while the Germans were speeding eastward along highly efficient railroads.

By mid-July the Austro-German combination had stabilized the front, and repeated counterattacks at Russian weak points had regained small parcels of land, particularly around Lutsk. Despite his lack of adequate reserves and ammunition, Brusilov not only held doggedly to most of the sixty miles wrested from the Austrians but repeatedly attacked. The fighting lasted until the second week of September, by which time more than 250,000 Austrians and Germans had been slain or wounded and nearly the same number taken prisoner. The Russians paid the appalling price of one million men. The Russian peasant often had no weapon or ammunition. Sometimes he charged with a bayonet tied to a stick and lacked the most common implements, even being forced to rip down barbed-wire barriers with his bare hands.

A trainload of captured Russian equipment and supplies waits for
transport to Germany. The waste and depletion of matériel and especially
manpower helped bring Russia to her knees.

German medics and a patrol in a desolated Polish village pass by a billboard advertising the shop of the locksmith and general mechanic Stanislaw Berger. The *Pickelhaube*, the spiked leather headgear worn by the men at right, was not replaced with helmets on the Eastern Front as quickly as on the more mechanized West.

The Russian Revolution

Czarist military policy alternated between massacre and stagnation. With the arrival of winter, more than a million soldiers deserted. Demoralization was so complete that deserters lived openly at home unmolested by the authorities. Corruption and inefficiency contaminated every segment of society. Army contractors provided only a portion—and usually of shoddy quality—of the supplies for which they were paid.

Such omens that his 300-year-old dynasty might be endangered did not, however, affect the Czar. Those who sought to enlighten him were ignored. When the President of the Duma warned that rebellion was sweeping the land, Nicholas II wrote the Czarina: "Again this fat-bellied Rodzianko has written me a lot of nonsense, which I do not even trouble to answer." Even the most conservative party in the Duma agreed that the Czar must be removed. The moderate Socialist Alexander Kerensky advocated an anti-Czarist coup "by terrorist means if necessary," and Chief of Staff General Alekseev began plotting to arrest the Czarina and force the Czar to introduce reforms. But events acted for him.

Early in March, 1917, strikes and food riots erupted in Petrograd. Troops were sent in but fraternized with the rebels. Wherever the regime turned for support, it found none and suddenly the autocracy collapsed before it could be overthrown. On March 15, the Czar sent his abdication to the Duma President he had so recently scorned.

A Provisional Government headed by moderates affirmed its loyalty to the Allies and pledged to continue the War. Workmen and soldiers organized councils, called soviets, and initially collaborated with the new regime; but they soon moved further to the left under the influence of Bolsheviks who demanded an end to the War and the abolition of private property. Germany sought a separate peace with Russia, in order to concentrate all its armies on the Western Front. To achieve this objective, Ludendorff, representing the German High Command, took a calculated risk to remove Russia from the War.

Except to hold their lines firm, the Germans ceased all military activity on the Eastern Front. Ludendorff looked with pleasure on the widening rift between moderates and Bolsheviks. He knew the unofficial truce prevented both factions from uniting for the common defense of Russia. Politically sophisticated German agents, disguised as soldiers, gathered at the front, where both sides fraternized in the warming sun. Russian soldiers simply ignored orders to fight.

To accelerate Russia's withdrawal from the War, Ludendorff arranged to transport Nicolai Lenin and a group of revolutionists across Germany from Switzerland to the small Baltic port of Sassnitz where they embarked for Malmö, Sweden. At Germany's request, the Swedish government provided transit to Finland, still a Russian province. "In the event of the Russians being refused entry into Sweden," read a directive from the Foreign Office, "the High Command of the Army would be prepared to move them into Russia through German lines." Lenin arrived in the Russian capital on April 16.

Russia shifted leftward slightly. A reorganized government in mid-May contained a majority of Socialists, including Kerensky as Minister of War. That Russia was bone weary and drained did not matter to the Allies who notified the new regime: No fight, no aid! France was particularly insistent on an eastern attack against the Germans. Shaken by mutinies, she feared—with good reason—defeat under large-scale assault. Kerensky, who had won his popularity largely as a radical orator, visited the front to raise morale and exhort the soldiers to fight, but his eloquence fell on deaf ears. The Bolshevik slogan, "Peace, Land, Bread" had a great deal more appeal than fighting Germans.

Kerensky's loyalty to the Allies was the undoing of democracy in Russia. He ordered an offensive to be led by Brusilov, the new commander in chief. Choosing Lemberg as the target, the general assembled 200,000 troops from crack Caucasian, Finnish, and Siberian regiments. Riding in the vanguard were the finest Cossack cavalry brigades. But no reliable infantry reserves were available.

Beginning their offensive on July 1, the Russians encountered little resistance from the Germans who assumed the truce still prevailed.

The Czar and his family.

Alexander Kerensky, Minister of War in the new provisional government, reviewing troops.

Revolutionary Russian soldiers pose
before their makeshift barricade in
front of the drugstore on Sergius Street
in Petrograd, now Leningrad.

More than 17,000 Germans were captured during the initial surprise, and 10,000 more seized in the following days. Lemberg had not been taken when the Austro-German armies braced themselves in the second week. Strengthened by newly arrived reserves, they counterattacked on a broad front using a vast array of field guns. It was too much for the Russians. Under methodical pounding, an orderly retreat became a wholesale rout with the Germans in hot pursuit. In less than a week, virtually all the territory the Russians had won during the Brusilov offensive in 1916 had been recovered. Before July ended, Russia was permanently out of the War.

Discipline at the front vanished. Desertions became so common that the army demobilized itself. At least eighty Austro-German divisions were still on the Eastern Front but all pursuit was halted. The German High Command assessed the situation, and took no measure that might unite the Russians. Peasant uprisings against landowners streaked across Russia; estates were seized without waiting for land reform; workmen expropriated factories; Russia was convulsed by chaos.

Whatever vestige of popular support Kerensky had after the July defeat vanished when he was unable to prevent civil strife, leaving a power vacuum into which Lenin moved on November 7. The Bolsheviks were a small minority and lacked public approval, but their source of strength was the soviets buttressed by armed Red Guards. On November 8, Lenin issued a peace decree. An armistice was signed on November 22, then peace negotiations be-gan in early December at Brest Litovsk, a Russian railhead occupied by the Germans.

The Soviet delegation, led by Leon Trotsky, balked at the German demands that Russia relinquish Poland and other western territory. Moreover, Trotsky believed that a German revolution was imminent and so addressed himself not to the delegation, but to the German working man. Pressed for a commitment by General Max Hoffmann, Trotsky stalled, then announced that Russia could not accept the German terms. His declaration of "no war—no peace" infuriated Hoffmann.

With no opposition, German forces then advanced deeper into Russian territory. Lenin needed no further prodding. On February 19, less than twenty-four hours after the Germans had marched, the Soviet leader sent a telegram accepting all the terms outlined at Brest Litovsk. General Hoffmann, however, advanced for another two weeks and his army moved to Lake Preipus and Narva, exposing Petrograd to invasion. Other Germans swept into the granaries of the Ukraine.

Convinced that the Soviet leaders would no longer stall for time, Hoffmann met again with them at Brest Litovsk on March 3. The Soviets gave autonomy to Poland, Latvia, Estonia, and Finland, while the Ukraine and other Russian territory would continue under German occupation. Trotsky's tactic of trying to outwit Hoffmann had been costly. Russia also had to surrender the region of Batum, Ardahan, and Kars to Turkey. (Eight months later a defeated Germany relinquished all the conquered territory.)

Red guards mass in Petrograd
to show their solidarity
and proclaim the revolution.

20. The Italian Front

King Victor Emmanuel III and
(right) General Diaz.

20. The Italian Front

Italy was a territorial bargain-hunter in both world wars. When she attacked defeated France in 1940, President Franklin Roosevelt denounced the act as a "stab in the back." But few realized that Italy's policy was quite the same in World War I, when she waited at the sidelines before joining the camp she judged most likely to win.

Prior to World War I Italy was a signatory to the Triple Alliance, a mutual defense pact that included Germany and Austria-Hungary. Although under no delusion about Italy, just before the outbreak of hostilities the Germans asked their ally's position. Because the Dual Monarchy would engage in an aggressive war against Serbia, Italy answered that she would invoke the defensive clause that exempted her from military action.

Austrian reverses on the Eastern Front in 1914 forced Germany to prop up her ally against the Russians, who were on the verge of crashing through the Carpathian passes and sweeping down the Hungarian plain. Another rash attack against Serbia was also costly to the Dual Monarchy. With each defeat, the Italians showed less inclination to remain neutral, and the German High Command feared that Italy as an Allied belligerent might tip the scales in crushing Austria.

To forestall this, Germany urged that Italy be given the territory she demanded as the price of her neutrality. As this territory belonged to the Dual Monarchy, Austria protested, but continued to talk. At the same time Italy was secretly negotiating with the Allies and these talks soon became more serious.

The Russian onslaughts had threatened the defeat of Austria-Hungary. This prospect chilled the Italians, for unless they formally joined the Allies before Austria fell, they would be unable to take part in her dismemberment. Another inducement was that the Allies were more generous with Austrian territory than was Austria herself. Consequently, in April, 1915, Rome signed the secret Treaty of London, declaring war a month later.

The pact stipulated that, in return for military aid to the Allies, Italy would be given the Tyrol, Trieste, Istria, a part of the Dalmatian Coast, and the Greek-populated Dodecanese Islands. She would also be allowed to expand her African colonies and share in the partition of the Ottoman Empire.

The Italians opened hostilities against Austria-Hungary on May 23, 1915, but a depleted treasury and fear of Germany curbed her military ambitions. With the consent of her new allies, Rome didn't declare war against Germany until August 28, 1916, when she felt more secure against reprisal. Berlin was not surprised at this double dealing, but throughout the Dual Monarchy, the Italian action was treated as treachery. Thereafter, General Conrad spoke of this enemy only as "perfidious Italy."

Italy's reverie of grandeur was interrupted

An Austrian machine-gun detachment takes a rest
before continuing to the front.

Mountain Warfare

Crack Alpine troops on maneuvers in the rugged terrain they are trained to cope with. Climbing these precipices seems sufficiently arduous even without Austrians to defend them.

Italian troops take up a position on a mountain. The lumber, laboriously carried to the top, was intended for defensive fortifications.

British armored cars supplied to the Russians were captured by the Austrians in Galicia and used against the Italians.

Austrian flame throwers on the Isonzo.

Stunningly beautiful and virtually impregnable the
Julian Alps rise a mile and more in the air.

Italian soldiers constructing a fortified
trench system high on the side of a
mountain.

by the realities of war. Economically the nation was a yoke on the Allies. She was poorly equipped to meet her military commitments, lacking both the means to produce heavy goods and the money to buy them. England had been sharing coal with France, whose mines in the northeast were behind German lines. Now she was compelled to ship the precious fuel to stoke Italian industry and ships, for the Italian Navy could bottle up Austrian submarines in the Adriatic Sea.

Still nursing its wounds from the Libyan War of 1912, the Italian army was far from battle-ready and its 870,000 troops lacked adequate equipment. Under a humane and flexible leader, perhaps the Italian army might have been made adequate. But General Luigi Cadorna, the commander in chief, did not meet this criterion.

General Conrad hurled a series of threats against Italy, but was powerless to carry them out. The Austrians were struggling to survive on the Russian Front, and could spare only 100,-000 soldiers to guard the common frontier (nearly as many manned these positions when Italy was neutral). Austria knew that any Italian assault would be an uphill struggle against entrenched forces protected by the Dolomite, Carnic, and Julian Alps. The Austrians also knew that any lessening in pressure on other fronts would release their troops, who could race downhill across the northern Italian plains with relative ease.

A topographical map of the 480-mile-long, curving mountain barrier on the Austro-Italian Front shows the problems that faced Italy in 1915. Any offensive or defensive operation along the southern and northeastern perimeters favored the Austrians. Cadorna knew that assault against the Dolomite or Carnic ranges would invite wholesale destruction. The Alps here are creviced with precipitous passes and defiles that can be scaled only by the most skilled Alpine troops.

In the northwest, the Trentino (part of South Tirol), bulged deeply and menacingly into Italy, with Austrian forces entrenched behind its jagged crests. Any Italian assault here would have to be a vertical climb up the high-walled Adige Valley only to meet ambush in the narrow Trento Ravine, or farther north at the even more rugged Brenner Pass.

To the east, the gateway to Trieste—Austria's only port on the Adriatic—was also barred by natural obstacles. These seemed to offer some hope of advance, but only in contrast to the two other sectors. Here the Isonzo River pours down the flumes of the Julian Alps, then flows sluggishly to form marshes, and finally empties into the Adriatic. Austrian strongpoints had been established on the east bank of the Isonzo at all available crossings.

At the center of these concentrations was the elevated and fortified city of Gorizia; to its north, was the Bainsizza Plateau; and south of the city stood the Carso Plateau, a sheer, barren, razor-sharp limestone cliff rising 900 feet above the sea.

Behind these barriers rose the cloud-scraping Alpine pinnacles garrisoned by the expert *Alpenkorps*. The Italian dilemma, one strategist concluded, was that the "Isonzo could not be crossed until the mountains were taken and the mountains could not be taken until the river had been crossed."

Having demanded Trieste, Istria, and other territory, the Italian government knew these would first have to be taken by armed conquest. Lacking easy alternatives, General Cadorna was compelled to mount offensives in the Trentino and along the Isonzo.

The Isonzo campaign consisted of eleven separate bloody and futile battles on a sixty-mile front between June, 1915, and September, 1917. To be sure, the Western Allies goaded Cadorna into these ventures. Great Britain and France believed that if Austria-Hungary could be forced to struggle on two fronts—against Russia in the east and Italy and Serbia in the south—the Dual Monarchy would be doomed. Even if the Allies miscalculated, the Germans would have to divert manpower from the Western Front to brace the sagging Austrian armies. But matters evolved quite differently.

Ignoring the mud flats and marshes along which the sluggish Isonzo winds its way to the Adriatic, Cadorna saw only the flat plain a short distance beyond. He paid no attention to the vertical alpine cliff guarded by the garrisoned citadel of Gorizia, strategically located where the Isonzo slows to form a flood plain of marshes and flats. In what was announced as "the first grand objective of the campaign," the Italians attempted to seize the sixty-mile-wide

THE AUSTRO-ITALIAN FRONTIER

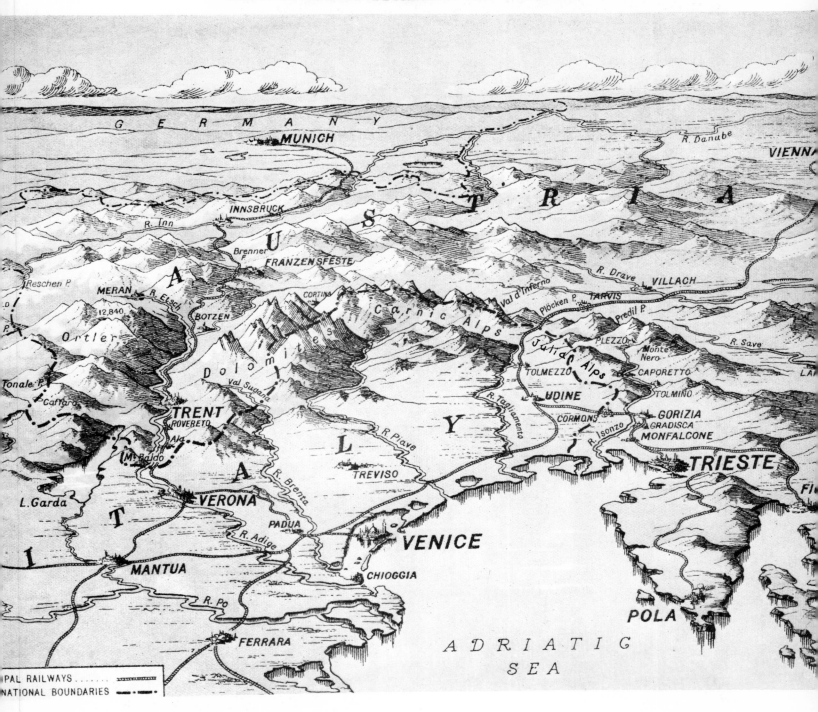

The problems facing the Italians are graphically shown on this topographical map. The Adige Valley with its rail line running from Trent to Innsbruck was suicidal; the Dolomites were far too rugged to attempt; this left the Julian Alps as the least difficult of three impossible solutions. After their final defeat on the Isonzo the Italians fled all the way back to the Piave before they were able to make a defensive stand.

An Italian mechanized unit brings supplies up a
makeshift mountain road. The ridged wheel would
prevent the vehicles from sliding sideways, but
even so the experience must have had its
frustrations and hair-raising moments.

bridgehead fronting Gorizia. Cadorna also decided to strike along the 125-mile Trentino front.

Command of the Isonzo sector was nominally held by Archduke Eugen von Hapsburg, but actually was in the hands of the Slav General Borojevic von Bojna, whose forces comprised skilled mountain fighters. Cadorna pitted two armies against these mountaineers in a fruitless endeavor to eliminate the Trentino salient. After a costly struggle, the rim of the salient was taken in 1915, but elsewhere the Italians met only adversity. Fighting along the Isonzo began on June 23 and varied in intensity, but the outcome remained constant. Trieste beckoned, yet to Cadorna it was as unattainable as Paris was to the Germans. Undaunted by mountains of Italian corpses, Cadorna kept attacking but could not budge the Austrians. Even if Gorizia could have been taken, it would have given him a Pyrrhic victory, for the city was the portal only to the knife-sharp palisades of Bainsizza and Carso.

The Italian two-to-one numerical superiority was inadequate to offset the advantages of the Austrian defensive positions. The bloodletting that began in late June continued through the summer and autumn with brief lulls for replacement of men, matériel, and supplies. When the sector became icebound at the beginning of December, the Italians could show only a few isolated dents in the enemy's line at tremendous cost to themselves.

The Austro-Hungarian Front was comparatively dormant during the winter of 1915–1916. But the warmth of the spring sun kindled in General Conrad the ambition to march on Rome itself. He assembled two divisions of *Alpenkorps* and, timing their attack to coincide with the spring thaws, swooped down on the unprepared Italians. The victorious Austrians chased the Italians across the plains of Lombardy, but the great success of the operation carried with it the seeds of its own failure. It prompted King Victor Emmanuel to request that the Czar begin an offensive, resulting in the attacks by General Brusilov and the removal of troops from the Italian campaign to cope with the Russians.

The Slavs of the Dual Monarchy's multinational army bore the Russians no ill will and fought them indifferently, sometimes to the point of sabotaging their own Teutonic officers. But their resentment at the Italian treachery was abiding, which was a factor in their success along the Italian Front. Once they had been transferred to the East, however, the remaining Austrian forces withdrew to the mountains. Cadorna took advantage of the situation to attack the Trentino, but his only achievement was a few square miles of Alpine rock. The remainder of 1916 saw only border skirmishes.

In the summer of 1917, the collapse of Russia left Germany and Austria free to mount a combined offensive against Italy. By September, General Otto von Below had formed an army of eight German divisions, including the superb *Alpenkorps*, and nine Austrian divisions. Below applied the new assault tactic that General Oskar von Hutier had devised to overwhelm numerically superior Russian forces in Riga.

Troop concentrations gave General Cadorna ample warning of the offensive, but he chose to ignore them. At the beginning of September, two Romanian officers deserted with detailed plans showing that the attack was to begin in the area of Caporetto. Cadorna still did little to prepare for the blow. He ordered the Second and Third armies to take defensive positions in depth, but didn't bother to supervise their deployment.

Cadorna's ability, whatever it may have been, was drastically impaired by his indifference to the welfare of peasants and workers, in or out of uniform. A Piedmontese count, the sixty-five-year-old general worked his soldiers beyond normal endurance and denied them even the most basic facilities for relaxation. His concept of military discipline was summed up in an old Piedmontese dictum: "The superior is always right, especially when he is wrong."

Lest any soldier forget, Cadorna issued disciplinary instructions to his commanders that began: "The Supreme Command desires that at all times and in all places, an iron discipline should reign throughout the Army." Then for rule infractions he listed barbarous penalties long since abandoned by civilized armies.

A Skoda-built Austrian 305-mm. mortar points its nose skyward with the Alps as background.

Cadorna's despotism brought about disrespect in his commanders. He seldom went beyond issuing general orders, which were sometimes ignored by subordinates who saw things differently. General Luigi Capello, commander of the Second Army, disregarded Cadorna's order for the defense of Caporetto and prepared instead for a counteroffensive near Tolmino, a village about ten miles southeast of Caporetto, thereby leaving a huge gap in the defensive line. Cadorna was touring other fronts and did not return to the Isonzo sector until October 19, five days before the enemy offensive began. Until then he did not know of the gap; no one had thought to notify him of it during his absence.

Capello had assigned his least reliable troops to the Tolmino front. Most were recent factory workers conscripted as punishment for participating in strikes to end the War, and now they were communicating revolution to other soldiers with their slogan: "This winter not one man in the trenches." As early as May, Italian attacks petered out when soldiers voluntarily surrendered to the enemy. On one occasion three entire regiments flung their weapons aside and marched behind a white flag toward the Austrians.

In the predawn hours of October 24, 1917, some 250,000 Austro-German troops crouched in readiness at Caporetto, well aware of the gap left by General Capello. Concealment was provided by sheets of frozen rain and thick fog. Austro-German guns, previously zeroed in on the Italian positions, began an intensive bombardment of smoke shells alternated with poison gas cannisters. Some shells emitted dense smoke or a vile stench, which made the defenders uncomfortable and careless about their respirators. Then they were smothered with mustard gas, against which Italian respirators provided no protection.

While the panic-stricken Italians milled about in blind, choking confusion, General Below began a slow rolling artillery barrage, inching forward at less than one kilometer an hour, closely followed by shock troops armed with grenades and light machine guns. When the fire had reached its range limit, the units poured through the gaps in the Italian line, bypassing pockets of resistance to encircle the survivors from the rear. While groping to escape, the Italians were deluged with high-explosive shells. They reeled back and the Caporetto Front crumbled.

By the afternoon of the 24th, Below's army had crossed the Isonzo and the Italians were in full rout. The Austro-German advances of the following day made clear that only an orderly retreat could salvage anything from the situation. But Cadorna waited two more days, and then it was too late. His order to withdraw was given on October 27, by which time Capello's twenty-five divisions had already been badly mauled. At almost every point of attack against trench lines, the Italians either surrendered immediately or, if time permitted, fled.

The Caporetto calamity ended when the survivors regrouped seventy miles back, behind the Piave River. Pitting sixteen divisions against the fifty-five commanded by Cadorna, the Austro-Germans retrieved, in one explosive assault, the few square miles of territory that the Italians had won in eleven bloody battles along the Isonzo at the price of one million casualties. Caporetto, sometimes called the Twelfth Battle of the Isonzo, nearly brought Italy to her knees. Her toll amounted to 10,000 dead, 30,000 wounded, and 295,000 prisoners, in addition to a mountainous loss of weapons and equipment. As in previous battles, thousands of Italians eagerly surrendered. Now, however, they cheered on their captors with "Long live Austria!" and "On to Rome!"

After the flight of the Italians to the Piave, the Allies rushed six French and five British divisions to shore up their partner. With these reinforcements, the Italians held firmly behind the Piave against the Austro-German troops. Finally, on December 26, the invader, his forces exhausted, withdrew. The failure to ensnare the Italians before they escaped rankled the Austrians and Germans, whose pursuit had been impeded by lack of railway or motor transport for their infantry and by the availability of horses only to pull cannon. The scudding Italians, on the other hand, were not handicapped by anything, having left all their equipment and heavy weapons behind. If the Germans and Austrians had been able to muster two or three fresh cavalry divisions and armored vehicles, Italy would have been out of the War.

Cadorna was replaced by General Armando

Diaz, perhaps not a better strategist but at least more considerate of his troops. In reorganizing the army, Diaz was aided by the presence of enemy troops on Italian soil; a resurgence of national unity swept over the nation. Factory workers abandoned their revolutionary dogma and declared a no-strike truce.

Having plucked Italy from the brink of disaster was scant comfort to the Allies. Her close call coincided with the prostration of Russia that released German legions for the Western Front. Italy had to be kept in the War at all costs. America had actively entered the conflict, but the full weight of her military might would not be felt until the spring of 1918. General Ferdinand Foch hastened to Rome to coordinate the operations of the Franco-British divisions with the Italians.

At a high-level emergency conference at Rapallo on November 7, the prime ministers of Great Britain, France, and Italy, and a special envoy of President Woodrow Wilson, met in a spirit of harmony. A Supreme War Council, chaired by Foch, was formed to contend with the Allies' critical military and political problems. It was the forerunner of the unity of command that helped accelerate victory in 1918.

Meanwhile the Allies took measures to protect Italy against another Caporetto. General Diaz' army was propped up with the British Tenth Army, three British divisions, plus two French Divisions, and the 32nd American Regiment of the 83rd Division. In the final months of the War, these combined forces handily defeated the dispirited Austrians.

The War is over for these Austrians, held prisoner in an Italian detention camp.

21. Cambrai-
Tank Warfare

British tanks with infantrymen.

21. Cambrai-Tank Warfare

General Sir Julian Byng, the commander of the British Third Army, was directed in mid-September of 1917 to organize an offensive to siphon German power from the Ypres sector. Byng and General Sir Hugh Elles, commander of the Royal Tank Corps, turned to a proposal made in August by Colonel J.F.C. Fuller, chief general staff officer, later a well-known military writer. Because tanks had proved worthless in the mire of Flanders, Fuller had searched for and had found dry ground where mobile armor could be deployed in large numbers and with immense impact.

He found his terrain at Cambrai, a town in northern France forty-five miles south of the Passchendaele-Messines battlefield. The countryside to the south and west of this city is compact, chalky, and fissured with narrow streams and small embankments. An irregular six-mile expanse between the Nord and Saint-Quentin canals, Fuller found, was suitable for tank maneuvering. Byng's objective would be the Hindenburg Line.

Nineteen divisions were at Byng's disposal for the attack. Prince Rupprecht of Bavaria, defending the sector, had six divisions, two of which were stationed between the two canals. Five cavalry divisions, consisting of British, Canadian, and Indian brigades, would exploit the tank breakthrough. The large forest of Havrincourt, immediately behind British lines, provided concealment for the massed tanks. To keep the enemy in the dark, every effort was made to ensure secrecy. Prior to the attack no tank was allowed to go closer than a mile to the German outposts.

As the British prepared for battle, their low-flying aircraft droned incessantly over the front to drown out the rumble of the landships as they moved about. Artists used the latest techniques of color-striping to camouflage the vehicles. Except for the officers, none of the troops knew about the tanks until forty-eight hours before the offensive. Even then they were not informed of the vehicles' actual function. In the event of capture before the surprise attack, no soldier could reveal damaging secrets—even under duress.

The main tactical purpose of the assault was to make a frontal smash into the enemy using mobile armor along a six-mile front, to bag all the Germans found between the canals, and to capture the town of Cambrai. There were no secondary objectives. The British were not intent upon a decisive breakthrough; the tactical strike was in fact a feint to divert German strength from their lines elsewhere. General Elles saw that the limited attack demanded a revised plan. Instead of restricting the tanks to the area between the two canals, he wanted to deploy them in a wide, steplike formation along a broad front as a shield for advancing infantry. His recommendation was rejected.

On November 20, at 6:20 A.M., daylight was

The whistle blows and it's "over the top" for these Canadians. The position of the hand of the lead man gives the appearance of that classic gesture of contempt—thumbing the nose.

still subdued, limiting visibility to about 200 yards. At that moment the engines of 381 tanks roared to life simultaneously and the vehicles lumbered forward along lanes that had been marked with tape during the night.

The thick barriers of barbed wire were flattened as the noisy tanks moved toward the front-line trenches. Each trench had been dug to a width of twelve feet, just to prevent tanks from crossing them, but Colonel Fuller had overcome this pitfall. All British tanks carried long fascines of brushwood tightly bound with chains which were dropped into the trenches and used as makeshift bridges. The British had dispensed with the artillery barrage that usually heralded an offensive and the Germans were taken completely by surprise. The troops in the outpost zone surrendered or fled, and before nightfall the Third Army had penetrated 7,000 yards on the six-mile front. The action was an undisputed success—British troops had seized enemy trenches at the unusually light cost of 4,000 casualties. German gunfire had destroyed 65 tanks and another 114 had broken down or tipped sideways into a trench, but about 7,500 German prisoners had been taken. Night fell at 5 P.M. with the assaulting troops holding the width of their salient. Without the aid of tanks, the positions that had fallen would have been almost unassailable.

Haig had achieved so few victories on the Western Front that he seemed completely at a loss to exploit the one at Cambrai. He was unable to advance without further reserves, and unwilling to relinquish the territory he had won. But if the British remained in place, they would be dangerously exposed to a three-sided attack, and the onset of cold, stormy weather would soon end the campaign season. Yet Haig's irresolution prevailed. He told Byng not to expect any reserves. British troops were needed to bolster the sagging fortunes of the Italian Army at Caporetto. Byng was thus euchred into the position of fighting a limited engagement with diminishing vigor and no fresh forces. (The transfer of the five battle-ready divisions to Italy was based on defective Intelligence or faulty judgment, for at a conference held on November 10, the Austro-German staffs had agreed to taper off operations on the Italian Front as the winter storms closed in.)

German prisoners in a "cage," as the detention pens were called. In the initial, successful stages of the campaign vast numbers of prisoners were taken by the attacking Allies.

Mounted artillerymen taking ammunition to the front pass by a forward first-aid station. Haig avoided such places as the sight of wounded men tended to make him "physically ill," his son later reported. He and his senior staff were in fact seldom seen in any forward area.

World War I Tanks

French Renault one-man tank.

A British light tank climbs out of a ditch.

French tanks ready to roll.

London's church bells pealed for the only time in the War to celebrate the Cambrai victory, which the home front did not yet know was only fleeting. Still it was a welcome change from the Somme and Flanders.

The Germans lost little time in bringing reinforcements from their Fourth Army in Flanders. Other reserves were en route from the quiet Eastern Front. As the Germans brought additional strength to Cambrai, the battle deteriorated into isolated, often confused skirmishes. The Canadians, as usual, kept in the van of battle. But the Third Army had lost its impetus for lack of reserves, while the replenished Germans could strike vigorously. In a massed counterblow on November 30, the Germans recaptured some of the ground lost on the first day. By the third day of December the British pulled back, reducing by one half their possession of the salient.

A blizzard halted all operations in the first week of December. Two weeks of fighting had cost the British 45,000 casualties, about the same number sustained by the Germans. More than 11,000 Germans were taken prisoner, to some 9,000 captured British. Most important, the tactical deployment of tanks at Cambrai demonstrated that when properly used, in sufficient numbers, mobile armor could turn the tide of battle.

Ludendorff's initial reaction to the German rout was confusion, but he soon recovered enough to order reinforcements rushed to the sector. Later, he said that the new weapon "had been a nuisance, but achieved no decisive results." In a more sober appraisal Hindenburg wrote: "The English attack at Cambrai for the first time revealed the possibilities of a great surprise attack with tanks . . . that they could cross our undamaged trenches and obstacles did not fail to have a marked effect on our troops . . . the infantryman felt he could do practically nothing against its armored sides. As soon as the machine broke through our trench lines, the defender felt himself threatened in the rear and left his post."

The jubilation in London turned to dismay as news arrived of the German counterattack and the subsequent British withdrawal. As the fresh German forces moved up, the British had seen their cavalry decimated and their infantry assailed on terrain that offered virtually no cover on which to stand and fight or from which to withdraw safely. When the British reverses at Cambrai were complete, a court of inquiry was called. As usual, it found that all was the fault of the junior and noncommissioned officers. The generals were, of course, blameless. (Battle records reveal that many junior officers were well aware of the imminent counterattack but that their warnings to senior commanders were ignored.)

Counterattacking Germans raid a British trench near Arras behind a screen of gas. By the time the campaign was drawing to a close, both sides were visibly played out.

22. The
Middle East

General Sir Edmund Allenby.

22. The Middle East

When Turkey joined the Central Powers on November 1, 1914, Britain's manpower in the Middle East consisted of one Indian brigade stationed on Abadan Island in the Persian Gulf to protect the holdings of the Anglo-Persian Oil Company. Seeking a more suitable base for operations, the brigade advanced northward to seize Basra, the main port of Mesopotamia (now Iraq) at the confluence of the Tigris and Euphrates rivers. The city fell to the British troops on November 22, but at the cost of sizable casualties.

Some months later General Sir John Nixon, senior officer of the Indian Army, moved with his forces from India's North-West Frontier Province to Mesopotamia, where he headed a corps comprising two infantry divisions and a cavalry brigade. Turkish strength amounted to 8,000 troops near Ahwaz and 18,000 at the Euphrates, equal to that of the British. The British, however, still underestimated Turkish fighting ability and paid little attention to the operational hazards that were peculiar to the feverridden, arid Tigris-Euphrates Valley.

Nixon assigned General Charles Townshend, in command of the Sixth Indian Division, to go after the main Turkish force, which was spread in varying strength throughout the region. Townshend advanced up the eastern bank of the Tigris and captured Amara on June 3 with negligible losses. Rather than defend a town lacking any strategic value, the Turks had withdrawn to regroup in greater strength.

Despite enemy harassment, the ovenlike temperatures, and disease, Townshend's task force plodded up the Tigris and took Kut-al-Imara in September, 1915, but the lack of adequate medical facilities caused many wounded men to die needlessly. Townshend continued along the Tigris encountering increasing resistance, and entered Al Aziziya in early October, when the river's depth drops to a muddy trickle. The cautious Nixon sensed difficulties in any further advance, and directed Townshend to halt his forces, but the latter's fate was already sealed.

To divert the public's attention from the Gallipoli misadventure, the British Cabinet wanted Nixon to capture Baghdad. A telegram on October 3 notified the commander that he "may march on Baghdad if he is satisfied that the force he has available is sufficient for the operation." It was a cagey ploy, for London well knew Nixon had little hope for success. If the enterprise failed, Nixon would shoulder the blame; success would redound to the government's credit.

Campaigning in unfamiliar terrain, Townshend's Indian soldiers came upon the Turks in the stoutly fortified ruins of ancient Ctesiphon, twenty miles southeast of Baghdad. Two days of fighting cost the 14,000-man Anglo-Indian army 4,500 casualties. Townshend's exhausted troops then retreated to Kut-al-Imara with a two-month food supply; their sole hope was to dig in and await reinforcements.

The Near East in World War I.

327

The pursuing Turks besieged Kut-al-Imara, beating off all attempts to relieve the garrison. In January, 1916, General Sir Fenton Aylmer suffered 6,000 casualties while trying to reach his comrades. Another effort in March cost Aylmer almost 5,000 more. Townshend now ordered 1,100 horses butchered to feed his starving men. Toward the end of April, the garrison faced annihilation. At Townshend's urgent radioed plea, Lord Kitchener granted permission to surrender, perhaps a dreadful mistake, for the wounded and emaciated captives were flogged savagely across the desert.

An unsuccessful Turkish attempt to capture Egypt in 1915 prompted the British to buttress their forces there against renewed attack, and England's failure at the Dardanelles had released Turkish troops for another attempt against Egypt. This time the Turks were beaten back at the Suez Canal, and advance units, which had crossed the waterway, were decimated. After subduing a local revolt sparked by pro-Turkish Egyptians in the spring of 1916, General Sir Archibald Murray then proceeded to march into the parched Sinai peninsula.

Murray's objectives were to protect the Suez Canal and prepare a means to strike at the Turks from the southwest. When the troops reached the Sinai in May, 1916, his men and a host of native laborers began the slow task of building a railway and water pipeline up the Sinai coast. Turkish sorties were beaten off as the project inched forward. By the end of 1916, Murray's units took El Arish where they built defenses to protect the rail and water lines. Finally in January, 1917, the lines terminated at Rafah on the Palestine border. Some twenty-five miles away lay Gaza, the Turkish-held gateway to Palestine, but no water supply was available along this stretch of desert.

Native revolts against the Turks in the Palestine-Arabia area gained momentum in June, 1916, when Husein ibn-Ali, sherif of Mecca, initiated a three-day rebellion and

General Erich von Falkenhayn and Djemel Pasha review troops in Jerusalem.

proclaimed the 150,000-square-mile province of Hejaz an independent kingdom.

In August, 1916, General Sir Frederick S. Maude was given command of the forces in Mesopotamia. His task was to plan a campaign for the capture of Baghdad and Murray was ordered to begin the invasion of Palestine by seizing Gaza in the spring of 1917. The British had superiority of more than ten to one, but they struck at Palestine without assuring themselves of an adequate water supply.

In the morning fog of March 26, 1917, Murray's 42,000 mounted and foot troops advanced by compass bearings toward a Turkish garrison of 4,000, entrenched behind natural stockades of tightly clumped, thorny cactus hedges. Several strongpoints were seized along ridges four miles south of Gaza, but the offensive began to falter as lack of water forced the two cavalry divisions out of action. Faulty staff decisions misled troops to retreat from hard-won positions. General Murray then tried to rectify the defeat by ordering foolhardy charges. Within a week the British retired with losses of 4,500 against 2,200 Turkish casualties.

At times, emotions influence history. Haig thoroughly disliked General Sir Edmund Allenby, commander of the British Third Army on the Western Front. Perhaps the latter's readiness to improvise strategy to meet changing needs incurred his superior's resentment. Ever alert to rid himself of an imaginative subordinate, Haig found his opportunity after the battle of Arras in April, 1917, which began successfully but foundered when German reinforcements proved too much for Allenby. Aware that Prime Minister Lloyd George needed a commander for the Middle East, Haig endorsed Allenby for the post.

Lloyd George viewed eastern Mediterranean operations with mixed feelings. He was pleased with Murray's advance into Palestine, but irritated at his failure before Gaza. Meanwhile, General Maude continued up the Tigris toward Baghdad. In a well-planned assault British artillery was coordinated with planes for spotting and light bombing, while supporting fire from a gunboat flotilla on the Tigris shielded a flanking attack beginning with two cavalry brigades followed by massed infantry.

The contest was brief and ended on March 11, 1917, when the sun-baked city fell. Maude reckoned the Turkish force at about 35,000 against his 120,000-man army. More than 9,000 prisoners were taken but no report is given of the rest who presumably were killed or fled. It was an expensive campaign, costing the British 40,000 casualties. Disease also exacted a high toll. General Maude himself succumbed to cholera.

To the British Cabinet, Jerusalem was the most prized jewel. The British knew that its capture would be both politically fatal to the Ottoman Empire and a boost to morale for England, compensating for the reverses on the Western Front. But General Murray's two attempts to capture Gaza in March and April ended in defeat. The second battle lasted less than three days, yet cost the British 6,500 casualties against 2,000 Turks. Murray then sank into inactivity. No other general officer in the Middle East met Lloyd George's criterion for the task. In accepting General Allenby, he told him: "I'd like you to capture Jerusalem as a Christmas present for the nation."

The road to Jerusalem was barred by a twenty-mile-wide Turkish fortified line, extending from Gaza to Beersheba. Unlike the Western Front's unbroken trench system, the Turkish defenses consisted of three equidistant bastionlike areas linked to a chain of outpost trenches. The right flank thinned out toward the Mediterranean, while the left reached into scrub brush and rocks in the Judean Hills. The British expedition hugged the coastal strip at the Palestine border where their rail and water lines lay.

Until Allenby arrived in June, 1917, to replace Murray, no one had quite known how to contend with the Turkish defenses. Unlike his predecessor, Allenby did not remain in plush lodgings in Cairo but lived in the field with his men. He quickly discerned that the first objective was Beersheba—the site of seven wells. Without these water reserves, his troops, horses, and camels could not survive the long, thirsty campaign to Jerusalem.

Beersheba would be seized by flanking assaults against the enemy's central strongpoints. Massed cavalry, followed by infantry, would race through the gaps to the enemy's rear and encircle Beersheba. Other columns would move leftward toward Gaza. Allenby had at his disposal mounted brigades of Australians and

Turkish officers captured by the British forces in the Tigris Valley.

Sikh marksmen clean their weapons. Although the Sikhs fought valiantly for the Allies particularly in the Middle East, they have received the least acclaim for their valor and accomplishments and remain among the War's unsung heroes.

New Zealanders, esteemed for their fighting qualities and horsemanship. These were reinforced by two divisions drawn from India and Salonika. In addition, every available camel and driver had been conscripted. Allenby's plan required time, preparation, and a *ruse de guerre*. D-day was scheduled for the end of October, when rainfall would preoccupy the Turks in their water-filled trenches.

The collapse of Russia and Romania released the finest of Turkish troops for the Palestine Front, and Enver Pasha, the Turkish Minister of War, wanted to use them to retake Baghdad from the British. He was overruled by General Falkenhayn who, after crushing the Romanian army, had been dispatched to mastermind the Turkish defenses. Falkenhayn foresaw that an Allenby defeat would allow the Turks to hold Jerusalem and preserve their mystique in the Islamic world. Also, the German commander was worried about a menace from the desert.

Abetted by British gold and warships in the Red Sea, Husein, the sherif of Mecca, had seized Islam's most sacred city with pro-British Moslem troops. He then led hit-and-run attacks against Ottoman garrisons along the Hejaz rail and telegraph lines, the Turks' only means of transportation and communication in western Arabia. Husein's success was largely due to the assistance of the twenty-nine-year-old Colonel Thomas E. Lawrence, an archeologist and innovator of guerrilla desert warfare. While digging in Palestine and Syria during prewar years, Lawrence had acquired an encyclopedic knowledge of the Arabs and their culture.

A resident of Cairo in 1914, Lawrence helped fan the fires of rebellion among Arab tribesmen. When Allenby arrived in the Middle East, Lawrence had already recruited guerrilla bands of nomadic desert tribes, and was busily directing sabotage and harassment against the Turks along the entire Arabian peninsula. His revolt began at Aqaba and spread northward, paralyzing Ottoman garrisons at the lower end of the Dead Sea.

The area was unpromising for military action. The only strategic objective in the desolate wasteland, where daily temperatures may rise to 140°, were the two oases on opposite shores at the southern end of the Dead Sea. A large Turkish expedition set out after Lawrence, who ambushed and annihilated his pursuers.

Meanwhile, Allenby was piecing his plan together. Because the Turks would continue to dominate the air until the rainy season, the majority of British troops were concentrated along the coastal zone before Gaza, to deceive the enemy into assuming an attack would begin there. About the same time, an English cavalry officer exposed himself—not dangerously—to a Turkish patrol, which fired at him. Pretending to be shot, he lurched precariously as he and his mount dashed away.

Upon reaching the scene, the Turks found an officer's dispatch case containing "secret" plans for the siege of Gaza. Allenby was delighted as the Turks began to shift and mass their strength toward the anticipated sector of assault.

Allenby assembled his forces for the third offensive against Gaza on October 31. British strength amounted to 75,000 infantrymen and 7,000 mounted troops against 42,000 enemy foot soldiers and 1,500 horsemen. The first blow was struck not along the coast at Gaza, but inland at Beersheba. A brief intensive artillery barrage blasted wide openings in the Turkish ranks, through which Allenby's cavalry forces rode and fanned out behind the defenders. The Turks were then routed by bayonet-charging infantry closely following the cavalry.

Before sunset Beersheeba and its wells were held by the British Army. Allenby now turned toward Gaza which also came under heavy gunfire from British warships. The combined assault overwhelmed the Turks a week later. Some 10,000 Turks were captured. Those not killed or wounded retreated a score of miles northward and regrouped, but again were given no rest. By mid-November they were cut off from the critical railway junction, where the Jaffa-Jerusalem line is joined by another railway leading south to Beersheba. The weary Turks made their last stand in the Judean Hills before Jerusalem, an historic defense site since biblical times. Then, on December 9, they suddenly ended all resistance and fled to the north.

General Allenby, the quiet conqueror, enters Jerusalem on foot to celebrate his "Christmas present" to the war-weary British people: the successful capture of that city.

Sir Edmund Allenby granted the Prime Minister his wish and gave England its Christmas present. The victorious commander entered the Holy City on foot clad in a simple uniform. His performance was in contrast to that made earlier by the German Emperor. The Kaiser had entered the city wearing a white cape bedecked with a Crusader's cross, riding an Arabian stallion. On another occasion an opening was chopped in the city's wall, as though breached by cannon fire, through which the monarch cantered.

The seizure of Jerusalem was England's only significant success in 1917, a year of reverses and soaring casualties. Allenby's coup provided the boost to morale anticipated by the Prime Minister and eliminated Turkey as an effective member of the Central Powers. British troops at Baghdad had little difficulty in holding the Turks at bay. Indeed, they felt strong enough to march northward toward Mosul. To save Enver Pasha's forces from crumbling altogether, Ludendorff sent another German army corps to the Middle East, but demoralization among the Turks was beyond repair. By June, 1918, General Liman von Sanders, who replaced Falkenhayn, recorded that deserters far outnumbered those still in the ranks.

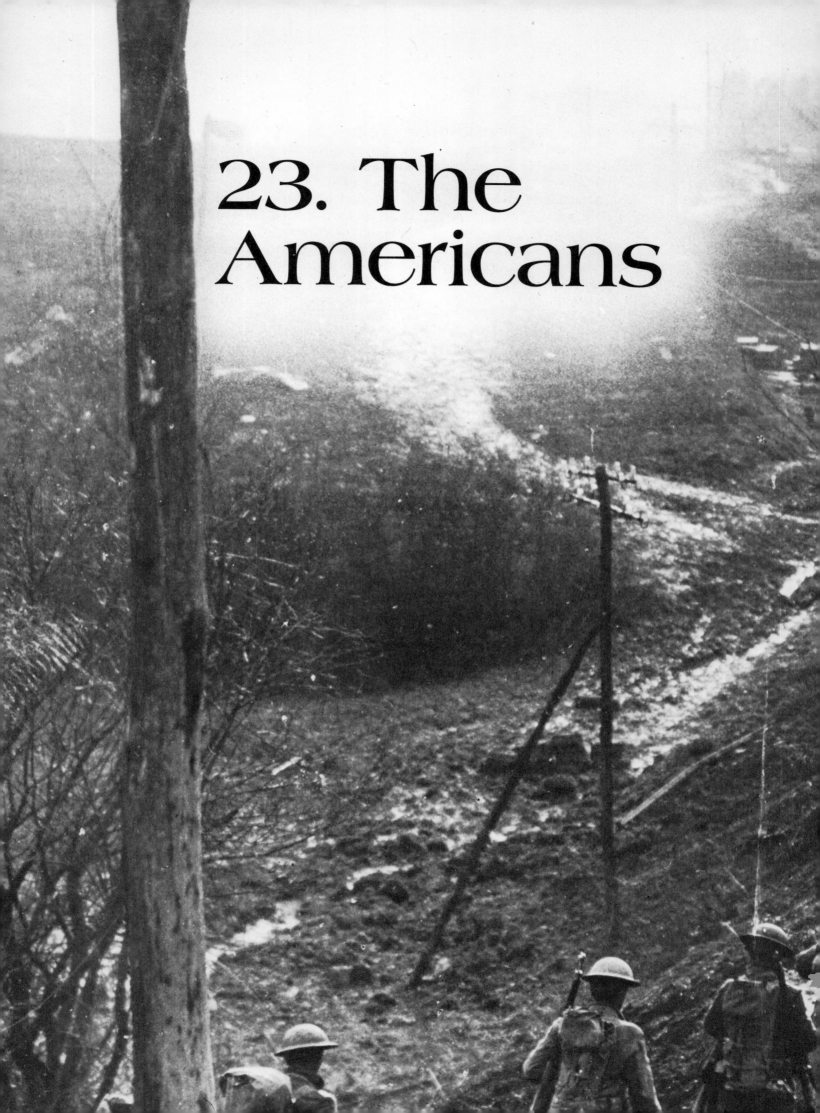

23. The Americans

Recruiting poster.

23. The Americans

American public opinion was largely neutral during 1914 but German ruthlessness brought about sympathy for the Allies. Washington's gradual involvement in the War began in 1915, when U-boats started torpedoing merchant ships carrying United States nationals. England's maritime blockade halted vessels for search and for the seizure of contraband, but German submarines sent them to the bottom without warning and every time a U-boat "victory" snuffed out American lives, antagonism toward Germany intensified.

Both sides waged vigorous campaigns to win American public support, but the secret service directors in Berlin were grossly misinformed about American temperament. Believing that the Americans, in their avaricious pursuit of money, would swallow any number of insults rather than fight a costly war, they were also convinced that the millions of German-Americans in the United States would refuse to bear arms against the Fatherland and would actually sabotage any such effort.

To prevent American war matériel from reaching the Allies, the German secret service plotted widespread industrial sabotage, including concealed delayed-action bombs on Allied ships timed to explode at sea, fomenting mass strikes, and blowing up munitions plants. With the exercise of caution and ingenuity, they might have attained some success, but the German secret agents in America proved to be incredibly inept.

Even the brighter ones were detected after only a brief operational period. Captain Franz von Rintelen, a German naval intelligence officer attached to the Washington embassy, for example, headed a group of saboteurs that planted bombs on Allied ships. But the British broke Rintelen's secret code and lured him to Germany in 1915 by a false message. When the Dutch ship on which he sailed entered British waters, he was seized by a boarding party, and upon America's entry in the War, was returned to the U.S. to serve a four-year prison sentence.

The Austrian ambassador, Konstantin Dumba busied himself with plans to paralyze steel factories by instigating strikes. He sent his government a letter describing his scheme in detail, then gave it to an American bound for Germany via Denmark. A British boarding party found the letter in a stop and search operation. It was dispatched to President Wilson, who demanded Dumba's recall in September, 1915, amid much publicity. Three months later the German military and naval attachés, Franz von Papen and Karl Boy-Ed, were linked with plots to dynamite munitions plants.

Such unfavorable publicity caused the German ambassador, Count Johann von Bernstorff, considerable anguish. He understood the American mind and temper. (His subsequently published correspondence with Berlin reveals his strenuous objections to U-boat warfare against neutral ships.) However, his recommendations were ignored in Berlin.

The first draftees march up New York's Fifth Avenue between Madison Square Park and the obelisk that marks the grave of the Mexican War hero Major General William Jenkins Worth.

With large sums of money at their disposal, the German propagandists spent lavishly and were often caught red-handed. They surreptitiously bought the New York *Mail*, a daily newspaper, only to have their ownership exposed. Whether they formed pacifist organizations or subsidized those already in existence, the money was usually traced quickly and publicly to German sources. Their most colossal blunder was committed by the secret chief of German propaganda in the United States, Dr. Heinrich Albert himself. On a torrid July afternoon in 1915, Albert boarded an elevated train in New York City. Seated directly behind him was Secret Service Agent Frank Burke, assigned to shadow the busy doctor. Albert was still absorbed in a newspaper when the train rumbled into his station. Not until the train was about to leave did he look up and realize he had to sprint out before the doors closed. In doing so he forgot his briefcase, which Burke promptly took.

Government officials were astonished at the incriminating contents of the briefcase and decided they deserved the widest publicity. The papers were made available to the New York *World* and published day after day, to the mortification of the Germans.

After the War, George Sylvester Viereck, an American of German descent employed by Albert in 1915, wrote: "The publication of the Albert papers was a German catastrophe. It dramatized German propaganda. Henceforth Allied propagandists could go as far as they liked. The stamp of propaganda was fastened upon the Germans . . . Albert's portfolio unloosed every half-hatched plan of the Germans. . . ."

Allied propagandists easily outpaced their adversaries. Neither the British nor the French instigated strikes or sabotage. Most of their operations were through the press. As England dominated the seas and the global network of cables under them, she intercepted and censored news with telling results. Moreover, the Allies were more imaginative. "The Rape of Belgium" played havoc with emotions in contrast to the trite "Invasion of Belgium."

Reports of German atrocities were embellished for the American public. The wholesale shooting of Belgian hostages, including priests, became the basis for blood-chilling tales limited only by the imagination of the writer. Stories that German soldiers gouged out the eyes of civilians, chopped off the hands of girls, or crucified captured Allied troops were widespread, although never supported by evidence.

When Allied inventiveness waned, the ham-fisted Germans provided fresh grist for their mills. In 1915 the Germans accused British nurse Edith Cavell of aiding the escape of convalescent Allied soldiers from occupied Belgium into Holland. That she had also nursed innumerable German wounded back to health went unmentioned—her German patients being forbidden to testify for her. She was convicted on October 11 and executed, an act that outraged public opinion on both sides of the Atlantic.

Edith Cavell served England more in death than in life. British voluntary enlistments had been sagging when news of her fate spurred thousands to join the colors—enough to form a full division. The German cause would have fared much better had she been simply sent home to England.

President Woodrow Wilson's many attempts to urge a "peace without victory" remained unfulfilled; neither side would accept it. Berlin was motivated by its favorable military position on the continent, and the Allies would not accept a German-dictated peace. Wilson was due for more disappointments before he realized that diplomacy without military might is futile. His protests against the loss of American lives at sea were brushed aside in Berlin and his declaration, "there is such a thing as a man being too proud to fight," deluded the German High Command into discounting America as an effective foe.

But unrestricted German submarine warfare was the deciding factor. On January 31, 1917, Berlin suddenly announced that starting the next day U-boats would torpedo without warning all vessels in the earlier-defined war zone. Germany, however, offered one "concession." One American steamer would be allowed to enter the British port of Falmouth—nowhere else—only on a Sunday and leave not later than the following Wednesday.

Markings on the vessel scheduled for the weekly crossing were detailed. The hull and superstructure must be painted in alternate red and white vertical stripes, each one meter

A German newspaper ad warns passengers of the peril of travel in the "war zone," the waters immediately around Great Britain.

Recruits with gas masks train with hand grenades before heading for Europe. Like baseballs, hand grenades can be thrown effectively by the left or the right hand.

British nurse Edith Cavell, whose execution by the Germans became a cause célèbre in America as well as in Europe.

wide. Each mast must fly a large red and white checkered banner—a kitchen tablecloth would do—and the American flag at the stern. Such a ship could proceed unmolested only if Washington guaranteed that she carried no contraband according to Berlin's published list.

Secretary of State Robert Lansing advocated an immediate break with Berlin, but Wilson found it difficult to overcome his pacific sentiments. He equivocated for three days before severing diplomatic relations. In his address before a joint session of the United States Congress on February 3, the President implied that perhaps the Germans did not really intend to carry out their warning. He then stated that any act, causing the loss of American life or property, might be met with force. After authorizing guns to be mounted on American merchantmen, he waited out the following weeks to see if the Germans would reconsider their threat.

Then another incident moved the United States closer to the Allies. A bizarre scheme had been hatched by German Foreign Secretary Alfred Zimmermann to embroil Mexico and Japan in war against America. At the outbreak of war, British Naval Intelligence had installed taps on all transatlantic cables. On January 19, monitors intercepted a coded German message that appeared to be a diplomatic communication. English cryptographers submitted the decoded missive, signed by Zimmermann, to Chief of Naval Intelligence Admiral William Hall. Hall read it and temporarily pigeon-holed it. He knew of Berlin's secret order to German naval commanders on January 10, ordering them to begin unrestricted submarine warfare the first day in February, and his sense of timing dictated that Zimmermann's message be withheld until the full impact of this order be felt in the United States. On February 23, the note was given to Washington.

Addressed to the German minister in Mexico, Zimmermann ordered him to enlist the Mexican government as a military ally against the United States if the U.S. refused to accept unrestricted submarine warfare. Besides generous financial assistance, Texas, New Mexico, and Arizona would be restored to Mexico. To strengthen the alliance, the Mexican president was to be requested that he invite Japan to desert the Allies and attack the United States.

Not surprisingly, a number of American officials at first suspected a hoax, but a careful check of the original cipher affirmed its authenticity. That Germany's foreign secretary accepted Mexico as a military power astonished Washington, for that nation was torn by revolution and was hovering on the verge of chaos.

The Zimmermann note was released to the Associated Press on March 1, and made banner headlines throughout the world. In a confession so rare as to be most perplexing, the German Chancellery in Berlin later confirmed the authenticity of the dispatch. Before America had recovered from the two directives—unrestricted submarine warfare and Zimmermann's plot—Germany committed the act that led directly to war.

America Becomes a Belligerent

President Wilson waited vainly for the German government to reconsider its threat at sea. Toward the end of February, the British liner *Laconia*, carrying American nationals, was torpedoed without warning. In mid-March the American vessels *City of Memphis* and *Illinois* were also sunk with further loss of life. Wilson then called a special session of Congress to recognize a state of war between the United States and Germany. Two days later the Senate passed a war resolution by a vote of 82 to 6; on April 6, the House similarly voted by a count of 373 to 50.

War with Germany was now official; diplomatic relations with Austria-Hungary were broken on April 8, but war was not declared until December 7. Diplomatic relations were also ended with Turkey and Bulgaria, but war was never formally declared against them.

Germany's collision course with the United States had been spearheaded by Ludendorff, who stood at the summit of military and political power in 1917. While the Kaiser still clung to his mythical status as Supreme War Lord, all decisions were made by Ludendorff, to the relief of his nominal superior, Field Marshal Hindenburg.

Few commanders on either side matched Ludendorff in ability as a military strategist. But in politics and diplomacy Ludendorff, in the words of the talented American newspaperman Edmond Taylor, ". . . counts among

On the Land

Sappers at Work: A Canadian Tunnelling Company
by David Bomberg, British, 1890-1957. The National Gallery of Canada,
Ottawa, The Canadian War Memorials Collection.

The Second Battle of Ypres, 22 April to 25 May 1915
by Richard Jack, English, 1866-1952. The National Gallery of Canada,
Ottawa, The Canadian War Memorials Collection.

Over the Top, Neuville-Vitasse
by A. T. J. Bastien,
Belgian, 1873-1955. The
National Gallery of Canada,
Ottawa, The Canadian War
Memorials Collection.

Canadian Artillery in Action
by Kenneth Keith Forbes,
Canadian, 1892. The
National Gallery of Canada,
Ottawa, The Canadian
War Memorials Collection.

Hand-colored copy of *The Engineer*
by Harvey Dunn.
The Smithsonian Institution.

the foremost wreckers of European civilization in his generation. Before he collapsed into his wotan-worshipping senility . . . he was to play a substantial role in pushing the Hohenzollern dynasty to its doom, in launching the Nazi nightmare on the world, and in assuring the ultimate triumph of Bolshevism in Russia."

Ludendorff's gamble of unrestricted submarine warfare seemed to yield the desired results. More than 1,300,000 tons of Allied and neutral shipping had been sunk in the first three months of 1917. Losses in April amounted to nearly 900,000 tons. Much of this success came from the stubborn opposition of the British Admiralty to adopting the convoy system. England, left with barely enough food to last six weeks, urgently needed American aid to combat the U-boat menace. Three days after the United States declared war, Admiral William Sims left for London where Admiral John Jellicoe, now First Sea Lord, confessed that "it is impossible for us to go on with the War if losses like this continue."

Unlike the admirals, Prime Minister Lloyd George was not hag-ridden by reluctance to innovate. George abruptly ordered the Admiralty to begin an experimental convoy in early May on the North Sea and Gibraltar routes. It was an immediate success. By the end of the month, maritime losses dipped below the 200,-000-ton mark. Before the convoy system, losses were as high as twenty-five percent; afterwards they were less than one percent. Beginning in the fall of 1917, England and America began building slightly more vessels than the former lost to enemy submarines, and soon they were destroying more U-boats than Germany could build.

Command of the American Expeditionary Force was given to General John J. Pershing who had come to public attention in 1916, when he led an expedition against the Mexican bandit Pancho Villa, in reprisal for a raid on Columbus, New Mexico, and the shooting of some Americans. After scouting the Mexican mountains and wasteland for nine months—often impeded by native troops—Pershing and his army returned to the United States. Several of Villa's aides were ambushed, but the Americans could never catch Villa himself.

Endowed with good judgment and common sense, Pershing, perhaps because of his back-ground in guerrilla warfare, was prepared to try new methods when old ones failed. He had graduated from West Point in 1886 and served in the cavalry against the elusive Apache chief Geronimo. He also fought and quelled the Sioux Uprising in 1890.

Pershing selected as his Chief of Staff Major James Harbord, a non-West Pointer who had risen through the ranks. With a staff of sixty officers, sixty-seven enlisted men, and thirty-two field clerks, Pershing sailed from New York on the liner *Baltic* on May 29, 1917. The commander was in Paris on July 4, and was given credit for the statement "Lafayette, we are here!" In truth, this dramatic phrase was uttered by Colonel Charles Stanton, as he stood before Lafayette's tomb.

The United States was meagerly prepared in April, 1917. With a population of more than 100 million, her military strength amounted to a mere 196,000 men of whom 77,000 were Army regulars, the rest National Guard. Military equipment was either obsolete or nonexistent. No separate air force existed—the Army's fifty-five planes, too rickety even for reconnaissance duty, were part of the Signal Corps. Sabered cavalry troops were the Army's elite, and not even a blueprint for a tank was being contemplated. The military chiefs knew little about corps, divisions, or brigade organization. Since the Civil War, the Army had maintained its antiquated regimental system.

No one in or out of the Army had had any training in trench warfare. The static lines on the Western Front were radically different from tactics used in previous wars. Current warfare was a numbing, gruesome contest of artillery, assisted by machine guns, hand grenades, and bayonet charges. Shortly after the United States joined the Allies, hundreds of British and French officers crossed the Atlantic to train the new troops in attack and defense, but the real training began when the Americans reached France.

Against strong opposition, President Wilson persuaded Congress to adopt compulsory military service for every able-bodied man from twenty-one to thirty-one, later changed to eighteen and forty-five. More than four million men were to serve in the Army, and 800,000 in the Navy. Pershing revamped his forces and determined that each American division

342

should consist of 28,000 men, about twice that of corresponding British and French sections. His order confirmed a widespread European notion that Americans do everything in a big way.

The only American-made artillery fired on the Western Front were four 14-inch naval cannons mounted on railway cars. All the others were French or British, as were the tanks. Nearly 4,500 tanks were ordered from automobile makers, but only a baker's dozen reached France—and they arrived after the Armistice. Similarly, American aircraft developed too late; so American aviators flew planes made by the Allies although some of these were powered with the British-designed DH-4 "Liberty engine" made in Detroit. Heavy weapons and related matériel were "bought" from the Allies and paid for in food and a wide variety of supplies.

With the nation's resources at its disposal, the Army embarked on a buying spree that staggers the imagination. The Army had 86,000 horses, but cavalry had not been used on the Western Front since 1915. Nonetheless, the War Department bought 1,000,000 horse blankets, 2,000,000 feed bags, 945,000 saddles, and 2,800,000 halters. More than twenty million mosquito nets were ordered but never needed in France. The miles of warehouses in France bulging with assorted useless items were too much for General Pershing. He notified the War Department to discontinue shipment of bathtubs, bookcases, floor wax, lawn mowers, office desks, stepladders, and spittoons.

The first American troops in France. American military leaders were still providing soldiers with campaign hats instead of helmets.

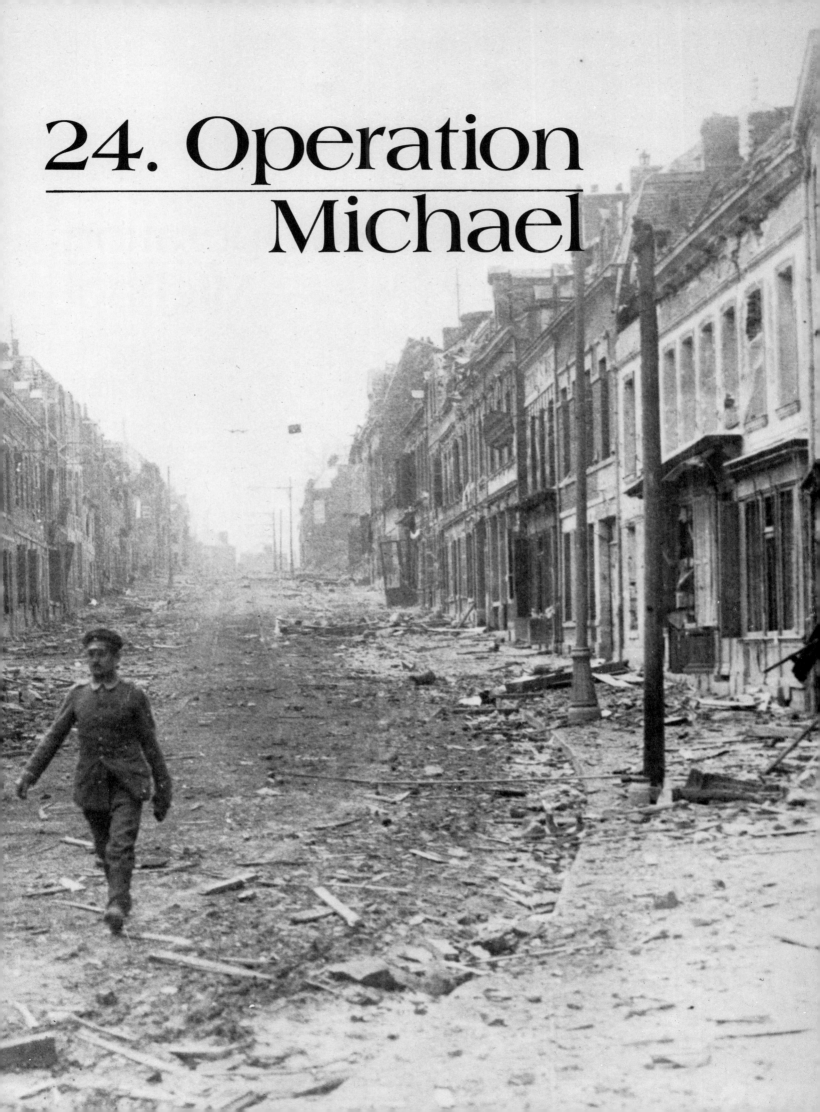

24. Operation
Michael

General Erich Ludendorff.

24. Operation Michael

Ludendorff resolved that 1918 would be the year of decision. He planned to concentrate all his available strength on the Western Front to crush the Allies or win a favorable peace before American intervention could decide the outcome. As Russia was permanently out of the War, troop trains rolled westward through the winter months leaving only a few divisions to ensure the shipment of grain to Germany, and to keep an eye on the still insignificant Red Guards.

High German figures, with few exceptions, reinforced each other's illusion that victory was inevitable. Addressing the Imperial War Council, Admiral von Holtzendorff guaranteed that German submarines would not let a single American soldier land in Western Europe. But even the long trainloads of Russian grain could not offset the Allied blockade's effects on the German people. Critical food shortages plagued the home front. Most Germans stolidly faced their fourth winter of war, but the patience of some had worn thin under privation. In January, 1918, about half a million factory workers in the largest cities struck against worsening conditions. The government wasted little time on negotiations; troops quickly sent the strikers back to work. Ludendorff then secretly ordered all army commanders to hold two battalions in readiness against civilian disturbance.

By mid-February, 1918, Ludendorff had ar-

rayed 178 divisions on the Western Front, but they were not greater numerically than the 173 Allied divisions. German forces in Belgium and France consisted of 1,232,000 infantrymen, 24,-000 cavalry, 5,500 heavy and 8,800 light field guns. Opposed to these were 1,480,000 Allied infantry, 74,000 cavalrymen, 6,800 heavy and 8,900 light artillery pieces. But the Germans were superior in infantry weapons for each division: 350 German as opposed to 64 Allied heavy and medium machine guns and 50 trench mortars as opposed to 36. Allied air power was nearly three times stronger—in the English sector 1,255 to 1,020 German and in the French zone some 2,000 to 470. But German tacticians offset this advantage by concentrating their aircraft where they were needed.

More than 125 miles of front were allocated to four British armies—from north to south, the Second, First, Third and Fifth—amounting to fifty-nine divisions that contained reserves and two Portuguese divisions. At least ninety-seven French divisions extended along a 300-mile front. Ten Belgian and five American divisions complemented the Allied force.

Throughout the winter the German soldiers had been trained in the tactics of infiltration that had been devised to capture Riga, and repeated at Caporetto. Momentum was stressed unendingly. Shock-troop battalions or smaller detachments, bypassing the strong resistance points, were trained to infiltrate gaps and thinly held positions. Resistance pockets would

French grenadiers in a quiet moment in the trenches. The box among the sandbags holds additional grenades.

Rubble of war—the hulk of a locomotive, destroyed and abandoned.

The Germans haul supplies forward
to exploit the breakthrough west of Saint
Quentin.

349

then be assaulted frontally by regimental reserves while the shock troops, fanning out, attacked from the rear. "We chop a hole," Ludendorff explained to Prince Rupprecht. "The rest follow. We did it that way in Russia."

Ludendorff had planned to inflict his most powerful blows on the British. England was the keystone of the Entente and her soldiers, untrained in the tactics of elastic defense, were expected to crumple under the German onslaught. Although this defense had been operative for at least a year, it was still a closed book to British General Headquarters. German training manuals, taken from prisoners and deserters, had been submitted to a board of British major generals for study and antidotal measures, but that this body had failed to grasp its import became evident in the next offensive.

Mobility for front-line battalions, according to the German instructions, was ensured by allotting only one third of their troops to hold strongpoints, while two thirds remained in dugouts or other rear entrenchments ready to repel the attackers at any point in their area. The British board of generals, however, reversed this system; they recommended that two thirds of the available British troops be assigned to front-line defensive positions.

Beginning March 10, the Germans shelled French defenses at Champagne and launched diversionary assaults against both Verdun and Reims. British air observers on that day reported massive enemy troop movements by train and road to the sector confronting the British Third and Fifth armies. Further, the observation of ammunition-dump construction and information given by deserters confirmed suspicion of an imminent offensive. German preparations were completed by March 19. The assault began on March 21.

The three German armies designated to break through the British front were General von Below's Seventeenth Army in the north, General Georg von der Marwitz' Second Army in the center, and General Hutier's Eighteenth Army in the south. Forces under Prince Wilhelm executed feints that were contrived to deceive the French into expecting an assault south of the Oise River.

Ludendorff planned to batter his way to the Somme on both sides of the provincial town of Péronne, after which the German right wing would sweep northward against the British flank. Known under the code name of "Operation Michael," the offensive was to begin on a fifty-mile front. The sector from the Oise to La Fère, to the immediate north of Saint Quentin,

German reserves and medics mass in Saint Quentin ready to take up their various duties on the front lines.

An old lady, her home no longer in existence, pauses to rest with her sole remaining possession on a street bench in Amiens. ▶

Operation Michael

An American machine-gun battalion. This was the battle in which Americans were first "blooded."

French soldiers throwing grenades at unseen enemies in a once wooded area of Champagne.

German dead in front of a strongly buttressed defensive fortification.

More German dead.

was assigned to the Eighteenth Army, while the front from that location to the Scarpe River near Arras was to be attacked by the Second and Seventeenth armies. German strength amounted to seventy-one divisions, but only thirty-two, with 2,500 pieces of artillery, were chosen for combat.

Facing the German Second and Eighteenth armies was Gough's Fifth Army, formed of twelve divisions sparsely spread along a forty-two-mile front, extending northward from the flank of the French Sixth Army to the Péronne-Cambrai road. General Sir Julian Byng was more fortunate. His army, with fourteen divisions to defend a front of only twenty-eight miles, confronted the German Seventeenth Army and merely the Second Army's right wing. The Germans were confident. "It need not be anticipated," wrote the Eighteenth Army's Chief of Staff, "that the French will run themselves off their legs and hurry at once to the help of their Entente comrades."

At 4:40 A.M. on March 21, 1918, thousands of German cannon and mortars, already zeroed in on the Fifth and Third army sectors, belched high-explosive and poison-gas shells steadily for six hours. In the fifth hour the bombardment was changed to a creeping barrage as thirty-two enemy divisions, supported closely behind by another twenty-eight divisions, began their assault in a fog made denser by acrid smoke and gas. Since German gunners were firing by map their accuracy was devastating.

British defenses and communications were already in shambles, much of the havoc caused by their failure to adopt the principle of elastic defense. Even small detachments of assault troops overpowered British strong pockets by attacks from the rear. At the end of the first day, the entire British front had crumbled. Twenty-four hours later, Gough's Fifth Army had been beaten back. To avert further disasters, Gough ordered the remains of his army to withdraw behind the Somme.

Allied dead in a trench close to Albert. The machine gun is a Lewis and at least one rifle is an Enfield, but the bodies are French. This may have been a joint effort. The French and British did fight side by side, but lack of a common language and interchangeable equipment hampered effectiveness.

Despite a partial loss of its front line, Byng's Third Army had area for defense in depth and was able to prevent the German Seventeenth and Second armies from gaining more than a fraction of the territory that had been taken from Gough. Because the two German armies did not meet Ludendorff's expectation of advance, he revised his tactics to exploit the progress made by Hutier's Eighteenth Army protecting the south flank of the Second and Seventeenth armies.

Hutier was ordered to fight along both banks of the Somme toward the coast, simultaneously deploying north and south to pound the British and French. Ludendorff surmised that the defense of Paris would be highest on the French list of priorities, while British primary concern would be to secure the Channel ports. These dissimilar interests would override any demand for joint action.

Hutier's initially good progress along the Somme's south bank was slowed when small,

separate French detachments came to support Gough's delaying action. A mixed British and French force appeared south of the Somme on March 25, under General Emile Fayole. At the same time six French divisions moved up but retreated toward the southwest before Hutier's advance, as though their mission was the defense of Paris. Their action suggests that Pétain's uppermost concern was indeed the availability of combat-ready troops for the defense of Paris. His own reserves were be-

German assault troops try to advance from one shellhole to another as their offensive begins to lose its momentum.

tween Soissons and Reims where he suspected a main German drive toward Paris would begin.

One of the deepest enemy thrusts toward the French capital was made by Hutier on March 27, when his divisions captured the town of Montdidier, some thirty-two miles from Paris. But exhaustion and insufficient supplies slowed up the Germans. Marwitz' Second Army chose Amiens for its goal but rear-line service groups, including two companies of American engineers, rushed forward and stopped him. Led by General George G. S. Carey, the quickly assembled force gave a superb account of itself. The Germans vainly thrust forward for three days—March 28–30—against the trench line held by Carey's force and after an equally futile second attack on April 4, wearily retreated.

Ludendorff's first 1918 offensive nonetheless was an outstanding example of tactical skill. His armies had overrun forty miles of territory in eight days, a record in the long war of static defense. The British, who bore the brunt of the battle, had suffered some 165,500 casualties; the French 77,000. Combined losses in prisoners were 70,000, and more than 1,100 field guns were captured. The usually reserved British were shaken when fast-moving German forces seized two million bottles of their whisky!

In a larger perspective, however, Ludendorff had won a doubtful victory. His loss of 239,000 troops, many highly trained in shock-troop infiltration, could no longer be made up. Germany's manpower shortage was critical, whereas American forces were steadily reinforcing the Allies. On May 25, General Pershing placed four American divisions, equivalent in manpower to eight French or British divisions, at Pétain's disposal. Because they lacked combat experience, the French commander sent them into quiet sectors to replace French divisions for action on the main front.

For the first time Ludendorff began to despair. He found "the resistance was beyond our strength. We must not be drawn into a battle of exhaustion." As the fighting tapered off, the Germans lost too much steam to chase the retreating Allies. When the panting British stopped to rest, many pursuing Germans also lay down nearby, too tired to fire their rifles.

Other cracks appeared in Ludendorff's military monolith. Rudolf Binding, the German novelist and poet, recorded in his war diary

scenes of drunken German troops looting near Albert: "Men were staggering. Men (who) could hardly walk . . . the streets were running with wine. Officers were helpless against the drunken mob." When the Germans "moved out of Albert the next day cheered with wine . . . ," Binding noted, "they were mowed down directly on the railway embankment by a few British machine guns."

Allied Unity of Command

The virtual destruction of the British Fifth Army and the general pounding of other units forced the Allies to make a long-postponed decision—establishment of a single command to shift reinforcements promptly wherever the enemy was strongest. Such authority was not vested in the Supreme War Council. Formed to prevent another Caporetto, it was powerless to direct Franco-British commanders to place emergency units at each other's disposal.

When Council leaders had recommended they be given control of thirty divisions as a reserve, Haig had quickly objected that he could not meet his quota. Explaining that, "I can deal with a man but not with a committee," the British commander proposed a mutual exchange between him and Pétain, an arrangement that had collapsed in battle. While the enemy hammered at Gough's Fifth Army, Haig had urgently pressed Pétain for aid that never came.

Pétain was afraid that the Germans might assault the front at Reims, break through, and head for Paris. He wanted his divisions available for a rapid withdrawal southwest to defend the capital. Haig replied that such decision would leave a yawning gap between the British and French armies, an opportunity for the Germans to fan out and destroy the Allied forces. Pétain was unmoved.

In a spirit of better late than never, British and French leaders hastily convened in the small town of Doullens on March 26. President Raymond Poincaré presided. British Secretary of State for War, Lord Alfred Milner, and Clemenceau conferred in a corner briefly, then with Poincaré. At the French Premier's suggestion, the Council announced that: "General Foch is charged with coordinating the action of the British and French armies at the front around Amiens." Haig joined Pétain in urging that Foch be invested with full authority over all Allied armies on the Western Front. On April 14, Foch was formally appointed commander in chief of all the Allied armies in France.

Haig's eagerness to subordinate himself to Foch effectively thwarted the British Prime Minister's intention to dismiss him. Convinced that "Haig was brilliant to the top of his boots," Lloyd George nonetheless had to tread cautiously. Conservatives in the House of Commons, whose support was vital to his career, fully endorsed Haig, who also enjoyed the confidence of King George. Haig's subordinate role now deprived Lloyd George of any convincing reason to remove him.

French soldiers in the trenches. The duckboards help keep them out of the mud, but the massed shovels suggests they had a lot of digging out to do. The archway cut through the barbed wire certainly made communications easier.

25. The Paris Gun

Gun muzzle.

25. The Paris Gun

Daytime air attacks on Paris became suicidal as the war trudged into 1918. The defense zones between the capital and enemy lines bristled with improved antiaircraft batteries and fast fighter planes. Nighttime raids by Gotha bombers were stepped up, but except for moonlit nights, accuracy was close to zero. Not only was the city blacked out, it was also ringed with antiaircraft guns that kept the raiders high and their aim erratic. An efficient warning system alerted everyone well before the planes arrived.

No cost was spared to safeguard Paris. To deceive German pilots, a mock-up of the city was built on both sides of a loop in the Marne to simulate the flowing Seine's contours. Prominent landmarks were added for easy recognition by enemy pilots. If the Germans were deceived, it was not for long.

Then on March 23, a few minutes after 7 A.M. a sudden explosion in a northern Paris street shook buildings and broke windows. There were no injuries and the incident was left to routine investigation. A second explosion twenty minutes later, one and one-half miles away, in the vicinity of the Gare de l'Est killed eight persons and seriously wounded thirteen others.

Soon the French realized the explosions at twenty-minute intervals were somehow caused by the enemy. An examination of metal frag-

ments found at the sites, and extracted from corpses, were too thick to be bombs. Ordnance experts agreed that the jagged metal chunks were from artillery shells. But the nearest enemy position was almost sixty-five miles away, and the heaviest cannon's known range was not much more than twenty miles. What the French had yet to learn was that German designers had developed three cannons, each with a seventy-five-mile range—the distance from Paris to the Saint Gobain Forest where they were placed.

To attain this distance, Krupp gunsmiths had built a barrel almost the height of a twelve-story building—118.2 feet long with an 8.26-inch diameter bore. Its 276-pound projectile was fired by 430 pounds of powder that stacked twelve feet high. A muzzle velocity of 5,500 feet per second propelled the shell more than twenty miles up, where it hurtled almost without resistance in the rarified stratosphere then arced downward toward Paris by gravity. Dr. Eberhardt, the inventor, applied mathematical calculations to determine the relationship of all factors—the projectile, amount of powder, three-minute air flight, and curvature of the earth.

A gun barrel of such extraordinary length is unable to sustain its own weight—however tough the steel, it inevitably sags a few inches near the muzzle. Eberhardt overcame this

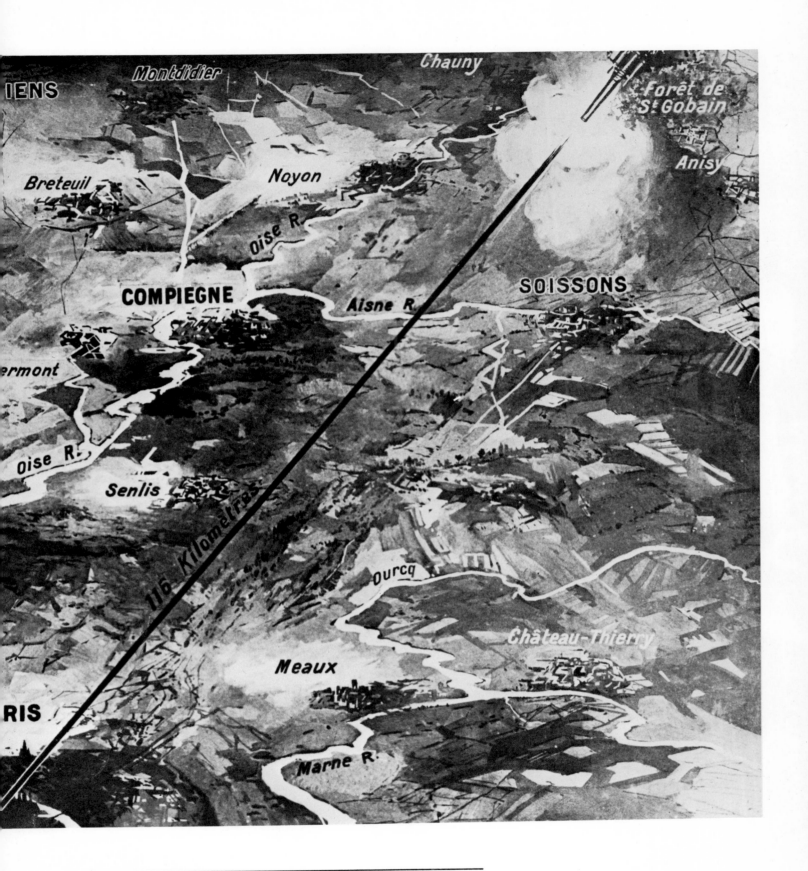

A schematic view of the range of the Paris gun: 116 kilometers, or about 72 miles, the distance from the Saint Gobain Forest to downtown Paris.

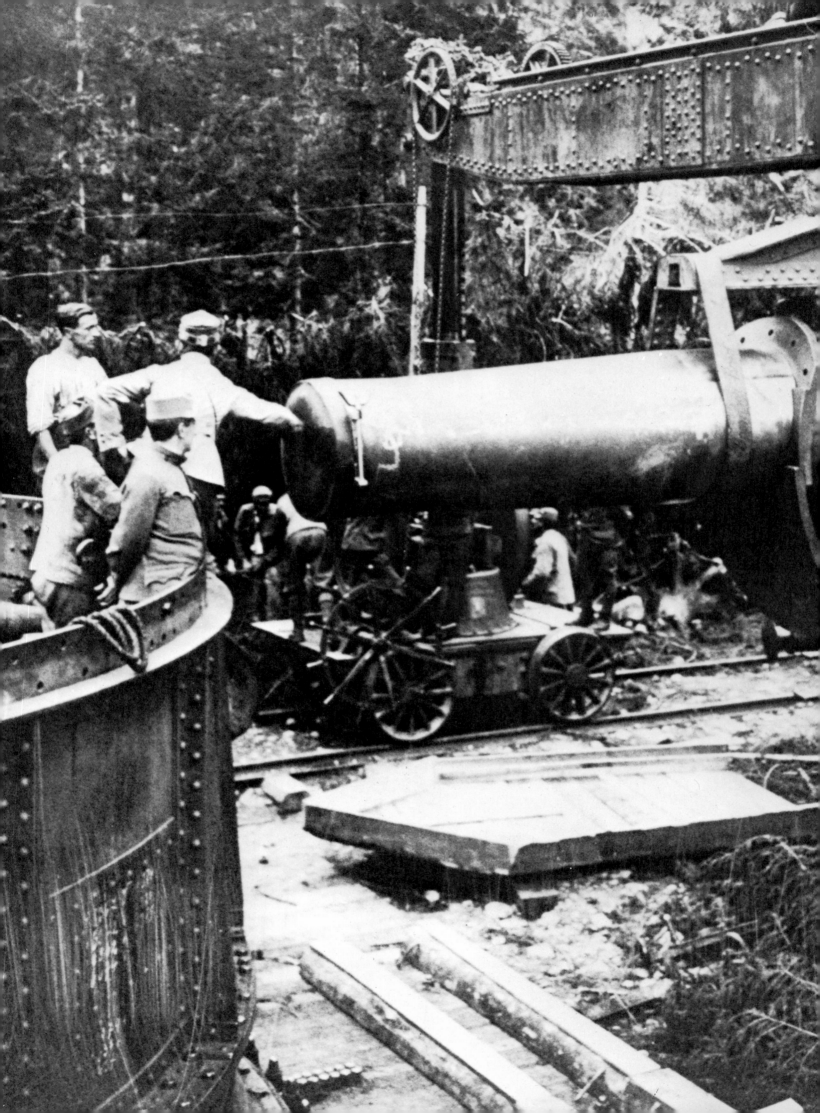

problem with a cantilever brace to support the gun barrel. Mobility was provided by flanged wheels designed to roll along railroad tracks. The whole monstrous affair weighed 375 tons; the guns alone 180 tons. The barrel was elevated at a constant angle of fifty degrees, and the range increased or reduced by modifying the quantity of gunpowder. A massive railroad turntable permitted the carriage and cannon to swing horizontally for directional changes.

Yet even Eberhardt's genius could not predict which section of Paris would be hit. Some days before the bombardment began, German secret agents were instructed to report where each shell struck but computations based on their reports could not aim even one shell at a strategic target. All fell indiscriminately on parks, public buildings, houses, and hospitals. And as though demonstrating its nonstrategic purpose, the Paris gun fired its most tragic shot on Good Friday, March 29. Churches were filled with kneeling worshipers at 4:30 P.M., when a missile ended its flight against the roof of the Saint Gervais Church in the center of Paris.

A huge pillar that supported the vaulted ceiling was shattered. Tons of stone crashed, killing 88 persons including 69 women and 3 children; 68 others were critically injured. A mass funeral on Tuesday, April 2, was attended by high government figures. Ludendorff ordered the Paris gun to be silent that afternoon, but the Kaiser jubilantly motored to Saint Gobain where he personally congratulated the gun crew.

One gun exploded and killed five crewmen. When the remaining two cannons were roughly located, the French moved up their most powerful artillery and rained shells on the forest. Anticipating such action, the Germans fired blanks in guns several miles from the secret site to confuse the French. Camouflage nets over the site prevented air observers from spotting the mammoth guns.

The Paris gun, the largest and most formidable cannon produced in World War I, was made only by Krupp. The biggest gun produced by Skoda was this 420-mm. coast howitzer, the equivalent to the Krupp "Big Bertha" siege gun used at Liège.

365

After fifty to seventy-five shells had been fired, the worn gun barrel was shipped to Krupp where it was rebored to a diameter of 9.15-inches. This arrangement allowed only one gun at a time on the firing line. When 180 projectiles had been fired in thirty-nine days, the guns were shifted to another sector from which the shelling of Paris was resumed. Every time the French came close to the new location, the Germans would again move.

By the end of July the Paris gun finally ended its brief reign of terror having launched some 370 shells at the capital. In the wake of the defeatism and mutinies of 1917, the French were alert to the hazard of tottering morale. Flying squads of workmen rushed to the site of each shell explosion, carted away debris, and repaved the street. To erase all possible scars of the Germans' random marksmanship, damaged public buildings usually were restored to their former appearance. No military installation was ever hit.

Parisians inspect a hole made by a shell from the Paris gun. For reasons of morale such craters were filled in quickly.

Two views of the gun:
an artist's conception of
one design, and a model
of the actual gun.

26. The Aisne Offensive

General John J. Pershing.

26. The Aisne Offensive

In exploring options for victory, Ludendorff decided the British could not survive another major defeat and prepared to strike at them in Flanders. Because the combined British and French troops in that area were strong enough to repulse any attack there, Ludendorff hatched a scheme to divert part of the French forces elsewhere, and thereby gain the Germans favorable odds. He chose the Chemin des Dames, the locale of General Nivelle's misadventure in 1917.

General Pétain had long feared that the Germans might attempt to capture the 15-mile-long steep ridge, but was finally lulled into assuming it would remain a "quiet sector." The French garrison was sharply reduced to buttress troops on other fronts, and four severely mauled British divisions were sent to Chemin des Dames for rest.

Ludendorff laid his plans carefully. Before clambering up the 300-foot bare incline, his troops first would have to cross the Ailette River and its surrounding marshland, pocked with water-filled shell holes. Upon capturing the ridge, the Germans would next have to cross the 200-foot-wide Aisne, and secure the south bank before Allied reinforcements moved up. Success depended on surprise.

Elaborate precautions were taken to disguise the preparations, especially from Allied planes which flew daily reconnaissance missions. All movements to staging areas were made at night, and no force larger than a battalion was

permitted to form or march during daylight. Cannon and horses were concealed in nearby wooded areas; the animals were fed and watered in small groups. Traces on the ground from nighttime activity were raked over. In forward areas, the wheels of wagons and gun carriages had "tires" made of sawdust bags to muffle sound. During the last night, as they assembled their bridges, the engineers worked to the welcome noise of croaking marsh frogs.

Artillery deployment was directed by Colonel Georg von Bruchmüller. Less than two weeks before the assault, Major Samuel T. Hubbard, chief of Pershing's Battle Order Section, warned that the enemy's next target would be the Chemin des Dames sector. A novice at combat intelligence, Hubbard deduced the Germans would select that area because it was virtually an Allied rest camp for the wounded and exhausted. The weakly garrisoned ridge, Hubbard added, was a clear signal that the Allies did not expect an attack there.

Foch and Pétain discounted Hubbard as a newcomer untested in combat, yet presuming to advise them in the complex profession of intelligence. Eventually Hubbard did convince Colonel de Cointet, Chief of French Intelligence. But like his predecessors at Verdun, Cointet could not persuade General Headquarters which went along with the view of General Denis Duchêne, the commander of the Sixth Army, whose zone embraced the Chemin des Dames sector.

Allied soldiers run for cover at the front north of Saint Quentin as a
towering explosion begins to rain down rubble and debris over them.

German reserves getting organized to move into the front lines. The lack of properly trained reserves in sufficient number eventually led to the failure of the campaign.

American marines of the 5th Regiment display a German trench mortar, or *Minnenwerfer*, captured at Belleau Wood and brought to a salvage station.

A medic and his assistant look over a wounded soldier in an impromptu field hospital. The wall charts are in French, but the helmet hanging on the wall is either British or American—perhaps a clue to the nationality of the patient rather than the doctor.

An aerial view of an artillery bombardment. The photographer must have been grateful to be in the air while this was going on.

A contemporary French sketch by Zingg shows infantrymen with gas masks and full field packs.

Duchêne's army was formed of seven French and four British divisions. The latter, filled with battered troops and raw recruits, occupied the eastern half of Chemin des Dames ridge; the French held the other part. Opposing the Allies were two German armies—General Below's First and General Max von Boehn's Seventeenth—consisting of seventeen divisions in the forward lines and thirteen divisions in the rear.

One hour past midnight on May 27, 1918, 4,000 German guns on a forty-mile front opened fire simultaneously on the French Sixth Army, smothering all of Chemin des Dames with shellfire and poison gas. Duchêne's entire command became disjointed in the first hours of the bombardment. His headquarters, ammunition dumps, communication centers, and railheads, located in forward areas, were hit by the first salvos.

Duchêne's tyrannical treatment of his subordinates and troops had earned him no loyalty. He also ignored Pétain's instructions to use the elastic defense in depth system and clung to the tactic of assigning most of his infantry to front defensive lines, where many became casualties even before the Germans advanced.

As the first light of dawn cast its glow over the fire and smoke, throngs of German infantry emerged behind the barrage. In less than an hour they held half of Chemin des Dames. Duchêne was left no time even to demolish the bridges across the Aisne—they were already heavy with Germans tramping to the south bank. By nightfall the Germans had overrun more territory than in any other day since trench warfare began, crossing three rivers—the Ailette, Aisne, and Vesle—to the village of Fismes, a distance of thirteen miles.

Ludendorff's timetable called for his diversionary thrust to halt at Fismes. As he had planned, Allied reserves were rushing to stop his forces and Prince Rupprecht was poised to strike at the depleted Flanders sector. But Ludendorff could not resist the lure of a possible spectacular victory; he allowed the attack to continue. As they rolled onward, German troops spread out to seize the pivotal rail hub at Soissons. By May 30, the Germans again reached the Marne at Château-Thierry, from which they had been driven four years earlier, thirty-seven miles from Paris.

The American 42nd Division sprawls over a French hillside. The National Guard units that formed it carried the colors of so many different States that the outfit was nicknamed the Rainbow Division. Its most famous member was its chief of staff, later divisional commander, Douglas MacArthur.

At French General Headquarters, Duchêne's reputation remained high until his beaten and demoralized Sixth Army left Paris exposed to enemy invaders. Thousands of his panic-stricken troops cast away their arms and uniforms, then vanished into civilian crowds streaming southward through the capital.

The French turned to General Pershing, who then assigned the American 3rd Division to Duchêne's Sixth Army. The raw division was then in basic training a hundred miles away. On June 1, the huge unit, having been sped to the Marne by rail and truck, received its first baptism of fire from combat-hardened Germans. For the next seventy-two hours the surprised then dumbfounded Germans were kept from crossing the Marne. German troops heading for Paris west of Château-Thierry had to contend with the American 2nd Division. It was a repeat performance. Bloody hand-to-hand combat stopped the attackers dead. Ludendorff ended the offensive June 6. It had been his outstanding tactical achievement on the Western Front.

The Germans received a severe psychological blow on May 28, when the American 1st Division seized the village of Cantigny. It was the first independent American operation, and the Germans were routed in a brief but furious battle that lasted slightly more than a half hour. The site was a crucial loss. Located on a highland, Cantigny afforded clear observation of Allied positions while shielding the German rear area.

Brigadier General James Harbord.

Belleau Wood

Among the Allied reserves rushed to the threatening German salient, forming a rough triangle bounded by Soissons, Reims, and Château-Thierry, was the 4th Marine Brigade of the American 2nd Division. The Americans were assigned to a battleline near Belleau Wood, northwest of Château-Thierry, where French troops were being routed from their vantage positions on the hilly slopes. On the evening of June 3, the retreating French met the marines several miles beyond the sector's outskirts. A French major came to Captain Lloyd Williams, told him what happened and urged that he retreat. Williams retorted, "Re-

Americans have a knack for making themselves as comfortable as circumstances will allow. Here, rearguard members of the 89th Division have dug quarters that are luxurious, compared to the muddy existence of trench life. ▶

378

Americans camp out in close quarters on the rear side of a hill at Belleau Wood during a lull in the fighting.

treat, hell! We just got here!" His words "spread like wildfire through the units," recalled one of his platoon leaders.

Belleau Wood, immediately south of the town bearing its name, was a dense growth of trees and tangled underbrush strewn with rocks and massive boulders that opened on wheat fields leading to the villages of Lucy-le-Bocage and Bouresches. The Germans had fortified the wood with a triple line of trenches that faced the villages. Mutually supporting machine-gun nests, arranged in a checkerboard pattern, exposed attackers to fire from all directions. Ravines, gullies, and lanes were covered by heavy Maxim machine guns for enfilading fire, and foxholes for sharpshooters were hidden behind closely entwined thickets. Rows of barbed wire protected the system.

An erroneous French report had misled Brigadier General James Harbord, commander of the Marine Brigade, to assume that Belleau Wood, except for the northeast corner, was free of Germans. Lacking the elementary caution that usually develops with combat experience, the marines neglected to reconnoiter the area.

At daybreak on June 6, the marines opened their attack. German gunners watched with disbelief as the men strode forward in four ranks—fifteen feet apart and sixty feet between ranks. Then chattering machine guns mowed them down. Yet the marines refused to acknowledge defeat. They repeatedly moved in and fought yard by yard for the area. Belleau Wood was well suited to sniper action, a skill common to many Americans.

After three weeks of fighting the leathernecks drove the enemy out of the Wood. Seldom had the Germans clashed with such combatants, whom they called in grudging admiration *Teufelhunden*, Devil Dogs. The 2nd United States Division counted 9,777 casualties; 5,183 of these were marines.

The Battle of Belleau Wood was not great by military standards, but its psychological impact was profound. Following in the wake of the victory at Château-Thierry, the Allies saw Germany crack under American blows.

At the direction of the French government, General Jean Degoutte, who had replaced Duchêne, renamed the denuded forest *Bois de la Brigade Marine*. Now owned by the United States government, the wood is maintained as a memorial to all American soldiers who fought in Europe during the War.

American marines man a small (37-mm.) howitzer in close combat.

An ejected case flies through the air as an American gun crew fires a French 75. Most of the artillery —as well as tanks and planes—used by the Americans were supplied by their allies.

27. Germany's Black Days

General Ferdinand Foch.

27. Germany's Black Days

Upon entering the conflict, the United States supported the Allies generously. Food and supplies shipped overseas rose to nearly a million tons monthly by the summer of 1918. But the long-awaited troop transports did not begin to arrive until the spring of 1918. Even then Allied military leaders underestimated both the fighting capacity and the industrial potential of the United States. Few disagreed with Foch when he predicted the War would last until the fall of 1919.

Most British and French writers in later years limited American combat participation to only a meager outline. Winston Churchill's great historical narrative *The World Crisis* is published in four volumes. If all his references to America's armed forces were placed together, they would amount to about ten pages. This is not intended to belittle. In a conflict that lasted well over four years Americans were in action only during the final six months, and American casualties were small compared to the stupendous losses of their allies.

At the outset American troops were brigaded with British and French armies. Pershing had agreed to this arrangement, but kept his plan to form an independent American army. With the support of President Wilson and Secretary of War Newton D. Baker, Pershing persuaded Foch, now generalissimo of the Allied armies, to consent and on August 10, a separate American command was formed. Initially doubtful of American fighting ability, Foch now admired his new allies. Pershing assented to Foch's request that the 77th Division continue under Allied Command. In the ensuing weeks, the American Army held nearly a fourth of the entire battle line—much greater than that held by the exhausted British.

Germany's last campaign began with Operation Michael on March 21 and covered much of the territory taken during the first major campaign in 1914. But as American manpower swelled Allied ranks, Ludendorff's drives became progressively weaker. His final attack, called the Second Battle of the Marne, started on July 15 and ended a mere two days later—four months of fighting in 1918 had cost the Germans 800,000 irreplaceable troops, whereas the Americans had handily replaced the combined Allied losses of 350,000.

Aisne-Marne Offensive

Germany was allowed no respite. Beginning on July 18, her army was pounded and forced onto the defensive. Foch planned his counter-thrust to reduce three enemy salients and to regain the railway lines that traversed the front, linking the strategic junctions of Amiens and Hazebrouck. The initial prongs were directed against the bulges formed during previous German drives—the Amiens salient from the first attack; the Aisne-Marne resulting from the second assault; and the Saint Mihiel that had existed since 1914.

Allied troops gassed by the Germans await medical attention in a rear-area
copse that, except for these soldiers, appears unscathed by the War.

American sharpshooters of the 38th Infantry, the "Rock of the Marne." They stopped two divisions of Germans in Ludendorff's last offensive at the Marne, totally disorganizing the attackers by their fantastically accurate rifle fire. In a letter found on the body of a German officer a few days after the battle, they were referred to as "the best marksmen in the world."

Four French armies were assigned to assail the perimeter of the Aisne-Marne salient. Facing the west side of the bulge were the Tenth under Charles Mangin, who had returned from limbo after his role in Nivelle's catastrophe, and the Sixth under General Jean Degoutte; next were General Marie de Mitry's Ninth and General Henri Berthelot's Fifth armies. Bolstering these forces were eight American, four British, and two Italian divisions.

Mangin struck first and early with twenty divisions, including two American and two British. His skillful use of 350 tanks in the drive toward strategic Soissons and the Soissons-Château-Thierry road threatened to disrupt German communications. Unable to resist Mangin's thrust, the Germans retreated, holding off Allied units by rear-guard action.

South of Soissons the American 1st and 2nd divisions drove deeply into the enemy salient, but stubborn resistance in tough hand-to-hand fighting delayed their advance. Then eight American divisions (224,000 men) joined in and squeezed the bulge flat, forcing the Germans back to the Aisne and Vesle rivers.

Driving the enemy from the Aisne-Marne salient brought jubilation to Paris; the city no longer faced the threat of invasion. In less than three hours on August 6, the Allies had seized and held the initiative. On that day a grateful French government gave Foch his baton as Marshal of France.

Amiens

Two days after the Aisne-Marne salient was reduced, Foch and Haig began to flatten the Amiens bulge. In this predominantly British offensive, Sir Henry Rawlinson's Fourth Army was supported by the French First and Third

armies under the command of Marie Debeney and Georges Humbert. They were buttressed by a formidable force—a Canadian corps of four divisions, an Australian corps of five divisions plus three cavalry divisions, and one American division. In addition their mobile armor included 600 tanks of the latest design and they had 2,000 pieces of artillery. Air support amounted to 800 fighter and bomber planes. Against this powerful force Ludendorff could muster only Marwitz's Second and Hutier's Eighteenth armies totaling twenty divisions which included teenagers and older reservists.

The Allies attacked at 4:20 A.M. on August 8. Rawlinson's large number of tanks enabled him to repeat the surprise that had worked with such telling effect at Cambrai and in subsequent tank assaults. No warning was given by a preliminary artillery bombardment. Intended to kill or stun, such shelling often backfired by alerting the defenders to dig in and await the onrushing infantry. Under cover of a rolling barrage, Rawlinson's armored column and the infantry suddenly moved forward. As at Cambrai, the clanking vehicles demoralized the defenders and in less than two hours the British had corraled 15,000 prisoners and about 400 guns. The attack even caught the higher echelons unaware; a divisional staff was captured while eating lunch. By nightfall the attackers had advanced nine miles behind German lines.

The relative ease with which the Allies penetrated its defenses revealed the plight of the German army. In the grip of depression, Ludendorff finally realized that victory was unattainable; even a favorable peace was no longer feasible.

"August 8th was the black day of the German Army. . . ," he wrote, ". . . morale was no longer what it had been. The enemy captured many documents of inestimable value to them. . . .

A French gas attack precedes the advancing foot soldiers as the Germans (upper left) are driven back by the reinforced and invigorated Allies.

In the Laon sector, infantrymen cautiously check for activity before advancing through the wall of a ruined building.

390

Retiring troops, meeting a fresh division going into action, shouted 'blackleg' and 'You're prolonging the war,'—expressions heard again. . . . Officers in many instances lost their influence and allowed themselves to be swept along. . . . August 8th also opened the eyes of the staff on both sides; mine were certainly opened." No longer scornful of the Americans, the General confessed that the odds were "bound to become increasingly unfavorable as more American troops came in."

Saint Mihiel

Since 1914 the Germans had held a wedge-shaped salient south of Verdun between the Meuse and Moselle rivers, protecting the key centers of Metz and the Briey iron basin, a rich source of ore for German steel. Stabbing sixteen miles into the French right flank, the salient severed both the Verdun-Toul and Paris-Nancy railroads. Its elimination was indispensable to any successful drive between the Meuse River and the Argonne Forest, the sector already selected as the next target. Clearing the Germans from the Saint Mihiel salient became the American Army's first action under its own command.

From its tip at Saint Mihiel, the western side of the salient extended diagonally across a wooded heights east of the Meuse; its southern side ran from Saint Mihiel to the Moselle,

American troops at Saint Mihiel warily move up under the protection of rifle grenades. When loaded with a grenade, the rifle butt was placed on the ground and braced with the foot.

The End Nears

Captured German officers.

An Australian division
assembled for review.

German prisoners await the next
move at a Canadian outpost.

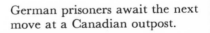
The church at Lucy-le-Bocage.

transversing the heights on either side of the rivers. Between the heights spread the Woëvre Plain, intersected by narrow streams, bogs, large ponds, and tracts of woodland that barred easy travel, particularly during rainy weather.

Pershing's final plans called for simultaneous thrusts against both sides, with heavier assaults on the southern border. Diversionary attacks would be directed at the tip. A force of more than 550,000 American and 110,000 French troops were assembled for the drive. Among the three United States corps and nine additional divisions that participated in the attack, two of the corps and none of the divisions had ever before been in combat.

The air service amassed 1,500 planes, the largest number ever assembled for an offensive, mostly provided by the French and British. About 400 French tanks were concentrated on both sides of the salient. More than 3,000 guns and 3,300,000 rounds of artillery shells assured the attackers that enemy positions would be closely combed by high explosives.

German defenses comprised eight divisions and two brigades in line and five divisions in reserve. Even though Pershing insisted upon painstaking measures for secrecy, the Germans became aware that the concentration of troops and matériel portended an attack. Anticipating an overwhelming blow they began a gradual withdrawal from the salient on September 11.

Next day at 5 A.M. the bombardment opened on the southern side of the salient. Three hours later a secondary barrage was launched from the west. Try as they might, the Germans could not fully escape the results of Pershing's careful preparations. Engineers blew up rows of barbed wire using special Bangalore torpedoes—long iron tubes filled with TNT. Others, armed with powerful wire cutters and axes, opened wide gaps in the dense skeins of barbed wire. Rolls of chicken wire, used by the advancing infantry as protective mats, were flung over entanglements.

Never before had attacking troops moved so fast through tangled snarls of barbed wire. This practical operation in American ingenuity amazed the French. A few days later hundreds of officers visited the scene to learn how it had been done. Pershing recalled: "One of these officers, after his reconnaissance, remarked in all seriousness that Americans had the advantage over Frenchmen because of their long legs and large feet."

To cut off his adversary's retreat, Pershing ordered a double-pronged converging thrust. Within twenty-four hours, the 1st Division from the south, and the 26th Division from the west joined forces at the village of Vigneulles. By evening the salient had been largely reduced. Only a previous agreement with Foch deterred the Americans from pushing on to Metz.

In less than thirty hours of fighting, German losses amounted to 16,000 prisoners, 450 guns, and about 200 square miles; their losses in men remain unknown. American casualties totaled 7,000 men.

A British detachment advances along a highway past a ditched and abandoned tank.

28. The Meuse-Argonne Offensive

Lieutenant General Hunter Liggett.

28. The Meuse-Argonne Offensive

Germany's skidding fortunes since August convinced Foch that victory *could* be won in 1918, not a year later as he had formerly anticipated. The Allied campaign was directed toward the collapse of the Hindenburg Line, which stretched from the coast northeast of Ypres to the Swiss border. (The battle itself did not extend east of Verdun.) The offensive, scheduled for September 26, was planned to seize or sever the rail lines on which the Germans relied for moving troops and supplies. Deprived of its transport system, the already weakened army would be further debilitated.

The railway that carried German troops and matériel to the front ran northwest from Metz to the key junctions of Mézières, Aulnoye, Maubeuge, Mons, Ghent, and Bruges, where numerous branches and spurs led to different sectors. Foch's plan was to seize the fifty-mile strip containing the two railway junctions of Mézières and Aulnoye, cutting off German withdrawal, thereby exposing them to piecemeal assaults. This maneuver was designed as a pincer action—a Franco-British advance to Aulnoye from the west combined with a Franco-American drive toward Mézières from the Meuse-Argonne in the south.

A successful Allied campaign in the Meuse-Argonne sector would overrun the rail system, and prevent all ground communication between the sundered enemy forces. Such a strike would compel the Germans to resume their broken contact by a roundabout, time-wasting route through Liège and the Rhine River Valley.

Ludendorff realized that under a fast-advancing onslaught, his forces could scarcely expect to withdraw in an orderly manner through the overcrowded bottleneck at Liège. Accordingly, the Germans proceeded to further strengthen the already very heavily fortified Meuse-Argonne zone. Every wood and village was converted into a mass of obstacles, and several defense lines were established behind the forward positions. Facing the sector assigned to Pershing, where rail lines were relatively near the front, a ten-mile-deep fortified trench system had been constructed.

The Germans had an advantage in that the Meuse-Argonne terrain was naturally adapted for defense. Directly east of the Meuse River rose the steep heights of Côtes de Meuse, an excellent position for artillery fire and an almost unassailable barrier to attackers. Argonne's bluffs and deeply creviced hills were connected into a bastion by miles of barbed wire snaked back and forth between defense lines, concrete machine-gun bunkers, heavy guns, and a variety of obstacles.

Midway between the Meuse and the Argonne rose the heavily fortified hill of Montfaucon with a panoramic view of the surrounding territory. The twenty-mile front had been so strongly buttressed that the only workable assault method was to punch salients in the lines on either side of Montfaucon, widen the bulges

A heavy French gun belches flame in the night.

Folded stretchers are stacked along the sides of the first of a line of ambulances waiting to be called into action. The tents behind them house a mobile field hospital where first aid or even emergency surgery could be performed. Seriously wounded men were then taken to a better equipped military hospital in a safe rear area.

by flanking attacks, then compel the defenders to retreat by threatening their rear.

Unlike previous French and British offensives which had been preceded by months of preparedness, the nine American divisions were moved to the front in barely a week. Only three had experience in attack, and four divisions were assigned artillery support by troops with whom they had neither served nor trained. Three more divisions were in close reserve. Transport snags arose in shifting troops the short distance from Saint Mihiel, allowing but one combat-tested division to be at the front on the day of attack. The Americans, however, outnumbered the Germans by eight to one.

The Meuse-Argonne was only one sector in a battle against the entire German line, with the Belgians and British attacking in Flanders, the British on the Cambrai-Saint Quentin stretch, and the French in Champagne, in the center. Combined Allied strength consisted of 220 divisions—102 French, 60 British, 42 American, 12 Belgian, 2 Italian, and 2 Portuguese. Except for the American units, all were undermanned. Upon deciding a plan of action, Foch was a man of enthusiasm. His battle cry was "Everyone in the fight," and he dispatched 160 divisions to the front and held 60 in reserve.

Against Allied forces, the Germans could scarcely muster 197 divisions—113 at the front and 84 in reserve. Aside from being seriously under strength, the army was a far cry from the once-proud force of past years. Reports of hunger from the home front aggravated the troops' own growing war-weariness.

Nearly 600,000 American troops entered the Meuse-Argonne battle zone during nighttime, while the French guarded outposts until the last minutes, successfully preventing the Germans from moving close enough to see what was going on. Supporting the Americans were 2,700 French-made guns (half of which were manned by French crews), 821 aircraft, and 189 small French tanks.

The attack was launched at 5:30 on the morning of September 26, after a three-hour cannonade. General Henri Gouraud's French Fourth Army was the first to advance, followed by Pershing's First Army. Movement was impeded by the thick morning fog, thousands of shell craters, barbed-wire entanglements, deep slippery ravines, and dense woods.

404

Tense infantrymen wait orders on a rugged hill. In addition to their rifles, American doughboys were equipped with short-barreled (sawed-off-type) 12-gauge shotguns, denounced by the Germans as an American war atrocity in violation of the Geneva Convention.

Sergeant Alvin York, awarded the Congressional Medal of Honor for his valor on October 8, 1914. With only his Springfield rifle and an automatic pistol he singlehandedly killed twenty of the enemy, captured a fortified hill, and forced the surrender of 132 Germans armed with thirty-five machine guns.

Top: A rifle grenade, aimed skyward. A fearsome device, the rifle grenade had considerably more range than the standard hand grenade, but demanded a good measure of skill to place with any accuracy. Bottom: Running for cover in a French village. The one-man tank is typical of many supplied to the Americans by the French.

405

Artillery

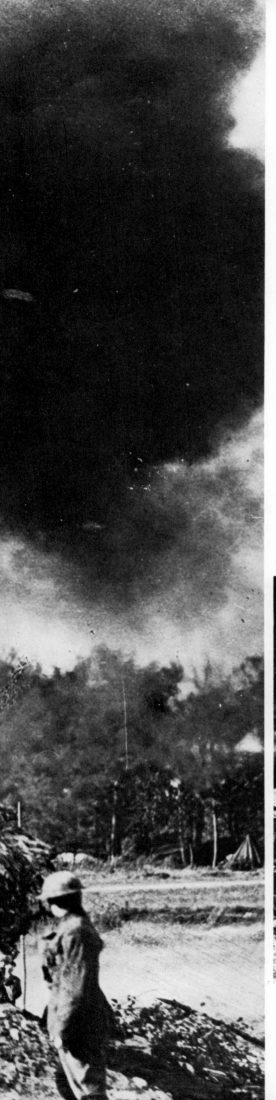

A 14-inch railway gun fires at its target some twenty miles away. Only four of these weapons were of American manufacture.

A French heavy field piece.

Before dusk the first line of defense had been taken by the Americans, who also had driven deep salients on both sides of Montfaucon, which was captured before noon the next day by the 79th Division of the V Corps. Except in the Argonne Forest, American troops also overran the Germans' second position on the same day. Meanwhile, Ludendorff hastily brought in seven more divisions from other sectors on the Western Front.

Stiffening resistance halted the drive by October 1, but, after experienced men replaced raw troops, the assault resumed on October 4. The Americans fought a dogged frontal battle for the next four weeks taking the third line of defense at a growing cost in casualties.

Contending with indistinct forms in dense and snarled underbrush was not a new experience to those many Americans who hunted game at home. They carried their knowledge of weapons with them. No firearm is more lethal in close combat than a 12-gauge sawed-off shotgun and German cries that the use of this weapon violated the Geneva Convention were ignored.

Growing pains in the army caused problems that Pershing quickly resolved by dividing his strength in two; command of the First Army was given to Lieutenant General Hunter Liggett, responsible for the Meuse-Argonne; the Second Army, assigned to Lieutenant General Robert Bullard, held the front east of the Meuse.

On October 31, the Argonne Forest fell to the Americans, who had progressed ten miles from their position of attack. That same day Gouraud's forces reached the Aisne River, twenty miles from his starting position. American pressure had forced Ludendorff to reinforce his tottering Meuse-Argonne front with twenty-seven of his best reserve divisions. In siphoning off so many troops to oppose them, the Americans considerably eased the burden of their allies on other sectors.

A German machine gunner, dead at his post on November 4, 1918, a mere week before the hostilities came to a close.

409

ERECTED TO COMMEMORATE THE HOMECOMING
OF THE VICTORIOUS ARMY AND NAVY
OF THESE UNITED STATES OF AMERICA · AND
IN MEMORY OF THOSE WHO HAVE MADE THE
SUPREME SACRIFICE FOR THE TRIUMPH OF THE FREE
PEOPLES OF THE WORLD AND FOR THE PROMISE OF AN
ENDURING PEACE · ANNO DOMINI · MCMXVIII

29. Armistice

The bottom of the barrel—
German recruit in 1918.

29. Armistice

The Allied blows against the Hindenburg
Line left the Germans groggy. Combat was
reduced to fierce rear-guard actions as the
German forces withdrew until almost all of
France and part of Belgium had been evacuated. German manpower was declining—about
thirty-seven percent of Allied strength. Only
one fresh division was in reserve at the end of
October, and more than 500,000 soldiers were
far from the front as congested railways reduced
military traffic to a crawl; many troops simply
deserted. Since that "black day" in August
when the Allies had flattened the Amiens
salient, some 300,000 Germans, exclusive of
casualties, had been taken prisoner and for
sheer lack of manpower the High Command
had been forced to strike thirty-two divisions
from the army rolls.

Ludendorff's authority slipped away as the
gains of the spring offensive were lost by
September. A double blow had hit him on
September 26, when Bulgaria dropped out of
the War just as the Meuse-Argonne attack was
launched. Two days later his nerves broke.
What began as a routine staff review of the
military situation turned into a fitful weeping
session with Ludendorff blaming everyone but
himself for Germany's plight. His embarrassed
subordinates shifted uneasily as his tirade
poured out. Finally, he toppled to the floor in
nervous prostration. That evening, still trem-
bling and barely able to make his blurred
words understood, Ludendorff advised Hin-

denburg to withdraw from all occupied Western territory and sue for peace on terms expressed in President Wilson's fourteen points,
which he seemed to have misunderstood. Hindenburg agreed and notified the Kaiser that
"the situation demands an immediate armistice
to avert a catastrophe."

Meantime, Germany's confederates were
tumbling. The Allied advances on the Western
Front revived the prospects of the Greeks,
Italians, Romanians, and Serbs, and confident
that the Austrian Army could no longer expect
reinforcements, they struck on their own
varied fronts. General Allenby, continuing his
triumphs in Mesopotamia, Palestine, and Syria,
ended the Ottoman Empire.

Germany and Austria were now fighting
alone. Reinforced by Allied troops, the Italians
struck at the Piave River, forcing the Austrians
from Italy. Disaffection spread throughout the
Hapsburg Empire, whose subject nations proclaimed their independence. Left in revolutionary tumult, Austria surrendered on November 3.

In casting about for a suitable spokesman to
deal with the Allies, the German government
appointed Prince Max of Baden Chancellor on
October 4, largely because of his liberal views.
Within twenty-four hours peace feelers were
sent to Washington via the Swiss government,
but President Wilson deferred his own reply
for two days without notifying the Allies; he
merely asked a few questions for clarification.

The last roundup. With the abdication of Kaiser Wilhelm and the
flight of Ludendorff fresh in their minds, members of the once mighty
German military machine await repatriation.

German Dead

A nonchalant American strolls down a
road strewn with German dead. The rolls
on the embankment are wattle, used to
line trenches and bunkers.

German skeletons disinterred in Belgium to
be returned to the Fatherland for
reburial.

Prince Max dispatched his second note on October 12, accepting Wilson's fourteen points in principle. He added that he spoke for the new German government and its people. President Wilson was in a receptive mood.

On that day, however, the passenger steamer *Leinster* was torpedoed between Ireland and England, with a loss of more than 400 lives, including a number of Americans. Wilson's anger rippled through his reply on October 14. He flatly refused to consider any negotiation while Germany followed its "illegal and inhuman practices."

Germany's situation grew more desperate by the day. Semi-starvation plagued Berlin and other large cities. An influenza epidemic broke out claiming thousands of victims, and scarcity of coal, gas, and other fuels threatened to aggravate it. As the home front saw military defeat, its faith began to crumble. No longer was the Kaiser revered as the All Highest. "Down with the Kaiser!" was a sentiment shared by rich and poor alike. Wilhelm was now seen as the major obstacle to peace.

The Kaiser tried to ride out the defeat by forcing Ludendorff's resignation on October 27. But it was later than he realized. The following day a naval mutiny erupted at Wilhelmshaven and spread to the High Seas Fleet in Kiel. Red flags flew from the masts of battleships, and thousands of sailors marched through the streets singing the *Marseillaise*. Officers were rare, and those encountered were disarmed and forcibly adorned with red cockades. By November 4, all of northern Germany was in a revolt that soon spread south and west; all the Rhine crossings were held by mutineers. On November 7, the German Armistice Commission under Matthias Erzberger, a leader of the Center Party and newly appointed Secretary of State, began talks with Marshal Foch in a railway car at Compiègne.

In a formal appearance at the Kaiser's headquarters in Spa, Belgium, on November 9, Hindenburg warned his sovereign that the German Army was now powerless to protect

Wearing the armband of revolution, mutinous German troops man a barricade in Berlin.

416

German troops on patrol during the revolt that
rocked the country at the end of the War. So
many soldiers participated in the uprising that it
was difficult to tell who was in revolt and who
was still taking orders from the Army.

Armistice Celebrations

Jubilation in Saint Louis.

Mobs congregate in Paris in front of the Opera to celebrate the coming of peace.

A "victory wagon" careens through the streets of Paris.

Open-topped buses travel up and down New York's Fifth Avenue in front of the Public Library.

Chicagoans throng the "Loop" to proclaim their relief and joy.

Rejoicing British wave flags before a Royal Air Force office.

him, adding, "I must advise Your Majesty to abdicate and proceed to Holland." In less than forty-eight hours the shaken Wilhelm accepted that advice. Before the jubilant Allies could mass for their invasion of Germany, a republic was proclaimed and the Armistice signed on November 11.

Germany agreed to evacuate all invaded territory, including the provinces of Alsace and Lorraine, seized from France in 1871. She also pledged to repatriate all Allied military and civilian prisoners without immediate reciprocity; and to surrender huge quantities of war matériel, including 5,000 pieces of artillery and 25,000 machine guns. German industry, however, was left intact.

The High Seas Fleet of ten battleships, six battle cruisers, eight light cruisers, and fifty destroyers was interned along with all submarines. Later the surface vessels sailed to the British naval base at Scapa Flow. The French expected to receive most of these as part of reparations, but in June, 1919, the German crews scuttled their warships while the British stared helplessly.

At Germany's collapse the generals retreated into the shadows, avoiding any role in the capitulation. No high-ranking military figure joined in the Armistice proceedings. Ludendorff decamped to Sweden clad in mufti and disguised behind dark glasses, afraid someone might kill him. Erzberger and his colleagues shouldered the burden of guiding Germany through the Armistice.

A subdued propaganda campaign stressed that Germany had not been defeated in battle, but that the High Command had sought peace to prevent further bloodshed and to end the hunger blockade against women and children. Later, when this fiction wore thin, the Army charged that it had been "stabbed in the back" by traitors on the home front. After all, the military asked, wasn't the Armistice Line on Belgian and French territory? (Under the terms of the Armistice, Allied troops occupied the Rhineland but not the rest of Germany.)

Ludendorff returned in 1919 and took up the cry, as did his political confederate Adolf Hitler. Few slogans struck a more responsive chord with defeated and embittered Germans than the "stab in the back" theme that became a pillar of Nazi dogma. Erzberger was an early victim of their drum-beating. In 1921 two former officers shot and killed him as a "traitor" for signing the Armistice.

Few agreed with General Pershing that confusing an armistice—negotiations through diplomatic means—with unconditional surrender was potentially hazardous. Addressing a letter to the Allied Supreme War Council on October 30, 1918, the American commander expressed his "opinion from the military point of view . . . whether or not Germany's request for an armistice should be granted.

"By agreeing to an armistice under the favorable military situation of the Allies," he observed, "accepting the principle of a negotiated peace rather than a dictated peace, the Allies would jeopardize the moral position they now hold and possibly lose the chance actually to secure world peace on terms that would insure its permanence. I believe that complete victory can only be obtained by continuing the war until we force unconditional surrender from Germany. . . ." Full military occupation of that nation was implicit in Pershing's proposals, which were received and ignored.

Twenty-seven years later, Pershing saw his vindication as the Allies rejected attempts by Nazi leaders to arrange an armistice. Instead, the chief of the German General Staff and the commander in chief of the German Navy, "acting by authority of the German High Command," were compelled to "surrender unconditionally to the Supreme Commander, Allied Expeditionary Force. . . ."

Car number 2419 D at a siding in
Compiègne. The Armistice was signed
in this car on November 11.

Chronology

POLITICAL

1914

June 28   Archduke Francis Ferdinand and his wife are assassinated by Gavrilo Princip in Sarajevo, Bosnia.

July 5   Kaiser Wilhelm agrees to aid Austria-Hungary if Russia and France interfere with her war against Serbia.

July 22   Germany warns Great Britain not to intercede between Austria and Serbia.

July 23   Austria issues ultimatum to Serbia.

July 25   Serbia's placatory reply rejected. Austria-Hungary severs relations and proceeds to mobilize; Russia warns she will mobilize if Serbia is attacked.

July 27   Germany rejects Great Britain's renewed offer to mediate.

July 29   Russia mobilizes.

WAR DECLARATIONS

1914

July 28   Austria-Hungary against Serbia.

August 1   Germany against Russia.
3   Germany against France.
4   Germany against Belgium; Great Britain against Germany.
6   Austria-Hungary against Russia; Serbia against Germany.
12   Great Britain against Austria-Hungary.
13   France against Austria-Hungary.
23   Japan against Germany.

Nov. 1   Russia against Turkey.
5   Great Britain and France against Turkey.

1915

May 23   Italy against Austria-Hungary.

Aug. 21   Italy against Turkey.

Oct. 14   Bulgaria against Serbia.
Oct. 15–16   Great Britain, France and Serbia against Bulgaria.
19   Italy and Russia against Bulgaria.

1916

Aug. 27–28   Romania against Austria-Hungary; Germany against Romania, and Italy against Germany.
30   Turkey against Romania.

Sept. 1   Bulgaria against Romania.

1917

April 6   America against Germany.

July 2   Greece against the Central Powers.

Dec. 7   America against Austria-Hungary.

WESTERN FRONT

1914

Aug. 2   German army invades Luxembourg.
4   Belgium invaded.
7   British troops land in France; French invade Alsace-Lorraine.
14   Battles of the Frontiers.
16   Germans conquer Liège.
20   Germans enter Brussels.
22   Battle of Mons.
26   Battle of Le Cateau.

Sept. 3   French government leaves Paris for Bordeaux.
5   Battle of the Marne.
13   First Battle of the Aisne, leading to the "Race to the Sea."

Oct. 9   Antwerp falls to the Germans.
11   First Battle of Ypres.

1915

March 14   Battle of Saint Eloi.

April 22   Second Battle of Ypres. Germans introduce poison gas.

May 9   Franco-British campaign in Flanders and Artois.

Sept. 25   Franco-British offensive in Champagne and Loos.

1916

Feb. 21   Battle of Verdun.
25   Fort Douaumont captured by Germans.

July 1   Battle of the Somme.

Sept. 15   British first use tanks on the Somme.

Oct. 24   Fort Douaumont recaptured.

Nov. 18   Battle of the Somme ends.

Dec. 12   General Robert Nivelle replaces Joffre.
18   Battle of Verdun ends.

1917

April 6   United States declares war against Germany.
9   Battle of Arras; Vimy Ridge captured.
16   Nivelle's offensive (Second Battle of the Aisne).
29   Mutinies erupt in French army.

May 15   General Henri Pétain replaces Nivelle as French commander in chief.

June 7   Battle of Messines Ridge.
25   First American soldiers reach France.

July 31   Third Battle of Ypres.

Nov. 6   Third Battle of Ypres ends; Canadians take Passchendaele Ridge.

Nov. 7   Supreme Allied War Council formed.
20   Battle of Cambrai; first massed tank assault.

1918

March 21	First German offensive (Operation Michael) to divide British and French forces.
23	Germans drive past Saint Quentin to the Somme; Paris shelled.
27	Germans capture Montdidier, thirty-two miles from Paris.
April 14	General Ferdinand Foch appointed Supreme Allied Commander.
May 27	Third German Aisne offensive leads to the Marne in four days.
May 28	Americans capture Cantigny.
June 2	Battle of Château-Thierry.
6	Battle of Belleau Wood.
July 15	Second Battle of the Marne; German offensive halted in two days.
18	Allied counterattack reduces German Aisne-Marne salients.
Aug. 8	Battle of Amiens.
Sept. 13	American First Army captures Saint Mihiel.
26	Final Allied campaign against Hindenburg Line.
27	Hindenburg Line is broken.
Oct. 4	Germany extends peace feelers.
27	General Erich Ludendorff resigns as German supreme commander.
Nov. 3	Franco-Americans drive Germans from Meuse-Argonne; Austria surrenders.
4	Revolt spreads in Germany; all Rhine crossings held by mutineers.
7	German Armistice Commission meets Foch.
11	Armistice signed at 5 A.M. Firing ends at 11 A.M.

EASTERN FRONT

1914

Aug. 10	Austrian troops invade Russian Poland from Galicia.
12	Austrian troops invade Serbia.
17	Russians invade East Prussia in first clash with Germans.
18	Russians invade Galicia.
26	Battle of Tannenberg.
Sept. 3	Russians capture Lemberg.
10	First Battle of the Masurian Lakes.
11	Battle of Rava Russkaya in Galicia. Russians drive Austrians back to Carpathian line and isolate Przemysl.
Oct. 6	Germans drive Russians back in Poland and Galicia.
12	Germans within ten miles of Warsaw.
21	Germans withdraw from Warsaw.
Nov. 2	Germans driven from Poland; Russians invade East Prussia.

1915

Jan. 31	Germans use poison gas for first time in Winter Battle of Masurian Lakes.
Feb. 28	Germans retreat from Upper Poland.
March 22	Przemysl falls to the Russians.
May 4	Austro-German offensive cracks Russian front between Gorlice and Tarnow.
June 2	Germans enter Przemysl.
22	Austrians retake Lemberg.
Aug. 4	Germans capture Warsaw.
20	Germans occupy all of Poland.
Sept. 5	Czar Nicholas II assumes command of Russian Army.

1916

June 4	Russian offensive south of Pripet Marshes.
Sept. 20	Austro-Germans halt Russian advance.

1917

March 12–15	Russian Revolution; Czar abdicates.
July 1	Brusilov offensive in Galicia.
Nov. 6–7	Bolsheviks seize state power.
Dec. 22	Trotsky begins peace negotiations at Brest Litovsk.

1918

Feb. 10	Trotsky refuses to negotiate with Germans.
18	Germans renew hostilities against Russia.
March 3	Soviet regime signs peace treaty at Brest Litovsk.

BALKAN FRONT

1914

July 29	Austrians shell Belgrade.
Aug. 12	Austrians invade Serbia.
16	Serbians rout Austrians at Battle of Jadar.
Sept. 8	Second Austrian invasion of Serbia fails.
Nov. 11	Third Austrian invasion of Serbia fails.
Dec. 2	Austrians enter Belgrade evacuated by Serbs.
3	Serbian offensive forces Austrians to again retreat across the border.

1915

Oct. 7	Austro-Germans invade Serbia.
11	Bulgarians invade Serbia.
14	Central Powers defeat Serbs.

1916

July 25	Remnants of Serbian Army arrive in Salonika.
Aug. 27	Romania enters war.
Sept. 1	Field Marshal August von Mackensen's Danube Army invades Romania.

20	Russian and Romanian troops stop the Germans.
Dec. 6	Germans rout Russo-Romanian forces; capture Bucharest and Ploesti oil fields.

1917 June 22	Pro-German King Constantine I of Greece forced to abdicate in favor of pro-Allied Eleutherios Venizelos as Premier.
Dec. 9	Romania signs Armistice with Germany.

1918 Sept. 14	Franco-Serbian armies move into Serbia.
29	Bulgaria signs Armistice.
Nov. 1	Serbs recapture Belgrade.
3	Austrians yield to Serbian terms.

ITALIAN FRONT

1915 April 26	Secret Treaty of London signed by Great Britain, France, and Russia, gives Italy generous territorial payment to join the Allies.
May 23	Italy declares war against Austria-Hungary.
June 23	First Battle of the Isonzo is launched; by Sept. 12, 1917, eleven battles are fought.

1917 Oct. 24	Battle of Caporetto; sometimes called the Twelfth Battle of the Isonzo.

1918 June 15	Battle of the Piave.
Oct. 24	Battle of Vittoria Veneto.
Nov. 4	Austrians sign Armistice with Italy.

MIDDLE EAST

1915 April 25	British and Anzac troops land on Gallipoli.
Aug. 6	British troops land at Suvla Bay.
Dec. 19	Anzac and Suvla Bay evacuation begins.
1916 Jan. 9	All Allied troops are withdrawn; Gallipoli campaign a total defeat.

MESOPOTAMIA

1914 Nov. 22	British capture Basra.

1915 April 12	Turkish attempt to seize Basra fails.
June 3	British occupy Amara on the Tigris.
Sept. 28	British capture Kut-al-Imara.

Nov. 22	Battle of Ctesiphon; Anglo-Indian army retreats to Kut-al-Imara.
Dec. 7	Kut-al-Imara beseiged by Turks. British relief drives fail.

1916 April 29	British at Kut-al-Imara surrender to Turks.

1917 Feb. 24	New British force retakes Kut-al-Imara.
March 11	British occupy Baghdad.

1918 Oct. 31	Turkish resistance ends.

EGYPT AND PALESTINE

1914 Dec. 18	Egypt made British protectorate.

1916 May	British start construction of rail and water lines on Sinai coast.
June 5	Sherif Husein of Mecca organizes armed revolt against Turkey.
Dec. 21	British take El Arish.

1917 January	Rail and water lines completed to Rafah.
March 26	First Battle of Gaza.
April 17	Second Battle of Gaza.
June	Allenby takes command of British forces.
Oct. 31	Beersheba falls to British.
Nov. 7	British win the Third Battle of Gaza.
Dec. 9	British capture Jerusalem.

1918 October 30	Turks sign Armistice.

SEA WAR

1914 Sept. 22	First British warships sunk by U-boat.
Nov. 1	Germans defeat British near Coronel, Chile.
2	British mine North Sea as war zone.
9	*Sydney-Emden* engagement.
Dec. 8	Battle of Falkland Islands; Vice-Admiral von Spee's German squadron is sunk.

1915 Jan. 23–25	Battle of Dogger Bank.
Feb. 18	Germans declare waters around Great Britain as war zone.
19	British naval raid on Dardanelles.

March	1	Allies blockade Germany.
	3	Allied landing in Dardanelles repulsed.
	18	Four British and French warships sunk attacking the Dardanelles.
May	7	*Lusitania* torpedoed.

1916

May 31	Battle of Jutland.

1917

Jan. 31	Germans announce unrestricted submarine warfare, starting February 1.

1918

April 23	British ships raid U-boat bases of Zeebrugge and Ostend.
May 9	British scuttle cruiser *Vindictive* in Zeebrugge canal.
Oct. 28	German naval crews mutiny at Wilhelmshaven; revolt spreads through High Seas Fleet.
Nov. 21	German High Seas Fleet sails to Scapa Flow and surrenders to British.

1919

June 21	German fleet scuttled by its crew.

Bibliography

Causes and Origins

Fay, Sidney B., *The Origins of the World War*. New York, The Macmillan Company, 1939.

Remak, Joachim, *Sarajevo*. New York, Criterion Books, Inc., 1939.

Seton-Watson, R.W., *Sarajevo*. London, Hutchinson & Co. Ltd., 1926.

East — West

Churchill, Winston, *The World Crisis*. New York, Charles Scribner's Sons, 1923–27, 4 vols.

Cruttwell, C.R.M.F., *The Great War 1914–18*. London, Oxford University Press, 1964.

Esposito, Brig. Gen. Vincent J., *A Concise History of World War I*. New York, Frederick A. Praeger, Inc., 1964.

Falls, Cyril, *The Great War 1914–18*. New York, G.P. Putnam's Sons, 1959.

Liddell Hart, B.H., *The Real War 1914–18*. Boston, Little, Brown and Company, 1930.

McEntee, Girard G., *Military History of the World War*. New York, Charles Scribner's Sons, 1937.

Taylor, Edmond, *The Fall of the Dynasties*. New York, Doubleday and Company, Inc., 1963.

Tuchman, Barbara, *Guns of August*. New York, The Macmillan Company, 1962.

Western Front

American Armies & Battlefields in Europe. Washington, U.S. Government Printing Office, 1938.

Asprey, Robert B., *At Belleau Wood*. New York, G.P. Putnam's Sons, 1965.

——— *The First Battle of the Marne*. New York, J. B. Lippincott Company, 1962.

Canadian General Staff, Army Headquarters, *The Western Front 1914*. Ottawa, 1957.

Farrar-Hockley, A.H., *The Somme*. Philadelphia, Dufour Editions, Inc., 1964.

Horne, Alistair, *The Price of Glory: Verdun 1916*. New York, St. Martin's Press, Inc., 1963.

Miller, Col. Henry, *The Paris Gun*. New York, Jonathan Cape & Harrison Smith, 1930.

Nicholson, Col. G.W.L., *Canadian Expeditionary Force 1914–1919, Official History of the Canadian Army in the First World War*. Ottawa, Roger Duhamel, 1962.

Pershing, Gen. John J., *My Experiences in the World War*. New York, Frederick Stokes, 1931.

Spears, Gen. Sir Edward L., *Prelude to Victory*. London, Jonathan Cape, Ltd., 1930.

Watt, Richard M., *Dare Call It Treason*. New York, Simon and Schuster, Inc., 1963.

Wolff, Leon, *In Flanders Fields*. New York, The Viking Press, 1958.

Eastern Front

Brusilov, Gen. Aleksei, *A Soldier's Notebook 1914–18*. London, Macmillan and Co., Ltd., 1930.

Churchill, Winston, *The Unknown War*. New York, Charles Scribner's Sons, 1932.

Hoffmann, Gen. Max, *The War of Lost Opportunities*. New York, International Publishers, 1925.

Knox, Major-Gen. Sir Alfred, *With the Russian Army 1914–17*. London, Hutchinson & Co. (Publishers) Ltd., 1921.

Pares, Sir Bernard, *The Fall of the Russian Monarchy*. London, 1939.

The Dardanelles

Moorhead, Alan, *Gallipoli*. New York, Harper & Row, Publishers, 1956.

Air Warfare

Bishop, William A., *Winged Warfare*. Garden City, Doubleday & Company, Inc., 1967.

Jablonski, Edward, *The Knighted Skies*. New York, G.P. Putnam's Sons, 1964.

Oughton, Frederick, *The Aces*. New York, G. P. Putnam's Sons, 1960.

Phelan, Joseph, *Heroes & Aeroplanes of the Great War 1914–18*. New York, Grosset & Dunlap, Inc. Publishers, 1968.

Reynolds, Quenton, *They Fought For the Sky*. New York, Rinehart, 1957.

Robinson, Douglas, *The Zeppelin in Combat*. London, G.T. Foulis & Co. Ltd., 1962.

Whitehouse, Arch, *Decisive Air Battles of the First World War*. New York, Duell, Sloan & Pearce, 1963.

Sea Warfare

Bacon, Sir Reginald, *The Jutland Scandal*. London, Hutchinson & Co. (Publishers) Ltd., 1925.

Hoehling, A. A., *The Great War at Sea*. New York, The Bobbs-Merrill Company, Inc., 1965.

Macintyre, Donald, *Jutland*. New York, W.W. Norton & Company, Inc., 1958.

Sims, Adm. William S., *The Victory at Sea*. Garden City, Doubleday & Company, Inc., 1920.

Scheer, Adm. Reinhard, *Germany's High Seas Fleet in the World War*. New York, Peter Smith, 1934.

Maps

Esposito, Brig. Gen. Vincent J., ed., *The West Point Atlas of American Wars*. New York, Frederick A. Praeger, Inc., 1959.

Johnson, Douglas W., *Battlefields of the World War: A Study in Military Geography*. New York, Oxford University Press, Inc., 1921.

Biographies

Barnett, Correlli, *The Swordbearers*. London, Eyre & Spottiswoode, Ltd., 1963.

Liddell Hart, B.H., *Reputations: Ten Years After*. Boston, Little, Brown and Company, 1928.

Acknowledgments and Picture Credits

The author is indebted to the following individuals and institutions for valuable suggestions, information, reference materials and cooperation in providing the illustrations for this book.

American Legion Magazine, New York: James F. O'Neil.
Australian War Memorial, Canberra: W. R. Lancaster.
Austrian Information Service, New York.
Belgian Consulate General, New York: Jan Hellemans, Consul, Philippe J. Berg, Vice Consul.
Brown Bros., New York: Harry B. Collins, Jr.; Meredith Collins.
Canadian Consulate General, New York.
Canadian War Museum, Ottawa: L. F. Murray.
Air Vice-Marshal Raymond Collishaw, Vancouver.
Cunard Line, Ltd.
Directorate of History, Canadian Forces Headquarters, Ottawa: S. F. Wise.
C. E. Dornbusch, Cornwallville, New York.
French Embassy, New York: Catherine Manteau.
Colonel G. B. Jarrett, Aberdeen, Md.
Heeresgeschichtliches Museum, Vienna.
Musée de la Guerre, Paris: Mme. A. M. Barthe.
National Archives, Washington: Josephine Motyleweski.
The National Gallery of Canada, Canadian War Memorials Collection, Ottawa: Major R. F. Wodehouse, Mrs. A. Armstrong, Allison Lang, Sherrill Moseley.
Smithsonian Institution, Washington: Daniel P. Stanton.
United States Air Force, Art & Museum Branch, Washington: Lieutenant Colonel Russell A. Turner II; William H. Winder.
United States Army Photographic Agency, Washington: Mrs. D. Traxler.
United States Marine Corps: Captain Crane Davis.
United States Military Academy, West Point Museum: Richard E. Kuehne.
United States Office of Military History, Washington: Joseph Ewing.
United States Office of the Secretary of Defense, Washington: Bettie Sprigg.
Yugoslav Consulate.
Yugoslav State Tourist Office.

All photographs courtesy of Brown Brothers with the exception of photographs on the pages noted below.

Australian War Memorial: 128–129, 147, 159, 194, 197, 211, 252, 265, 280–281, 324–325, 328, 350, 352, 353, 371, 385, 395.
Austrian Information Service: 39, 118, 227, 269, 303, 304, 305, 311, 364.
Author's Collection: endpaper maps, 307,
Belgian Consulate, New York: 54, 59, 109, 130, 227, 339.
French Embassy Press and Information Division: 32, 48, 62–63, 64, 65, 69, 71, 74, 75, 77, 79, 132, 135, 164–165, 170, 171, 175, 178–179, 183, 240, 245, 248, 261, 262, 272, 273, 278, 286, 342, 347, 352, 367, 384, 407, 416, 417.
Grosset Art Studio: 17, 49.
Jarrett Collection: 167, 240, 241, 243, 248, 367.
Musée de la Guerre, Paris: 101, 174, 375.
National Archives: 40, 57, 58, 73, 93, 94, 120, 131, 143, 185, 192, 200, 203, 206–207, 213, 229, 234, 239, 244, 245, 246, 266, 267, 283, 314–315, 323, 344–345, 348, 351, 354, 360–361, 363, 368–369, 373, 375, 388, 391, 401, 405, 406, 408, 414, 415.
Royal Canadian Air Force: 240, 241.
Smithsonian Institution: 240.
United States Air Force: 235, 241, 249.
United States Marine Corps: 374, 380.
United States Military Academy Museum: 169.
Yugoslav State Tourist Office: 14, 15, 305.

Index

Page numbers in *italic type* refer to illustrations.

433